Walking on Water

Walking on Water

Edwin Taylor

The Pentland Press
Edinburgh – Cambridge – Durham – USA

First published in 1999 by
The Pentland Press Ltd
1 Hutton Close,
South Church
Bishop Auckland
Durham

ISBN 1-85821-697-4

Typeset in Bell 11/14
by Carnegie Publishing, Carnegie House, Chatsworth Road, Lancaster
Printed and bound by Bookcraft Ltd, Bath

*This book is dedicated to my late wife Anne,
for fifty-two years of marriage and for her
companionship on my travels in search of water;
it has been a great pleasure to have seen
so much together.*

Contents

Contents

Illustrations

Foreword

DOWSING WORKS. As yet there is no scientific explanation – but in due course no doubt there will be one. Meanwhile this ancient practical art remains a gift given to the few and a mystery to everyone. There could be no better practitioner than Mr Edwin Taylor whose inherited dowsing skills and inherent charm have brought great benefit and pleasure to the many thousands of people he has met up with over a long working life. He has respected and honoured those skills as a truly natural professional in the knowledge that in an over-analytical world some God-given mysteries enhance and enrich the lives of all of us. Having benefited at first hand I am doubly delighted to write this Foreword.

Lord Vinson of Roddam Dene,
Northumberland. Spring 1999.

Dowsors

Moses was the first one,
When he smote the rock,
And lowsed oot aal that wattor,
And gave the Israalites a shok,

And Midas wes a clivvor buggor,
Aal he touched was gold,
But Edwin Taylor – canny lad,
He waddent just be told!

He had two bits of whalebone,
And it seems a daft like thing
But the dozey buggor went an dowsed,
And found a wedding ring!

If only he would use his art
In a mannor like thats reet,
The Harold Wilson – wet a shyem,
He'd be in Downing Street!

For if wor Edwin got to work
Wi' whalebone at the ready,
And went and dowsed Fort Knox for wer,
The economy would be steady!

Noo Jonah was a leery buggor,
Sorviving the whale's belly,
But Edwin – just a bit of bone,
The buggor 'll be on the telly!

So hears to aall the dowsers,
Wherever they may be,
So let them dowse a pot of gold,
For poor buggor's like ye and me.

Taylor Family Tree

John – Ann (Stephenson) Taylor
1736–1818

Married 7 Nov. 1767
John: Died 30.10.1818 aged 82: Ann: Died 1.7.1823 aged 88
Both are buried at Lanchester.

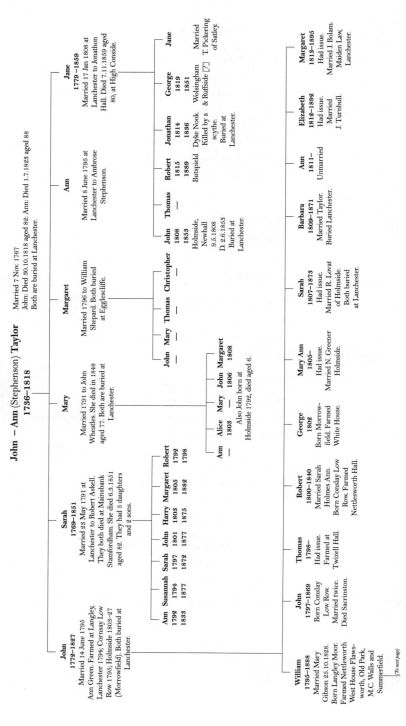

John
1772–1827
Married 14 June 1795
Ann Green. Farmed at Langley,
Lanchester 1794; Cornsay Low
Row 1795; Holmside 1803–27
(Morrowfield). Both buried at
Lanchester.

Sarah
1769–1851
Married 23 May 1791 at
Lanchester to Robert Askell.
They both died at Mainsbank
Stamfordham. She died 6.3.1851
aged 82. They had 5 daughters
and 2 sons.

Mary
Married 1791 to John
Wheatles. She died in 1848
aged 77. Both are buried at
Lanchester.

Margaret
Married 1796 to William
Shepard. Both buried
at Egglescliffe.

Ann
Married 8 June 1795 at
Lanchester to Ambrose
Stephenson.

Jane
1779–1859
Married 17 Jan 1808 at
Lanchester to Jonathon
Hall. Died 7.11.1859 aged
80, at High Conside.

Jane
Married
T. Pickering
of Satley.

Ann
1792
1833

Susanah
1794
1877

Sarah
1797
1872

John
1801
1877

Harry
1803
1875

Margaret
1805
1882

Robert
1792
1798

Ann
—

Alice
1803

Mary
—

John
1806

Margaret
1808

Also John born at
Holmside 1792, died aged 6.

John
—

Mary

Thomas
—

Christopher

John
1808
1853
Holmside,
Newhall
9.5.1808
D. 2.6.1853
Buried at
Lanchester.

Thomas
—

Robert
1815
1889
Butspield

Jonathan
1814
1836
Dyke Nook.
Killed by a
scythe.
Buried at
Lanchester.

George
1819
1851
Wolsingham
& Ruffside [?]

William
1795–1888
Married Mary
Gibson 25.10.1828.
Born Langley Moor.
Farmed Nettleworth
West House Flaws-
worth, Old Park,
M.C. Walls and
Summerfield.

John
1797–1869
Born Conslay
Low Row.
Married twice.
Died Sacrinston.

Thomas
1798–
Had issue.
Farmed at
Twizell Hall.

Robert
1800–1840
Married Sarah
Holmes Ann.
Born Conslay Low
Row. Farmed
Nettlesworth Hall.

George
1802
Born Morrow-
field. Farmed
White House.

Mary Ann
1805–
Had issue.
Married N. Greener
Holmside.

Sarah
1807–1873
Had issue.
Married R. Lovat
of Holmside.
Both buried
at Lanchester.

Barbara
1809–1871
Married Taylor.
Buried Lanchester.

Ann
1811–
Unmarried

Elizabeth
1812–1892
Had issue.
Married
J. Turnbull.

Margaret
1813–1895
Had issue.
Married J. Bolam.
Maiden Law,
Lanchester.

[To next page]

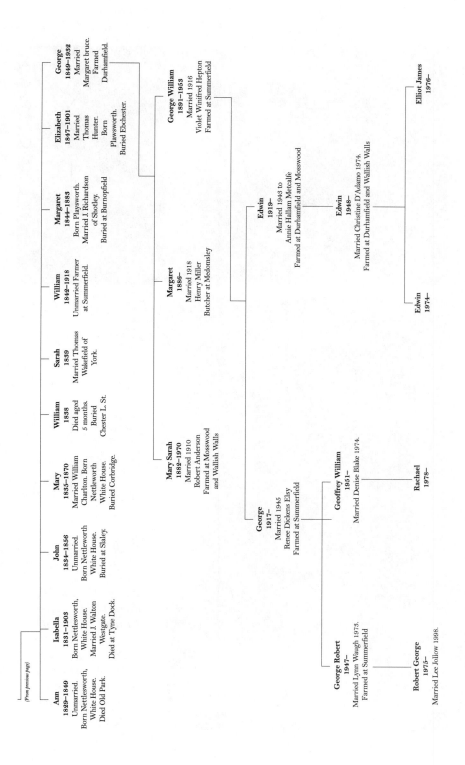

(From previous page)

Ann
1829–1849
Unmarried.
Born Nettlesworth,
White House.
Died Old Park.

Isabella
1831–1903
Born Nettlesworth,
White House.
Married J. Walton
Westgate.
Died at Tyne Dock.

John
1834–1856
Unmarried.
Born Nettleworth
White House.
Buried at Slaley.

Mary
1835–1870
Married William
Charlton. Born
Nettleworth
White House.
Buried Corbridge.

William
1838
Died aged
5 months.
Buried
Chester L. St.

Sarah
1839
Married Thomas
Wakefield of
York.

William
1842–1918
Unmarried Farmer
at Summerfield.

Margaret
1844–1883
Born Playsworth.
Married J. Richardson
of Shotley.
Buried at Burnopfield

Elizabeth
1847–1901
Married
Thomas
Hunter.
Born
Plawsworth.
Buried Ebchester.

George
1849–1932
Married
Margaret bruce.
Farmed
Durhamfield.

Mary Sarah
1882–1970
Married 1910
Robert Anderson
Farmed at Mosswood
and Wallish Walls

Margaret
1886–
Married 1918
Henry Miller
Butcher at Medomsley.

George William
1891–1953
Married 1916
Violet Winifred Hepton
Farmed at Summerfield

George
1917–
Married 1945
Renee Dickens Elsy
Farmed at Summerfield

Edwin
1919–
Married 1943 to
Annie Hallam Metcalfe
Farmed at Durhamfield and Mosswood

George Robert
1947–
Married Lynn Waugh 1973.
Farmed at Summerfield

Geoffrey William
1951–
Married Denise Blake 1974.

Edwin
1948–
Married Christine D'Adamo 1974.
Farmed at Durhamfield and Wallish Walls

Robert George
1975–
Married Lee Jollow 1998.

Rachael
1978–

Edwin
1974–

Elliot James
1976–

Above: *Edwin (3),
Edwin (1), Christine,
Edwin (2), Elliot*

Left: *George Taylor
and Margaret Taylor,
Grandfather and
Grandmother of the
author*

Introduction

OR THE contents of this book, I have selected from my experiences as a water dowser, with a view to handing on the wide range of different requirements of those people who call on the services of a water diviner.

At the beginning of my dowsing career in 1949, it was difficult to find any written accounts of the experiences of a dowser who had been successful to a degree that would warrant sharing those experiences with the beginners of my generation. There are a number of people today who are offering their services to teach students in the art of dowsing, but thanks to the many ways in which dowsing can be applied, covering all techniques and applications is nigh-on impossible – it is indeed a marathon task to master one alone.

After forty years of dowsing for water, I am now able to write about facts, as they appear to me through my experiences, rather than conjectures. I say this because simplicity, and the application of common sense, are paramount; water divining requires neither rites nor rituals, and those that seek to make a performance out of a gift leave themselves open to scorn and ridicule. I have recorded faithfully in my diaries the results of hundreds of invitations to find that precious liquid, water, and even after these hundreds of successful wells, it remains a very satisfying feeling to find another. I still marvel at the accuracy of my results, proving time and again that dowsing for water, whilst science cannot explain it, really does work.

I have gone through all the stages of water divining, from the beginner to the expert, and as I have found myself, there is always something left to learn. How I began is explained in detail, followed by advice for intermediate and advanced dowsers – though, of course, advancement in water divining comes through experience and not just through reading a book.

A considerable portion of the book relates to the practical day-to-day dowsing that I have undertaken over the years, and discusses the variations from one dowse to the next and the small, but valuable, pieces of knowledge gained from each which build up into the cloak of confidence known as experience.

Chapter I

He Who Would be a Dowser?

WAS BORN at Summerfield Farm in the parish of Shotley, Northumberland on 9 May 1919 to a family who, as records show, have farmed in, or near to, the Derwent Valley since the 1700s, and very probably long before that. It is not surprising that water divining, linked as it is to the health and well-being of the country, should be in the blood of one whose family background is so steeped historically in the country way of life. After all, my clients over the years have, by and large, been country folk who farm, own and care for the land and it has been a great advantage to me that we have been able to talk the same language, understanding, as I do, the practical need for a water supply.

I am sure that this similarity of interest between the two parties gives some measure of confidence to the farmer who wishes to drill for water on my say so – people are always more relaxed with one of their own kind and, I feel, not knowing the ways of the country would be a very great disadvantage for a prospective dowser. The drilling operator can get water without a dowser, but not every time, and not every time is not good enough for me or for anyone who is spending the £5,000 or so that it can take to sink a well to give a good supply of water. Anyone contemplating dowsing for water as a career must realise that there is a need for only a small number of professional dowsers in the British Isles. However, that I am called to dowse for water over 300 miles distant suggests that there are not many dowsers to choose from. Dowsing has not been my profession, but I have been prepared to devote a considerable amount of my spare time to it, and unless one is willing to do that, as with any skill, there is much less chance of success.

My professional life has been as a landowner and farmer who has

3

George William Taylor,
the author's father

taken great interest in the livestock side of the business. Until 1972, I was in partnership with my brother and was fortunate that his main interests lay in the machinery: a true partnership. When my son, Edwin, married in 1972, I formed a partnership with him and as he too was skilled with machinery, I was able to continue with my love of livestock.

My great liking for farm animals dates back to the days before school and I recall seeing the lambs born in March when I was nearly five. Starting time in those days was 5.30 a.m. – daybreak – and I remember putting on my clothes, sitting on the window sill looking out of the bedroom window, and listening for 'Old James', the ploughman, to appear. This was the signal for me to sneak down the stairs to join him in the lambing shed to see what lambs had been born during the night. In my pre-school year, this was a regular morning activity.

Violet Winifred Taylor,
the author's mother

Later on during lambing time, I was sitting the Scripture examination at the Snods Edge village school, Shotley Parish, taken by the Rural Dean of Corbridge. Part of my interest in finishing the exam was that after it came a half-day holiday and I would be back home to the farm early. It was on this day, 21 April 1928, that the Dean came into the classroom and said, 'What happy event has been announced this morning on the radio?' Answering his own question, he told us that a princess had been born to the Duke and Duchess of York. That little Princess is now our present Queen, and on Her Majesty's birthday each year, I always remember the day she was born and how I heard.

In September 1930 I entered my calf for showing, and myself in the hand-milking competition at the local agricultural show at Edmondbyers. At that time, all the milking on the farm was done by hand, and once we children had picked up the art of hand-milking, we were often called upon to help out during busy times. At the show, whilst my calf was unplaced, I was the very proud winner of the red rosette for first

Prince and Molly, Old James, Brother George and the author

Brother George and the author (with stick)

The author on Molly

The author in 1930 with first YFC calf

prize in the hand-milking competition, and told by the judge that I was correctly squeezing the teats of the cow rather than pulling them to draw the milk.

The Shotley Branch of the Young Farmers Club (YFC) was formed in 1931 and I joined the year after at the age of thirteen. In the early days, all the members took on rearing their own calf, keeping records of the food and its cost. The calves were sold at Hexham Auction in October and a new calf purchased to begin the cycle again; it was my first step towards looking after livestock.

When I was fourteen years old, 'Old James', retired leaving a gap that I was destined to fill. My father talked to the headmaster, who said, 'Edwin would be of more use on the farm!' so I left school on my fourteenth birthday rather than at the end of the summer term. My working life began on 9 May 1933, and in the autumn my father showed me how to plough with our two Clydesdale horses, Prince and Molly. I was to walk behind the plough holding the cord that went to each

8

horse's head, and tied to the bit in each horse's mouth, whilst I also guided the plough by holding the handles at the back. First the plough and then all the other two-horse implements on the farm landed in my lap: the binder for the grain harvester, the reaper for the hay crop, the harrows for making the seed bed, the drill plough for the root crops, and so on . . .

When I started work, it was a time of great hardship, and farming too was at its lowest ebb. A ploughman's wage was sixteen shillings a week, and I was given pocket money of half a crown a week until I was seventeen years old. Having said that, there were still good times to be had and we were never unhappy – I never knew what the word bored meant, a word on the lips of many children today. The main forms of transport for me at that time were bicycle or shanks's pony, and this was how I attended the YFC events, meetings, stock judging competitions, the cinema and the village dances. I passed my driving test at seventeen, the second year after its introduction. My brother had passed his test in the previous year so at last we both had wings for longer journeys. In 1938, a new Ford 8 could be bought for £100 and petrol, in today's money, was 6.5 pence per gallon. One acre of good, fertile land could be purchased for less money than the cost of dinner for two these days!

During the thirties, farm staff were found and employed by going to the 'hirelings' held in the larger market towns in November and May. Both male and female workers were available to hire for a term of six months. The remuneration would be worked out between both parties and included board and lodgings in the farmhouse. A female worker would also act as maidservant to the lady of the house and the wage for six months was usually about £7. As few women work on farms today compared to then, I will recount the week's work for a working girl on the farm.

Monday was washing day undertaken with a poss tub and a poss stick. I well remember the sound of the poss stick hitting the clothes in the bottom of the tub. Tuesday was butter-making day and involved churning the week's cream and turning the handle of the churn until the cream turned to butter floating in the churn milk. The churn milk was fed to the pigs and the butter made into half pound pats for sale. Wednesday was baking day, when both brown and white bread was made in large-sized loaves. Thursday was market day, and my mother and father took their T-Ford, loaded up with eggs and butter, into town to sell our goods and to fulfil their own shopping list whilst the maid completed various household chores. Friday was used to clean up for the weekend, and the maid would wash the stone floors, polish the brass, refill the paraffin lamps and clean the surrounding glasses. As well as working in the house, the girl would help with the milking twice a day and operate the cream separator, taking the cream off the milk for making into butter on Tuesdays. She would also be responsible for feeding the hens and gathering the eggs twice a day, and at haymaking time and harvest, she would make the teas and take them to where the men were working in the fields. At the weekend, there was time for a break from work, and the boys and girls from neighbouring farms had a chance to meet up and go for walks, bicycle rides and to the 'Picture Hall'. I remember seeing Bing Crosby in *Pennies from Heaven* in about 1934, whilst sitting in the picture hall on wooden bench seats. We did have one unfortunate experience with a girl hired from the hirelings, as some mothers would hope to get six months paid work from their daughters when they found out that the girls had become pregnant. We hired one girl onto Summerfield Farm and I recall my mother having a serious talk to the girl; I think she suspected what was up and work on the farm was quite hard especially if one was pregnant. About three months later in August, I was cutting grass for hay, sitting on the reaper seat drawn by two horses, when I noticed a van drive into Summerfield Farm at great speed and with some apparent urgency. Rather as I suspected, it turned out that the girl was being collected and taken back to her mother in Newcastle-upon-Tyne. We never found out what happened to her or her soon-to-be-born child.

I found my time behind the plough gave me the chance to think and I noticed things that I would never have known about otherwise. In my first month as a ploughman, the words of Robert Burns, a ploughman and poet himself, became plain to me: 'Wee bickering beestie, what trembles I' thee breastie'. As the plough turned over the stubble furrow, suddenly the mouse and its warm winter nest of straw and leaves were upturned together with the winter supply of grain. The 'panic in thee breastie' of that small creature was then laid bare for all to see, and the mouse would run blindly and aimlessly into the furrow bottom, its world in tatters.

Whilst there was little we could do for the mice, we did have the time to help some nature as we worked. The lapwing or plovers would make simple nests of dead grass on the ground after the land had been ploughed, and lay up to four eggs in it. When the land was dry, we would bring the harrows to level the land and prepare the seedbed. The birds would sit tight as I approached each nest as they were used to me walking behind the harrow from one end of the field to the other. Eventually they would take flight as I came too close for comfort, and I would just pick up the nest and contents, move it to the ground now harrowed and continue working the land. When it came to rolling the land, I would just pick up the eggs and return them as soon as the roll had passed. These activities did not take very long and the birds would return to their nests within a matter of minutes. Today, with fast-moving tractors, there is no time to do this, another way of life that is now past.

Being the second son in a farming family, I was eligible to be called for active service when war broke out, but since agriculture was a reserved occupation and my medical examination determined that I had a 'lazy eye', I was told that my services would be more important at home on the farm. The 3rd of September 1939 was the end of an era in the agricultural world and the use of the horse, as a beast of burden, ended overnight. Farmers were instructed to plough large areas of land which had not been ploughed for many decades and put every effort into food production. We received £20 per ton of wheat, a massive increase from £3 19s 3d per ton before war broke out, brought about because Great Britain could no longer rely on the import of corn under the threat of German U-Boats. Life in the country had to adjust to the needs of wartime, and I remember vividly the changes as a teenager. The blackout was the first sudden change, a serious offence if ignored, and so the glass windows of the outhouses on the farm were lime washed to stop the light from showing through. The headlights on cars were very small with a shield above them, intended more so that another motorist could see your vehicle than for you to see where you were going! Moonlit nights were taken advantage of to travel but the petrol coupon allocation for the private car was very small so we did not journey much. Another problem on long journeys was that all the road signs had been taken down in case of invasion! We soon got used to these restrictions, but I recall German heavy aircraft droning over the farm for hours on their way to, and return from, dropping bombs on Glasgow and Clydeside.

In the summer of 1941 at an annual dance at the Cooperative Hall in Consett, I first met my wife Anne. I was introduced to her by mutual friends and remember her looking very smart. She worked in an upper-class dress shop and I will recount one of the rare times I was in a dress shop too! It was the early 1960s and I was in London for a number of meetings. As a joke, or whatever, Anne said I should bring her back a nice dress from London – knowing full well of course I was not the sort to go shopping! However, I was walking down Regents Street, passing Dickens and Jones when I thought I would have a try at surprising her. As I entered the shop, a young lady came forward, I think sensing that I was on unfamiliar ground and asked if she could assist me. I remember saying, 'I certainly hope so!' and that I wanted to buy a special dress for my wife, realizing at that point that this was an adventure full of risk! The young lady asked me what size. Here I drew a blank but suggested we walk about the store and see if I could point out a girl of similar size and stature. That accomplished, I bought a blue dress with white ovals on it and when I arrived home with my Dickens and Jones parcel, there was some panic. Anne simply could not believe I could have bought the right size but the dress fitted perfectly and she treasured it for years.

We were married at the peak of the War in December 1943, and were to have the good fortune to spend nearly fifty-three years together. We planned to spend our honeymoon in Whitby on the East Coast, and the only way to travel there was by train from Newcastle to Whitby via Darlington. On the day before we were due to set off, the 4.00 p.m. train from Darlington to Whitby was hit by a bomb whilst in Darlington station, and we were somewhat concerned that this was a fine start to our honeymoon! However, in those days, folk were very resourceful and so by the next day, a coach was organized and we were ferried around Darlington to resume our journey by train, gas masks and all.

In June 1946, my aunt, who lived in the farmhouse at Durhamfield, decided to move to a cottage on Mosswood Farm to be closer to her sister who lived in the farmhouse there. This opened the way for Anne and me to begin our farming life together, and we moved into Durhamfield Farm, just as my grandfather had done in 1891, together with the same breed of cattle that he too had taken with him from Summerfield: Dairy Shorthorns. I remember well our first day at Durhamfield after moving, when we hadn't even had time to wind up the clocks. Through the novelty and excitement, we were up before the larks with a welcome from the cloudless sky, the warm June air and the smell of the country-side. They say that 'it is a rich man indeed who can get pleasure out of the simple things in life' and so we did. We settled down quickly with a new sense of freedom and the delights of new challenges together. Anne began with keeping poultry and laying hens to provide eggs for us and for sale to others. She also kept turkeys, geese, ducks and cock chickens for the Christmas market – all free range before there *was* any other way. *My* first move was to organize moving the Shorthorns from Summerfield to Durhamfield, a distance of half a mile. First, however, I had to build a new byre to house the cattle, as the original byre at Durhamfield only had room for eight cows. In those days, eight was the optimal number for hand-milking, but my herd was three times that size. I considered putting the building out to tender, but this would have proved costly and prolonged so I thought, If you want a job done well, do it yourself – and I did. I knew the cattle could not be moved until the following year because we could not start building the byre until the last of the winter frost had gone – around the following May, so I drew up the plans and submitted them to Hexham Rural District Council and began assembling the materials required. We were fortu-nate to have sand and gravel already on the farm on the bed of the river Derwent, and I had two moulds made with which we could make concrete blocks. We made twenty-four blocks per day which were ready to use after three days. The foundations were laid in April 1947 and my diary entry of 17 April reads: 'Working on byre foundations. Drainage and floors levels true.' On 4 June, I ordered the spouting and steel roof sheets. We started making blocks a week later only to run out of cement, which was very difficult to buy in those days, on 27 July after using three tons. By 2 August we were up to the eaves and the steel roof went on ten days later. They say where there's a will, there's a way and that is how I built my first byre. On 20 October 1947, a good year after we had initially moved in, we walked the Shorthorns with the aid of a border collie to their new surroundings at Durhamfield and it was very rewarding to have planned such a move and seen it to fruition.

When December came that year, Anne started for the first time to prepare the birds for sale, oven dressed, some for private clients and the remainder for the local butcher. I had learnt to pluck birds when I was a child and was well acquainted with the procedure; Anne soon picked up the technique. Whilst we prepared for Christmas, little did she and I know that our first winter at Durhamfield was going to be the most severe in living memory, starting, as it did, with a snow covering before the New Year was in. This first snow fall remained until 19 January when the winter really set in with heavy falls of snow, strong winds and severe temperatures. The winds came in from the east, heralding more heavy snow storms and giving true meaning to the old phrase 'wind from the east, neither good for man nor beast'.

We were prepared for winter as in any year, but not for this extreme. After a further week of lowering temperatures and drifting snow, the roads were well and truly blocked. Most livestock farmers keep a pocket diary to record servicing and due dates for their animals, sale dates and prices, and usually the weather for comparison with previous years. Re-reading my diary of fifty-years ago, the entry for 20 February 1947 is as follows: 'Rosemary 3rd with milk fever. Not possible for vet to come. Heavy snow, all roads blocked. Calf sick. Durhamfield road full of snow again'. The water supply to the farm and house was now frozen solid and we had to get water from the spring. We had no electricity at that time, so no television, and the radio was powered by a battery which lasted seven days and had to be recharged at a radio shop. The lighting was provided by paraffin lamps and candles, there was no telephone and we were truly snowed in! Looking back on that experience, the greatest need was for warmth and all we had was a log fire and a hot water bottle, but no central heating and no electric blanket – no wonder we never forgot the winter of 1947. The snow lasted well into March and my diary records us sowing corn on 13 March that year, four weeks late.

When we had thawed out, 1947 also saw me become more involved in cattle breeding and, at the same time, through the introduction of artificial insemination, there was a trend towards breed improvement throughout the cattle breeding societies which had begun to compete with one another. Beef breeds were aiming for quality beef, whilst the dairy breeds were aiming for higher yields of milk and butter fat. This year therefore saw the first dramatic change in farming where the Dairy

Shorthorn, a dual-purpose breed, producing both beef and dairy products throughout the British Isles, began to be replaced by single-purpose breeds producing either milk or beef. This once worthy breed's demise was accelerated by the introduction of the Milk Marketing Board which guaranteed, for the first time, the income of farmers who were involved in milk production. The financial impetus was thus provided to breed a cattle which would maximize milk production, and the MMB set up breeding centres throughout the country run by breed representatives. In 1948, I was elected onto the advisory committee of the MMB Shincliffe Cattle Breeding Centre and through the new technique of artificial insemination, the Shorthorn was served with Fresian semen, a breed known for its milk production, and so the Fresian strain began to take hold as the Shorthorn was bred out. In the space of fifty years, the Dairy Shorthorn went from being a common sight on the hills to having rare breed status.

I found that not only did I care for the welfare of the land and the livestock, but also for the people living in the area, and to that end I have been a parish councillor for thirty-three years, as were my father and grandfather before me. In a country district, the thought is to maintain and preserve, and not to see party politics take over, and it is a pleasure to see meetings conducted in a manner where the aim is to resolve the item in front of the Council to the benefit of all.

When I started farming in 1946, it was with 320 acres. By 1972, when I was in partnership with my brother, that area had grown to 1,400 acres. Since we both had sons, we then divided the estate equally to form new partnerships and now, when all the leased and rented land is taken into account, we farm just under 2,000 acres. My two grandsons, Edwin and Elliot, both now in their twenties, are also becoming active in farming and so it seems that the tradition of the Taylors farming in and around the Derwent valley will continue into the next millennium and beyond. Elliot is also interested in water divining and has been with me several times to locate water for clients. He knows my methods and I was very pleased when he asked one day: 'Grandad, I have dowsed and found a supply, will you check to see if I am right?' It pleases me greatly to say he too has the gift.

My other interest dates back to pre-war when an ageing uncle asked me to assist him with the management of the 130 acres of standing timber at Mosswood. This included measuring the felled timber for sale, thinning the crop at different stages and planting young trees in an area that had been clean felled. I took great enjoyment out of forestry work, especially in the great beauty of the south-facing hillside of the Derwent Valley where the timber has been grown and managed for a long time. The woodland was part of the Belsay estate belonging to Sir Arthur Middleton. The History of Northumberland mentions the Belsay estate in 1260 and the woodland had been part of that estate for 662 years until my Uncle Robert purchased it in 1922. I inherited this woodland thirty years ago and it was a pleasure to carry on the management of land that I knew so well.

Tree planting is popular across the country and never more so than at Mosswood where an annual effort is made to plant some trees each year. Of the softwood conifers, we have planted Scotch Pine, Norway Spruce and Douglas Fir and the hardwoods tend to be Oak, Ash, Sycamore and Beech. For decorative purposes Willow is planted – a vigorous grower beside streams.

My love of woods is reflected in my interest in antique furniture and when my brother George and I divided the family estate in 1969, the sharing was made much simpler by George's wife, who liked a more modern style. Old furniture suits Mosswood Farm better as the house is referred to in local history back to 1600. We were lucky, in that our likes differed, but the dividing of a family estate can spoil valuable sets by splitting them up. One such occasion comes to mind when my two aunts split the family dining chairs to have five each. These beautiful chairs dated from the William and Mary period and though one aunt sold hers, I still have the other five, another part of a long family history. My wife and I have many family pieces of furniture that date back 300 years or more, including this very table that I am writing on which could date back to 1690. If only it could talk, it could tell a wonderful tale – eight generations of the Taylor family have had tea around this old, oak, gate-legged table.

One of the earliest family members was John Taylor (see family tree), and in J. W. Fawcett's *Tales of Derwentdale*, published in 1902, which is now out of print and hard to get hold of, he gives the following true tale of the discovery of hidden treasure in Dipton Parish.

The Lowd Farm Money Pot

In the commencement of the nineteenth century, the farmer who lived at Lowd or Loud Farm, near Catchgate, was named John Taylor. John and his wife Ann, or as they were best known, Jackie and Nannie, were a hard-working couple, toiling early and late to earn the necessities of life for themselves and their large family and to make both ends meet. The farm being a large one, a couple of men servants were kept to assist in the work. One day, one Spring, at the period above mentioned, having sent the servant men to Running Waters, near Coxhoe for lime, Jackie went to take up 'furs' (i.e. furrows) in a tillage field. The land being wet necessitated his having to place one of the draught horses before the other, tandem fashion, and to have someone to lead the 'fore', or first, horse. His wife, Nannie, consented to do the latter task, and as they were going up one furrow, the plough caught hold of something in the bottom, which stopped the progress somewhat suddenly. In the exertion of the horses to pull the plough through the obstacle, it tore off the cover of some kind of vessel, and exposed its contents, at which Jackie called out 'Ho'd, Nannie, ho'd, she's a' here' (i.e. hold nannie, hold, she's all here). The trove proved to be a hidden treasure in the shape of an old kail-pot filled with guineas. The discovery was kept a secret in the neighbourhood, and Jackie having some trusty friend in London, sent the old guineas to him, and he getting them changed into the current coin of the realm, returned the same to the finder. After this, Jackie Taylor and Nannie are said to have 'nivver leuked ahint them' (i.e. to have always done well). Shortly after the discovery, they left the Lowd Farm, and went to reside at Worland Green, near Holmside, where they died; Jackie in 1818 and Nannie in 1823 and are buried at Lanchester. With a portion of the money obtained from the treasure trove, Jackie made himself a landed-proprietor, purchasing a couple of farms in the neighbourhood of Cornsay – one North Low Row and the other Hill Top – besides some other property, which passed to his offspring, and have since been sold to different parties.

Beginnings

My introduction to dowsing began after the War, and by that time I was married and had moved to Durhamfield Farm as my Grandfather had done in 1880. In 1949, after our son was born, a relative from Canada called in on a rare visit to see the family and babe in arms. Joe Anderson was a farmer from the Mid-West, and having seen the value of dowsing in Canada thought he would demonstrate the method to me too. Little did I know at this stage that his kindness would spark off an inherent desire to which I would devote a large part of my life. Not knowing the art of dowsing at that time, I did not fully appreciate the implications of his advice but, on his departure from my farm, I hastily picked up the piece of fencing wire which he had roughly fashioned into the shape of a V.

Joe Anderson ('on the rocks') Paisley, 1949

I retraced the steps of my impromptu tutor and found that I too had the ability to respond to those unknown influences that were making the rod move. My enthusiasm to pursue these hidden mysteries was now on course to discover the art of the real masters, and their ways of achieving success.

Several months went by during which time I developed the feel, and the strength of the pull on the rod. By now I needed to know more of what it meant and so I became a member of the British Society of Dowsers, gaining valuable information from their quarterly journal and lending library where I concentrated my choice on the written experiences of the master dowsers. It is their methods on which I based my dowsing career.

I now began my self-training because though the basics can be handed down, dowsers are individuals in their methods and each instinctively adds to the given methods in their own fashion. This training was self-planned: to dowse in reverse. I first located a spring of water running out of the ground and began dowsing, tracing it from the surface underground, recording as I went, depth and quantity.

It is my opinion that you cannot teach a fellow friend to follow your steps exactly in the ancient art of dowsing. We seem to be a breed of people with an inherent nature to be individual in our own ways in life, and the trait of dowsing shows that same individuality. You can only really spark off the enthusiasm in someone to be a dowser, and then only by their own study, practice and determination will they succeed; this even holds for the top 8 per cent to whom the skill comes naturally, as born dowsers.

My beginnings as a water dowser were not fashioned around any one individual but many, and I have collected and selected from a wide range the methods which have resonated with me as a dowser and have helped me ever since. During my many years of dowsing, I have found that when I talk to other water dowsers, it is sometimes difficult to compare notes; though we can all locate water underground, the methods we use are very, very different. Whilst I am all in favour of individuality, I do have some concerns about the complexity that some dowsers build into their techniques, perhaps because I am at a loss to fathom the real techniques from the surrounding wrapping. In my opinion, if one has worked to build the gift, whilst it may not always be pleasant, one should be able to dowse come rain or shine in wellies or barefoot, up hill and down dale. I make no apologies for being devoted to the simple, practical approach.

Perhaps this is a good point to outline some of the instruments used in dowsing, the all-important medium between the dowser, the water and his success or failure to locate it. The choice of instrument is very personal and depends on the application, as those looking for water tend to use the V rod whilst those practising medical dowsing, the pendulum. Before the time of plastics, perspex, brass rods and crystal pendulums, the simple hazel rod cut from the hedgerow had to suffice, and it was often cut from the site where water was to be found; you might say that nature had placed it so. When a dowser becomes a regular at marking well sites, the rod becomes part of him. I know only too well what this feels like for in 1989, whilst dowsing on the Isle of Man, I lost mine. It had been quite a busy day as I was seeking water on five different sites and at the end of the day, I realized that I had mislaid the rod which had been a part of me for forty years. The feeling was like losing part of oneself and I was overjoyed when two weeks later, packed carefully in a cardboard tube, my rod was returned to me by post; it had been left on the front window ledge of the farmer's

White bull, 1st Prize; Roan Cow, 2nd Prize; Great Yorkshire

Land Rover. My rod fits neatly into the inside pocket of my coat and on many occasions clients have asked me whether I have forgotten to bring it – they are most surprised when I retrieve it from inside my coat. I also believe that becoming attached to one particular rod is beneficial to the dowser as the rod seems to 'learn' with the dowser and produce subtler movements for the dowser to interpret.

I find that the rod is the best for water dowsing as it is little affected by wind and rain – even if these conditions are uncomfortable for the dowser! The rod can also be used to detect field drains and pipes, and I teach these skills to students from time to time for the Agricultural Training Board. I usually find that within the student group there is one born dowser who takes to the skill like a duck to water, and one for whom dowsing is out of his grasp, the remaining students lying somewhere in the middle. I always carry a supply of hazel rods to hand out as most people do not come prepared! When looking for a suitable rod, I look for one which is roughly Y-shaped with each branch about eighteen inches long – it is also important that the two arms are of a similar thickness – around half an inch. I remember cutting one such rod for the late, and much missed, Michael Bentine from trees planted some 220 years ago at Mosswood. Holding the rod to get the correct tension is a knack, and finding the point of balance so you can walk with the rod prepared to react is the first skill to be mastered. Some of the dowsers find that the brass angle rods are easier to master, and are rather more adept at finding drains and pipes with these.

Hazel has been widely used throughout Britain for centuries for its suitability to coppice, and in the art of basket making. Hazel rods were also used for making sheep hurdles and in the steel industry where they were called corf-rods and used for making corres, or baskets, by which coals were lifted from the coal pits. The smaller hazel rods were used by blacksmiths, twisted in such a manner as to hold their hot chisels whilst they worked, and called, for that purpose, chisel rods. In 1773, records show that 960 bunches of corf-rods were sold for 5d a bunch. In 1829, the price was 9d a bunch for 1,054 bunches. These were cut from the woodland at Mosswood Farm.

As I mentioned before, I spent a long time practising on springs of water which come to the surface. First I would find out by dowsing which direction the spring came from, estimate the quantity the spring should yield and then measure the spring to see what actual amount

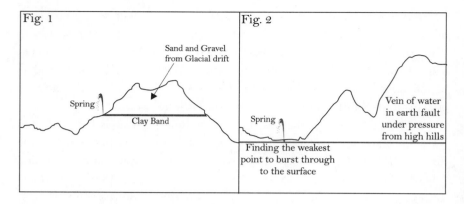

it was producing. If the measured quantity of the spring does not match the amount predicted by dowsing, it could be surfacing under pressure. As fig. 1 shows, some springs are being fed by two sources, the second being a deeper vein where water is forced to the surface under pressure, and comes out at this weak point in the ground. The rest of this vein is likely to continue on its journey and come out elsewhere. I also tracked the springs back to practice depthing, very revealing as to where the stream comes from.

Springs are Nature's way of supplying clean water to the countryside, and very effectivly too over the length of the British Isles. There are two types of spring, one for the cottage dweller, or a field trough for farm livestock. For the larger farm, or outlying villages there are springs to match their needs. Spring one is simple and very effective formed by glacial drift of thousands of years ago, see fig. 1.

The larger yielding spring will produce more, and will be more dependable from drying up in a dry summer, and can be fed from far distant places. The quality of the water in this category having a higher quality, and generally a less chance of drying up in summer time, see fig. 2.

As you climb to higher ground, the depthing should get deeper, except in some cases where the strata dips with the fall of the ground so one needs to be prepared for variation.

I found over the years that clay bands in the strata would play havoc with my depth measurements, but not seem to affect the estimate of quantity. Clay can also be troublesome when it contains bands of water-holding sand. When this is found, it means extra cost for the client as the borehole will have to be sleeved to a greater depth than is usual. I have not discovered yet why clay causes these results but maybe one day this anomaly will become clear. I will continue to add the depth of the clay to the dowsed depth until the reason is found.

I am currently in the midst of a clay-like problem with two dry holes after drilling through 'Mudstone.' My usual dowsing method gave very clear signs of a good result but this stone appears to act like clay and is unpredictable in depth. In East Yorkshire, the 'Mercia Mudstone' covers a large area. Mudstone is the most difficult of rocks to dowse in to find a water supply. It has the same effect as clay to the dowser. The dowser can not pick it up or find any way of its presence.

When mudstone was formed it was on the move like red hot mud flooding valleys and low ground, in places reaching 600 ft in depth. A borehole should have to drill through mudstone and into other rock on water bearing strata.

I can find a vein of water under the mudstone and get measurements of depth without the mudstone. I do warn clients when drilling through bands of clay to add to my depth forecast the thickness of clay in the drilling.

In my fifty years of dowsing it has only been in the last four years I have had this experience, on these occasions I have had that unfortunate experience. It will affect my success by less than 1 percent.

The beginner can also be affected by wishful thinking and distracted by little bands of water which would be of no use to a farming client. Over the years, I have tuned my dowsing reactions to filter out the smaller streams unless I specifically need to look for them. I rely on a very definite and strong pull of the rod.

I have found that keeping notes is a vital part of dowsing. I make notes not only of the location, depth and quantity of the water found but also of advice given and received. If you are called back to a drilling site, some wells being drilled many months after a survey, then the value of one's notes becomes truly apparent. They are also a detailed reference to your experiences, from which, over time, you can review and draw more conclusions than separated accounts allow.

I like to go to a site with a 'clean sheet' and not to be told where the local dowser said there was water or where the old well was. This enables me to draw my own fresh conclusions and not be influenced by the thoughts and recommendations of others. When I first started,

I visited old wells on farmsteads where a dowser had been before in order to practice. Over the years, I found where perhaps the beginner dowser had been the wells were often characteristically sited on the edge of the stream rather than in the middle. This mistake is easy to understand in retrospect; the dowser felt the pull of the rod sure enough at that point, but failed in the interpretation. For a successful result of the drilling the bore must be mid-stream.

Advancing

There is no profession where a demonstration of confidence is needed more than when a dowser is carrying out his survey – 95 per cent of clients needing the services of a dowser will only do this once in a lifetime and so the end result is as important to the client as it is to the dowser. We need to remember that the client is very conscious of the cost of drilling a well and, in many cases also conscious that the technique which he is employing is not explained by science or even accepted in most hydrological circles. Thus it behoves the dowser to be quietly confident and to represent with integrity this ancient profession.

I have found it pleasant and useful in the past to take a friend with me on a site survey – they can talk to the client whilst I am working and many clients want reassurance of my success rate or to try to understand how dowsing works.

Veins that turn out to be 4yds wide or less can also be disappointing and should be avoided for drilling unless there is no alternative. It is really better to aim for 7yds or more, and for irrigation purposes, the veins need to be 50 or 60 yards wide. As a general guide, the country cottage requires about 2,000 gallons of water per day approximating to veins 3yds wide, the farmer with livestock between ten and twenty thousand gallons per day approximating to veins 20yds wide, and the arable farmer with a requirement for crop irrigation, somewhere in the region of 250,000 gallons per day from a vein 60yds wide and over. I have found also that a vein of, say 19yds wide which enters a farm on one side will usually exit the farm many acres later but still at 19yds wide. If the vein you find on another side of the farm is not of the same width as the one you are trying to trace, it is very probably not the same one at all as in my experience they tend to keep their 'width identity'.

Let us take first the request for dowsing at a country cottage site. From the new dowser's point of view this might seem the easiest of the three categories, but experience has taught me that because such cottages usually stand in a small area of land the chances of success can be restricted. I am often called in by intending purchasers who would like to know if any water is available inside their cottage boundaries. The country cottage without water is likely to be an expensive proposition in terms of piping mains water onto the site. Sometimes the vendor of the property also owns adjoining land and may allow you to dowse there too, but this is not always the case. I had an instance where a vendor said 'no' and so I was forced to do a search within a very small area indeed, no more than 45yds square. The land on which the cottage stood had originally been the playground for a country school in the foothills of the Cheviot range in North Northumberland. On the day of the search, meeting the owner on site, it did not take much time to locate the only chance of water, though I have never had to make use of such a small vein, only 5yds wide, before. The vein was found under the dividing wall between the boys and girls playground at a depth of 75ft, and the well when drilled produced 3,000 gallons per day to the delight of the client. This example shows that what can appear to be the most simple dowse can often be the most difficult.

The second category takes into account the requirements of the farmer, landowner or estate manager and they have some specific needs which should be borne in mind whilst dowsing. The first requirement is the location of power by which the water can be drawn out of a borehole. It is cheapest and therefore preferable to locate a suitable vein not too far from the power source. Obviously this is not always possible but it should be remembered that it is both expensive and inefficient to take power to a proposed borehole miles from anywhere. Secondly, the water will need to be stored and piped to its intended use so once again it makes good financial and common sense to locate a vein as close to the proposed storage site as possible. It has been my experience that an ample supply of water should be found on any farm within two hundred yards of the farmhouse and its buildings. If advantage can be taken from the siting of the storage tank, so that the water can be gravity fed to the farm or water troughs, then I also look for this. I have been to farms to dowse where the farmer will say, 'We will have to find the water near to the storage tank!' and I always reply that it is much easier and cheaper to find water near to the power and pump it to the storage tank than the other way round!

The third group of users are much more demanding on both the water underground and the dowser. These users need significant quantities of water for irrigation, factories or farm irrigation and racecourses and the number of veins able to fill that requirement are likely to be reduced in number from that which would suffice the first two categories. Finding 250,000 gallons a day is indeed a tall order but I have found 450,000 gallons a day from one borehole, so one should not be downhearted. It seems to me that Nature, in all her wisdom, has provided much wider water veins in the areas where irrigation is needed. One of the advantages of stipulating such high volumes of water is that the client is likely to be prepared to site the power wherever it is required, so the choice of area to dowse from is less restricted. I also tend to give the farmer as many alternatives as possible so that with such a high requirement for water he can choose the best one, or ones, to suit his purposes. The best borehole is not always the one with the highest yield, depending also on its physical location, and so a balance is drawn in this category between accessibility, power and yield. It is often wise to try and site boreholes where two veins cross so that the cumulative yield will be much higher.

If water is not available in large daily quantities, the next step to help provide the required gallonage is to place a small reservoir on the farm, topping it up throughout the year in readiness for the summer months and peak growing season. With experience and careful thought, it is amazing what can be achieved.

Farms that need irrigation are generally 500 acres or more and this is a lot of land to cover in one day! However, at this size the farm usually has roads or tracks through it and I make good use of these. I have found that dowsing whilst being driven around the farm in a four-wheel drive, preferably a Land Rover, allows me to cover the farm and locate as many veins as possible from which we can choose later. Yes, dowsing whilst being driven works just as well! When I feel a response from the rod, I ask the driver to stop the car and then get out and dowse in the normal manner over the land, noting width, depth and quantity and marking same on a map of the fields. I generally physically mark about eight alternative sites, and it gives an interesting picture of how the water lies hidden beneath the land.

I should add at this point that marking the site clearly is extremely important. It is also the moment of no return for the dowser. The point where you have done your best, surveyed methodically and await the judgement of your mark to reveal success or failure. There is nothing further to be done, the site is marked and despite the wish to succeed, the wheels have been set in motion. I can still remember the feeling after my first 'professional' dowse when the time between marking the site and drilling went very slowly, the longest six months of my life. As a beginner, I tried to play safe and marked the point where two veins crossed and water was found at both levels within two or three feet of my predicted depth. I knew then for me that dowsing worked and I have never looked back. If it had been a failure, my life would have been very different.

Students setting out on a similar course can be assured that dowsing does work, but there is also much skill in the interpretation of your results. Whilst the marker placed midstream on a vein can be moved along the vein to a convenient place for drilling, the marker placed where two veins cross is much more restricted – an area of one foot square may be all one has to play with. I have found often that neither the man doing the drilling nor the client takes seriously the importance of drilling at the exact place I have marked. It is not helpful to have the client place a stake on your marked site that the cattle can uproot or a stone which sheep will push over. I have had several clients who have drilled 'roughly' where my marker was, or used to be as they remembered and have found no water. As my reputation is at stake, if you will pardon the pun, I now always ask for a spade before I set out to dowse, and then take off a grass sod about eight inches thick and securely knock into the bare earth a stake of three inches by three inches. In a hard rock or roadway where this is not possible, I make a mark on the ground with indelible spray paint.

When I am out on a dowsing survey, a pocket notebook is a must – leaving things to memory is not a policy I can encourage. I note the details at every stage in a survey and then transfer my notes to a desk diary for reference when I get home. Many times I have had clients who would like me to give them the details once again, sometimes years later. When the client rings in this way, I note the gist of the conversation and advice given in my book too; this is all part of the survey and the dowser-client relationship in my view. When keeping notes, I use Ordnance Survey maps and ring in red all the places where I have dowsed for water and the clusters on the map after all these years show how word of mouth recommendation works! Perhaps I should add that I have been lucky enough never to have had to offer my services as a dowser to any of the clients over the years, they have all come to me.

As I have said, drilling a borehole can reflect an investment of £5,000 or more to the client and this cost has to be balanced against the installation of a mains supply and mains water charges. Sometimes clients want to see what water is available on their site before choosing the mains water option, but of course there are many for whom mains water is ruled out by the very remoteness of the site. In the past, remote and widely distributed sites have depended on surface water running in land drains, rivers or from natural springs, (see spring fig. 1) but even for the country cottage, the increasing use of dishwashers, washing machines and the introduction of en suite bathrooms have all contributed to the added need for water. With the average yield of my dowsed wells being around 15,000 gallons per day, the ability to obtain clean water from under your own land, and the cost savings involved, have proved a very popular option.

I have always been interested in geology, and this interest has gone hand in hand with my dowsing. I use the One Inch Geological Maps to enlarge on sites of particular importance but, in the main, it is the Geological Survey 'Ten Mile' maps that are of the most use showing, as they do, the structure of the land beneath my feet. These maps have been of particular use in the north-west of Yorkshire where you can expect the drilling to be into limestone. This rock is the one I fear most to let dowsers down, as there are so many fissures in the rock that can carry water at some time of the year and yet be dry at other times. It seems that throughout the seasons the quantity of water is constantly changing, and thus sometimes you can dowse water flowing and other times, not at all!

By contrast, in the regions where there is sandstone such as the Vale of York, you might expect to find water without the aid of a dowser. This is possible, but where the dowser comes into his, or her, own is the ability to judge the quantity of water to be found in a fissure. The Triassic sandstones such as Bunter Sandstone are found widely in northern England and tend to yield large quantities of moderately soft water. The Millstone Grit and Coal Measure regions at Huddersfield for example, can also yield large quantities of water from boreholes, and once again the dowser should get a very high success rate dowsing on this ground.

I would add a note of caution to the dowser in regions where underground water would be expected to be plentiful: wishful thinking can still strike! In County Durham once, where the rock is Millstone Grit, an unfortunate driller cum novice dowser thought the very same – after drilling a very expensive dry borehole 280ft deep, I was called in and found the water, a plentiful 14,000 gallons per day, just two feet from the dry hole at 230ft.

Chapter II

Dowsing Experiences

Like a fish to Water

DURING the last ten years, I have been asked to locate water for several fish farms in Scotland, the North of England and on the Isle of Man. Fish farming, like any livestock farming, carries with it some risk in that the weather can be unseasonal and livestock struck by disease, but at least with livestock farming one is in charge of the land on which the animals are raised. With fish farming, the river water in which the fish live often comes off the hills and thus there is no control over the quality of water; it is the sudden pollution of that water that is feared the most. Often, by the time pollution is detected, it is too late to save the fish and a pollution source can be difficult to trace and even more difficult to prove for compensation. Whilst the National Rivers Authority takes great pains to explain to farmers and factories what effect pollution can have on the river life downstream, the only true safeguard against this problem is to have one's own water supply. Borehole water also has other benefits: it is generally drawn at constant temperature making it suitable for hatcheries and young fish and it does not contain wild fish which can spread disease into farm fish colonies. My first visit to a fish farm, in October 1987, was to a large salmon enterprise on the coast of Argyll, on the road from Lochgilphead to Oban. The fish were contained in raft-like enclosures, according to age, which floated on the sea though tethered strongly to the land. I was concerned at the distance Oban was from my home but as the proprietor had already called in one dowser to no good effect, I felt I had to accept the invitation. In order to be fresh for the survey, I stayed overnight at Oban – a town I know well as a gateway to the Island of Lismore and the site of an auction where I have purchased Highland cattle in the past. When I met the owner, he was very disappointed at having a dry borehole and his confidence in dowsing had been greatly reduced. He needed water for a fish hatchery and felt that if sufficient water was available, he would expand to a freshwater fish tank on the land he had adjoining his factory.

After I had outlined my method for the survey, I asked if I could begin by checking the dry borehole which, at 200m depth through very hard rock was a very costly failure. My reason for checking was to try and understand the other dowser, which was difficult as there was no water anywhere near the dry borehole. I began therefore by scanning the area and felt one jump of the rod, the only one it seemed to chose from in that area. I was soon on the edge of the vein and it measured 51yds wide and 183ft deep. At this early stage, I was very relieved to find that there was some water to be found. I moved on to the larger field and as the highway ran along the length of the field at about a third of a mile distant, I asked the proprietor if he would drive me along the road whilst I dowsed in the car. This he did and though we travelled the entire length of the field, we found only one vein. Stopping at the gateway to the field, I now knew where to go and make my quantity measurements – luckily this second vein, 28yds wide and 100ft deep ran exactly across the first vein and so we could drill where the veins crossed.

On 12 November, the proprietor telephoned me to say they were drilling as advised and were at 100ft and were yielding an estimated 14,000 gallons per day and should they continue to drill. I replied that No. 2 vein was a bonus, that the real yield was to be obtained from No. 1 vein at 183ft and so they should keep drilling. Although I never did hear the final result, and whether they did indeed drill down further as I advised, I am sure I would have heard if there had been anything amiss! One event that pointed to a successful conclusion at this farm was that my name was passed on by this client to another fish farmer at Selkirk.

The proprietor of this farm wanted borehole water for another reason entirely: cost. He felt that with the rising cost of water in his area, if there was any pollution of the river water he was using, he would have been forced to use the metered mains water – a very expensive option for his operation. He had calculated that the cost of drilling a borehole would be quickly surpassed by the cost of using mains water and also

Dowsing on the Isle of Man

that any change in the legislation of Scotland, where boreholes can be sunk without National Rivers Authority permission, might prevent him from drilling in the future. The requirement at this fish farm was much higher – the owner needed half a million gallons per day. This daily usage set me thinking for I had only once in hundreds of wells found water to satisfy this level of quantity. Much to my delight the first vein I found was 50yds wide and 75ft deep; a good start at least. This one also ran very conveniently under the entire length of the fish tanks so I marked a spot to drill closest to the power point. The second vein was found to the west in a turnip field, 25yds wide and 60ft deep.

There were unfortunately no more veins of any value so I began to scheme out the alternatives to make the best use of what was there. I felt that the first vein could yield up to half the requirement and that a second well could be drilled on that vein too. I suggested that the second vein was used to fill a large reservoir in the turnip field, and using that reservoir, the owner could obtain the quantity of water required. The fish farmed on this site were trout and I was kindly given some to take home – quite delicious, I can recommend them to anyone.

My final example of dowsing for water for fish farms is from the Isle of Man where, once on site, I soon realized that there was no large

Dowsing on the Isle of Man

quantity of water to be found. I found four veins: the first, 4yds wide and 10ft deep; the second, 8yds wide and 10ft deep; the third, 11yds wide and 8ft deep and the fourth and final vein, 11yds wide and 10ft deep. I recommended the fourth vein as, although the others were easier to access, at 101ft deep, it should have been out of the risk of pollution.

Watersports?

Water is needed for a variety of reasons in sport. On the golf course, the greens need to be watered and no doubt the clubhouse needs a supply of clean water too. I have also been called out to racecourses and polo grounds where the courses and grounds need to be kept in good condition. In general, the most important factor is cost and usually with large areas in which to find water, there is a good chance of finding an economically viable supply. To date, I have dowsed at five golf clubs, one of which was Slaley Hall Golf and Country Club near Corbridge. The course, professionally designed is situated in a heavily wooded area and highly praised by my golfing friends. On 22 August 1985, I surveyed the site for water to supply the Hall, the houses within the grounds and the greens when necessary. I found two veins of water near to the Hall: the first was 19yds wide and 90ft deep, the second was 10yds wide and 72ft deep. The two veins happened to cross at a very convenient place so I marked that as the drilling point of choice and also a second point on the first vein. When the bore was drilled at the crossing of the veins, in the words of the drilling foreman, 'They found a lot of water' but they had to drill through 19ft of gravel which began to fall into the bore. They pulled out and moved to the second point on the first vein but found the same problem. They asked me to return about a year later and my first reaction was to move away from the Hall area where the glacial drift had settled. I moved on to higher ground and found two more veins of water which were not connected to the ones near to the Hall. The first was 39yds wide and 160ft deep and the second was 20yds wide and 75ft deep. They drilled within days of my survey and found water at 66ft for the second vein and at 170ft for the first, which was near to my prediction.

After the unfortunate results of drilling through the gravel near the hall which collapsed in the borehole, and had been proved adequate in yield of water, there was only one thing to do. That was to locate water on another site. I moved about a half mile to the south of the estate and on to high ground to miss the danger of gravel. It was now very pleasing to me to find the prospect of a good result in a place that had advantage over site one. To find water on high ground meant it would gravitate to any part of the property, which has now proved an advantage having golf as the main enterprise.

Where the two veins crossed was an ideal place to drill the bore. I was not present at the drilling but in the evening I called at the borehole and had a most interesting experience. I knew that water was at two levels in my forecast, one 66ft down, and the other 170ft, quite a distance apart. I put my ear to the borehole and heard the wonderful sound of a gusher where the water from the 66ft vein was falling down to the level the water had risen to. It was a sound worth recording. The yield from the bore was test-pumped at 60,000 gallons per day, of very high-quality water.

As a strange coincidence, whilst I was writing for the book about Slaley Hall, I received another request to locate water for the Cleveland Golf Course at Redcar. On Tuesday, 5 January 1993, I made the round trip of 126 miles to Redcar to carry out this survey. Like all such trips to dowse, I cannot predict much about the site until the rod reveals its secrets. In that north-east part of Yorkshire, before it became part of Cleveland, I could only recall that there was a large area of sandstone underground making it more likely that we would find water in that porous rock. This club needed 7,000 gallons of water a day though more would have been welcome and as they already had a storage tank with power suitable for containing such a supply, that was where I started my survey. There was also a plan, proposed by Redcar council, to build on the site of the original clubhouse and site a new clubhouse between the golf course and the sea. I scanned the site to get the direction where the water lay and within a minute I was on my way towards the water vein. I am always interested in the first find on any site as it gives me a guide to the pattern that follows. I arrived at the edge of the vein and onwards to find that it was 33yds wide and my immediate thought was: If there is no other, this will certainly do! I crossed the course and from where I was standing, I could see the 7,000-gallon tank and the vein looked to be running very near. I depthed the vein and it measured 129ft deep; my next task was to see how near to the storage tank the vein actually ran. By good fortune, the vein passed under the tank and this was another point in its favour. I marked two points to drill and these can be seen on fig. 3. After this, I went to the area of the proposed new clubhouse and found a second vein better than the first at 36yds wide and 120ft deep and running under the site of the proposed clubhouse.

The two sister veins have many similarities; the earth faults are side

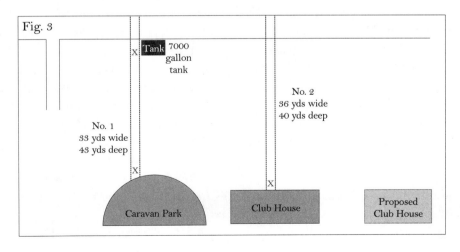

by side and of similar depth and yield potential. it is not often that you find veins where you want them but on this occasion the drilling points could not have been better positioned. Cleveland Golf Course has been in existence for over one hundred years and a very high percentage of its members play regularly; certainly whilst I was there it was Ladies Day and very well attended. Apparently, because it is so close to the sea they hardly ever lose a day to bad weather and members of golf clubs in the surrounding area come to Cleveland when their own clubs are closed.

During the 1980s there was a considerable increase in the number of farms resorting to irrigation, particularly in the eastern side of Britain where the rainfall is much less than other parts of the country. It came as no surprise therefore to be asked down to Berkshire for another assignment and I assumed it was for crop production. I hoped the weather would be kind for the long journey of over 300 miles and, on trips such as these, I always take my wife with me and our friends, Eric and Nell Christopher; the ladies can go shopping in pastures new and Eric helps me by carrying my marking canes whilst I dowse the site. We planned to stay overnight in Windsor, but even in February the town was booked up and we stayed over the river in Eton instead. At 10.30 the next day, I met the estate manager, Charlie Bullen, and after looking at the plans of the estate, I formed a strategy for the impending survey. My curiosity was aroused on learning that the water was not for crops but for polo greens and paddocks. As it had rained quite heavily overnight, gumboots were needed by the morning and I was not far from the estate office when I picked up my first sign of water. A strong pull of the rod led me over the grass to site No. 1 on the survey. When I came to the edge of the vein, Eric marked it with a cane and after thirty strides I reached the other side of the vein. It depthed at 120ft and I felt that with such a good start I should try and find if there were any veins that crossed over or under this one. I had not walked very far before my wish was granted and No. 2 measured out to be 32yds wide and 150ft deep. Charlie Bullen put in the stake that marked the middle point of both veins and I was very pleased to have found two good veins with such potential.

The remaining part of the survey was to assess the water supplying the two large ponds, a field apart. Charlie Bullen wanted to know whether the water could be used to irrigate the land near to the ponds i.e. where the water came from, and how much of it was available. Using my normal technique, I located a vein of water 11yds wide running 45ft under the first pond. The second pond also had a vein 11yds wide and 45ft deep running under it and it is in my experience very rare to have such symmetry. Having marked out the points to drill in these fields too, a scheme could now be worked out to irrigate the green. The only unfortunate part of this dowse was that I was surveying out of season and so there was no polo to watch but there were plenty of polo ponies in the paddock, winter coats on, watching me!

Water for the Factories

In the mid-1990s, when water privatisation was the trend, the cost of water for factories rose sharply and during the low rainfall of 1995, many factories were restricted as to how much water they could take. In Yorkshire, some of the factories had their water supplies cut off entirely and several of my recent clients were affected by these shortages in this way. Factories making wool and fabrics or processing hides for the leather trade need large quantities of water and some of these have been forced to call in the services of a dowser to locate other sources. I say *forced*, as calling in a dowser is far more natural to county folk than those in the town. A real case of 'needs must when the devil drives'.

Since the shortages in 1995, I have been called to factory sites in Leeds, Bradford, Dewsbury, Halifax, Wakefield, Brighouse, Holbeck, Ossett and Normanton and it has always amazed me that such large yields of water have been found within the factory's boundaries. An example of this would be a factory in Leeds city centre where on my recommendation a borehole was drilled and a water yield of 288,000 gallons of water per day recorded.

Mineral Water for Bottling

On 12 October 1990 I received a telephone call from George Henderson Esq, of West Town Farm, Sorn, Mauchline, Ayrshire, for me to find a large supply of water with a view to going into the mineral water industry, and installing a bottling plant in his farm buildings. I agreed that I would go and do the survey, and that I would fix a date with him within the week.

The following day I received a letter from Prof. Cedric Wilson of Edinburgh, Chairman of the Scottish Society of Dowsers. Would I give a talk to the Society on Saturday the 3rd of November? After I had agreed with Prof. Wilson to go to Edinburgh on 3 November I called George Henderson and asked if it would be convenient to do the survey on the morning of 2 November, which was agreed.

It was a very fine autumn day with the colours of the trees at their best which made the journey to Sorn very pleasant, a distance of over a hundred miles.

Mr Henderson's plans were told to me but all important was where was the water and what was the quantity? I began my dowsing in the farmyard and was fortunate to find a good vein running under the farm buildings. I will call it No. 1. It was 30m wide and 102ft deep. With quantity being important I marked the vein at three places about 40m apart, to be able to drill three times on the same vein if it carried the best water for the purpose. Vein No. 2 was the spring that supplied the farm and was issuing a very good yield of clear water, but the point of issue was very high risk area for pollution because both cattle and sheep were drinking near the spring. My advice to overcome the problem and at the same time make use of the large quantity of water was to drill and take the water before it got to the point of pollution. So vein No. 2 was treated as an underground supply and measurements taken accordingly. It was 42m wide and 132ft deep. Four drilling points were marked on the vein, and the depth marked at each. It was very noticeable from the spring to the first depthing that water was being forced to the surface under pressure.

Vein No. 3 is unlikely to be related to 1 or 2. And when it comes to the time of testing the various waters for the quality looked for I hope it gives Mr Henderson a wide choice. The crossing point of 2 and 3 is a mark for drilling and will produce a blend of the two. That point should not be drilled until the others are fully valued. It could let 1 into 2 to disadvantage.

The National Trust

The National Trust own large areas of land throughout the British Isles and like many other landowners let their farms to tenants to farm the land.

In the Northumberland and Durham region there are many places of great beauty and interest to visit, such places as the Roman Wall, Wallington Hall, and areas of the Northumberland coastline with superb natural beauty. It is within the boundaries of such places that I have had the privilege and pleasure of locating water to supply farms and the Housesteads Roman Camp reception area, 2.5 miles north of Bardon Mill on the A69.

My first survey to find water for the National Trust was in August 1972, to supply a mainly stock farm in the heart of Northumberland one and a half miles north of Scots Gap. The main supply they were depending on was a well 16ft deep and yielding very little. I located a vein of water within the farmyard boundary, which was 10.5yds wide and 100ft deep and I forecast that the yield would be in excess of the requirement. I marked the point to drill and hoped that all would be well.

On 19 October I received a telephone call from the drillers that they had drilled beyond the predicted depth without water – what should they do? I replied saying I would come now and would be there in about half an hour. I arrived on site and first checked to make sure the drilling point had not been moved; it was correct. I rechecked the width to see if there was any change; it was as before. I next checked my depthing and found that my divining had wanted to go down at 33yrds. I decided to resist the node's desire to go down and carry on to where it did go down strongly at 180ft. I repositioned my findings to the drillers and advised them the water was still there but at a greater depth of 180ft or thereabouts.

I got word of the result within days, which was very satisfactory water found at 180ft and yielding 7,000 gallons per hour, sufficient to supply a village. From that day in 1974 I always resist the rod to make sure. I find at each change of strata there is a flick of the rod.

My second survey was near to the Roman Wall on 24 April 1974 at High Shield, Bardon Mill. I remember the day well as the time of the year when the lambs are born on the higher ground. The sun was shining with quite a lot of heat in it and the baby lambs were responding by basking in ecstasy in those early hours of life.

To meet me for the survey was a young agent fairly new to the National Trust. I felt sure he was a non-believer in the art of dowsing and he was soon to admit that by saying, 'You will find water anywhere if you drill.' To which I replied, 'If what you are saying is true, why waste your time and mine on this survey?'

I began my survey and quickly found a vein of water running under the farmyard. The site was later drilled and proved to be a satisfactory result with a good supply of water.

In June 1978 I did a survey to locate water at Housesteads, one of the more famous camps on Hadrian's Wall. It is reported by the tourist industry to be one of Britain's major attractions. The water was found very near to where it was needed at the entrance of the A69. The result of the drilling was a very good supply of water found and I am proud to boast that people from all parts of the world are drinking pure clear water found by my divining rod of over forty years.

Hot Bank and Bradley Hall are two farms near to the Roman Wall and Housesteads. On the day of my survey, 29 May 1985, I had arranged to meet the National Trust's building manager at Bradley Hall. When I arrived at the meeting point I was surprised to find David Leach, Agricultural Editor for the *Newcastle Journal.* He had heard all about the survey for underground water and asked Mr Glover if he could come and see what a dowser does to locate and mark out the place to drill.

The following is his report of the events of the afternoon in his words as published in the *Newcastle Journal* on Saturday, 1 June 1985:

Ganton Hall, Ganton, Scarborough

It was on the 25th April 1990 I received a telephone call from Mr Rigley owner of the Ganton Hall Agricultural Estate along with his other interests which included the running of an agricultural enterprise with his son in South America. He said he needed water for irrigation and he was looking for a dowser to assist him in locating an amount of water that would fit in with his needs. I said to Mr Rigley that I had located water for several schemes on the Eastern side of Britain and that I would be very pleased to carry out the survey and that I would telephone on Monday the 7th of May to fix a day suitable to us both for the survey. The date agreed was the 14th May at 10:00 a.m.

On a survey of this kind where I know before that it is for irrigation it can be quite demanding on both time and energy and with that in mind I thought it would be advisable to stay over night within a few miles of Ganton Hall, instead of travelling over one hundred miles before the dowse. Many times on such an occasion as this to stay over night I take my wife and a farming friend and his wife. The ladies will do some shopping and I have someone to carry my markers. It is a matter of combining business with pleasure, also company seems to shorten the journey.

We had stayed in Scarborough for the night and began the day refreshed, my friend and I arriving at the appointed time for the survey which looking at the plan of the farm and forming a plan of action. I thought it better not to plan too far ahead until we see what we find and if a pattern is forming in depth or quantity.

We boarded the Range Rover and planned to travel through the farm on a farm track which nearly crossed all the land in an East-West direction. I would do my dowsing from the front passenger seat and on arrival at any influence of a water vein we would stop and I would do three things − establish direction of flow, potential yield and depth to water. I would make notes of all that could be of value which would go onto a plan of the farm for assessment at the end of the survey. At this early stage of the day I was pleased to find that Mr Rigley was a believer in the art of dowsing and that his faith in it was strengthened by the use of it in South America where a good water supply was so important in the ranching of large herds of cattle.

I am now at the point where the first sign of water is felt and the dowsing rod is telling me we are approaching water and could we stop. I appointed my rod towards it and the rod went down to show me what direction to walk to meet it at right angles. I now know direction of flow. I now walk to the edge of the vein, the rod firmly dips and goes down; that point is marked. I walk over the vein stepping out in metres and you come to the other side which you mark and record it in your notes. On this one on my notes it is my No. 1 the width is 50m (each step as I walk being a metre). I then walk on to where my rod goes down again, which equals the depth at 45: the depth of my No. 1 is 189ft a very good start to the survey. The following will not give details as in No. 1 method. A plan of all sites will be shown when complete. And a X at point to drill. Site No. 2 was not so heartening but worthy of recording – it was 28m wide and 132ft deep. If at the end of the day and you knew more about the others which are to come you may discard No. 2 but not at this early stage of the survey.

Site No. 3 was marked on a vein of water 60m wide, and 210ft deep. No. 4 was on a vein 34m wide and 112ft deep. Site No. 5 was 70m wide and 189ft deep. This one has a very good potential to yield a large quantity. No. 6 was again good measuring 68m wide and 180ft deep. No. 7 25m wide no depth taken. No. 8 another good vein 68m wide and 159ft deep. A pattern is now forming with large quantities of water available. For the next survey we are crossing over the Malton to Scarborough Road to see what was available on the north side. Site No. 9 ran under the road and could be drilled at both sides whichever side it was needed. It was 42m wide and 135ft deep. Site No. 10 was a vein 53m wide and 150ft deep. Site No. 11 was 62m wide and 246ft deep. Number 11 was the only one that the flow line was different also the depth to be such deeper strata. As these two veins crossed and were both good the drilling point was marked where the midstream of both crossed.

There were sufficient sites marked to make our a scheme for irrigation in the fertile valley of the River Derwent which rises on the Whitley Moors flows south through West Ayton, then westward to Malton. Ganton Hall with its farms and land lies between the River Derwent to the north and the sharp rising chalk hills of the Yorkshire Wolds. The land in the valley is starved of surface water hence the reason to install a scheme to irrigate. When looking at the plan of the different veins of water and their flow lines it stands out that the water is flowing out from under the chalk hills.

On the 21st June 1990 I received a telephone call from Mr Rigley of Ganton Hall requesting me to return to Ganton Hall. He felt that he was spending many thousands of pounds on this scheme and he wanted to get it right. Also that he had consulted with one of Britain's senior geologists who was willing to come to Ganton Hall on the same day that agreed to be there. We agreed that meeting to be the 24th June at 2:00 p.m.

On the 24th June we met as arranged. I was introduced to Mr

J. A. Hawley (geologist). I was delighted to find his willingness to work with a dowser. Mr Hawley said a geologist could indicate the area to expect to find water but the dowser had the ability to pinpoint the site to bore.

Mr Hawley's advice to Mr Rigley was to go up onto the chalk hill which he thought would enhance the chance of getting more but it will need the dowser to find it.

My plan of action was now simple. I had all my facts to work on from my first visit. The map showing the choice veins which were coming out of the chalk. At this time we were still in Mr Rigley's office. I explained what my views were. No. 3 and No. 5 were the choice veins of the survey which ran from under the chalk. When we get onto the top of the chalk hill, I will hope to find both and mark them. We journeyed alone through the farm land passing the places that I dowsed at the previous visit and now to climb about five hundred feet to the top of the chalk. I had a fairly good idea of my bearings I thought whichever of the ones I found before would tell me where I am on the map. As we travelled over the chalk hill, I felt the pull of water and asked to stop. I got out, found the edge, walked across and the width was that of number five being 70m. I found midstream and we marked the place to bore. The depth from the hilltop was considerably deeper than number five in the valley. I now knew where to look for number three and within minutes I found it and identified it and marked the drilling point at midstream. This survey had so many different experiences that it should be one that was listed to go onto record.

Chapter III

The Failures

 HE QUESTION is bound to arise, sooner or later: 'Do you have failures?' The direct answer is yes, and I doubt if any man could be 100 per cent correct and remain so.

My concern about failure is to see what went wrong, learn by my mistakes and not pass them by but say what a dowser said to me: 'We are bound to get failures.' I am not lying down to failures – there are known causes for them:

1. When clay is being drilled through at the time of sinking a well it affects the depthing and the direction. Where clay is considerable allow quite a lot more on the depth prediction.

2. Wishful thinking can trick a dowser, for example if you listen to a client who tells you where pipes and drains are and a dowser said it was there, this you must be beware of. It is better not to accept any information until after the dowsing survey is complete.

3. Inexperience – if for this reason you should not be dowsing. I know that experience is the great teacher but not at the expense of others. The average cost today of sinking a bore is about £5,000. No dowser is going to be willing to claim himself to be an able dowser without a success rate. It is a hard climb. 'Success will breed success.' Creep before you walk is a must with dowsing. I have had failures and if you have a conscience you will not let a person spend his time and money to improve your knowledge.

For the benefit of dowsing this could be the most important chapter in the book for a dowser to declare his failures and passion to others hard-earned experience that may cushion the effect of others.

Failures happen with drillers too. I have many times been to dry boreholes and never have I found one over water. I have seen at least three which have been within three feet of a vein of water. There have been dry boreholes where I was called in to mark a site for a second drilling and where water was found.

I have also followed other dowsers where the vein chosen to drill was very inferior to other veins on the site and would have been a failure. This is not good dowsing. The dowsers in this category should not mark sites when they are not water dowsers.

In 1953, after I had found many water supplies successfully I came up against my first failure, which was very hard to live with. It was important to me to know more about the cause. A house was being built on the outskirts of Kendal, in Westmorland at this time, now in Cumbria since the boundary changed.

I had heard about the risk of dowsing in limestone and where other dowsers had failed. Maybe this one was lost cause before I begun. On my first survey of the site I found that a dowser had been there before me and a large hole was dug into solid limestone, about 18ft deep and dry. Looking back I should not have taken on the challenge. The hole was not on water to me and was 10ft away from a vein on the strength of the vein being there and not as deep as 18ft. I advised the owner, a Mr Crabtree, to dig from the inside of the wall 10ft and he should find the fissure with water in it.

I wrote a letter about the well to the geological survey office at Manchester and received the following reply:

E. Taylor Esq.   Geological Survey Offices
                                         Manchester, 13
                                         6th March

Dear Sir,

Well 1.5 miles SW, of Kendal

At the above site there may be several hundred feet of limestone, underlain by a basement conglomerate resting on the Kirkby Moor flags. Water if any will be restricted to fissures in the limestone and these are most likely to be water bearing towards the base where saturation conditions may reveal.

If the well already made has been a failure it is most unlikely that conditions will be much different 10 feet to the north of it. The water supply prospects at this site are poor but it would require a banchable several hundreds of feet deep to test the site properly.

Hoping this information will help you.
Yours faithfully, John R. Corp
Principal Geologist

In a letter to the British Society of Dowsers at the time of the Kendal well I read the following with interest:

A survey at Kendal on limestone. On my first visit I marked out a place showing the vein. when I was asked to go again the influence had changed being three feet less.

I can now answer this question. Six years ago at a farm in the North Tyne Valley where I had been to eleven years before (I keep all my notes), at that time a particular vein was 7yds wide; on the visit of six years ago it was one yard wide in a very dry period.

I bear out the facts of the Kendal limestone which would be unsafe to rely on. I became very much wiser through being involved with the Kendal well and other dowsers take heed.

In October 1985 I was asked to find a water supply for Mr Rodger who lives in Melrose in Southern Scotland and farmed near the town of Selkirk. I did the survey and found a vein of water 25yds wide and 129ft deep. Prospects looked good by the measurements. Shortly after I heard that the drilling had been a failure with a dry bore. My response to the information was a telephone call to Mr Rodger saying I wanted a satisfied customer and that I would journey to Selkirk to see the reason why.

It was so important to me to find out what had gone wrong. I went prepared to depth it again, and see that the drilling was done where I had marked midstream on the vein. All was as should be by my record book. I lowered a small steel weight tied to a fine cord down the bore and when it touched the bottom of the bore I put a knot in the cord at ground level, drew it out, laid it out on the ground, stepped along the cord and found that it was not down to the water. Mr Rodger was a farmer, a builder and well driller. It was not difficult for him to return to the bore and go deeper.

Had I not returned to that failure to correct it in my book it would have remained on the failure list. Since the redrilling of Mr Rodger's No. 1 I have marked the site for twenty-five successful boreholes which have been drilled by Mr Rodger's machines.

I had an experience where the driller had gone beyond my depthing and were going to give up and pull out. I went to the drilling, and checked that everything was as it should be. In my method of depthing, by walking away from the vein of water when you have travelled the same distance from the vein as the vein is from the surface, the rod will go down. I have also found in that distance, while depthing at the changes of stratas, there is a pull on the rod. I reached my depthing and tried to resist the point of the previous one; it did work and the prediction of depth was now 30ft deeper and found the water at that depth yielding 168,000 gallons of water per day. Not accepting failure paid off again. The farm was the property of the National Trust for whom I have found several good supplies since. If that first one had remained a failure the other drilling may not have been done.

Stand Hill was a dairy farm situated between Jedburgh and Melrose, a very fertile and well-farmed unit corning very good quality limestone. A mains water supply was in use on the farm which was becoming more and more costly especially with the likelihood of change in the Law of Scotland.

Mr Shanks, the farmer, thought a borehole would be a great saving. I did the survey and found prospects of a very good yield of water. The drilling was done and he telephoned to say he had not hit water. I returned to the farm to find that the drilling had been done to my estimated depth and he called it a day. I was very disappointed about his decision not to go a little further. This one remains a failure.

Three years ago I had done a scheme similar to the one at Stan Hill which proved a saving of nearly £3,000 per year on water charges.

Harry Lund was dairy farming in the West Riding area of Yorkshire. He lived at Spinning House Farm, Bolton by Bowland. He called in a Yorkshire firm of well drillers for advice on sinking a borehole. When Mr Lund asked them about having a dowser, their reply was that he did not need one.

The drillers were given approval to do the drilling and the borehole was sunk to over 200ft resulting in a dry bore. I was called in urgently because the drilling machine was still on site. My services were needed and I responded to the urgent call and agreed to do a survey on Thursday, 9 November 1989. On arrival I checked the dry bore to see if water was there. In my view there was no water under that bore.

The next task was to do the survey on ground near to the farm and in easy reach of electric power. I found my No. 1 vein near to the farmhouse, measuring 18yds wide and 100yds deep. My No. 2 vein ran under the farm buildings and was 12yds wide and 130ft deep. These two veins did cross not far from the dry bore. I now felt more confident in marking out the point to drill with two chances to find water at two levels. I then wished Mr Lund good luck and travelled home.

Two days later I received a telephone call from Mr Lund saying the men had stopped drilling and pulled out. All they said was that they did not want to waste any more of his money. It was very puzzling for me to understand the thinking of the drilling foreman when it was on their advice in the first place. I knew Mr Lund was keen to see the result and so was I. Over the next day or two I did think a lot about the driller's motive to pull out when the prospects were good. It would have been very embarrassing to the drilling foreman to be succesful on my advice after he said he did not need a dowser. We will never know. Sadly Mr Lund was the loser.

Forestry Commission

It was on 6 April 1967 I received the following letter from the Area Land Agent of the Forestry Commission.

E Taylor   Hexham, Northumberland
                                                            6th April 1967
                                              Slaley Forestry Water Supply

Dear Mr Taylor,

I wonder whether you would be able to help us locate an auxiliary water supply in Slaley Forest, about five miles south of Hexham. Present supply to our properties is rather unreliable and it would be helpful if we could feed from another source.

If you could come over perhaps you would like to suggest a date and time to meet at this office.

Yours sincerely
R Raban-Williams

Monday 10th April was the day we agreed to meet at Saley Post Office and then go on to Low Trygill Farm. I heard from Mr Raban-Williams what scheme he had in mind. He told me what a poor supply it was and realised the Forestry Commission would have to spend a sizeable amount of money to get a reliable supply, so could we go onto higher ground to see what we could find.

I knew by our conversation that he did not expect some easy solution was out there, as there would be new pipes to lay, new tanks to build, and it was quite possible that there would be a borehole to sink to get the quantity. I said at this stage of the survey I always check the present supply to make sure there is no more water in the spring.

We then went to where the spring was rising and it looked hopeless. I then tried my divining rods over the vein and I saw signs of more water there than they were getting out. I then advised before going to further expense to get a man with a spade and follow the water into the ground for about four feet to make sure what was there. He put a man to dig but at 3 p.m. that day I was not near to the telephone – the message was: 'Have dug in and it is dry'. It was one hour later I got the message and jumped in my car to head for Slaley Forest. On arrival I crossed some woodland to get to the spring and in the ditch was water flowing 4ft deep and 6ft wide. It had burst out after he telephoned.

When the yield of the spring was measured at Low Trygill, Slaley Forest, it was over 10,000 gallons per day at a depth of 5ft.

On 9 November 1970 I received the following letter from Mr R. Raban-Williams, Area Land Agent for the Forestry Commission.

West View
Bellingham
Northumberland
7th May 1970

Mr Taylor
    Shotley Bridge

Hamsterley Forest Water Supply

Dear Mr Taylor,

You may recall that you very kindly helped us with finding water supplies at Work Forest and Slaley Forest about three years ago. I wonder whether you would be able within the next few months to spare us a day to see if you could locate supplies at our Hamsterley Forest which lies about four miles south of Walsingham. The existing supplies are from springs in the forest and these are in some ways inadequate and I was hoping that we might either get an increased quantity from the existing springs, or possibly locate new springs.

I would mention that the improved supply that you divined for us at Slaley has been highly successful and we have had no water shortage since then.

Yours sincerely
R Raban-Williams.

The dowsing for spring water was surveyed during the first week of June 1970 and I received the following letter:

E Taylor Esq,

West View
Bellingham
8th June 1970

Hamsterley Water Supply

Dear Mr Taylor,

Many thanks for such an interesting and worthwhile day last week.

I have now been working out the most effective and cheapest methods of getting a good supply of water to all the various properties but very stupidly I did not take any notes of the quantities available.

If possible could you tell me what the estimated quantity would be at:

1. The spring on the Church Commission land – I think you said about a half a million gallons a day.

2. The spring at present supplying Bedburn Camp. You said that we should strike the main flow of water at a depth of 9 feet. Do you think we could intercept this if we dig down two or three yards to one side of the present spring – if we dug where the

water is coming up at the moment it will mean a very muddy supply at the camp.

3. The proposed Caravan site field where you estimated a depth of between 41 and 51ft.

Provided there is sufficient quantity the cheapest way of connecting all properties would be from the present camp supply which would only mean digging 9ft and laying not a very great length of pipe to supply both the Camp and the Holdings and the Caravan Site. I am in any case having this analysed for purity.

Yours sincerely,
R Raban-Williams.

The Bedburn Camp spring was dug and water was found at 8ft yielding 50,000 gallons a day. A very satisfactory result without any great expense.

The success of my dowsing in the early link with the Forestry Commission led on to my connections with many later schemes, several at the time building the Kalder Reservoir where many farm supplies were destroyed and had to move to higher ground for new sites. It seemed very odd for a water diviner to be called in on the site of Britain's largest man-made lake.

The Forestry Commission are the principal owners of the land where Kielder Water is sited, also its surrounding area which is the large expanse of Kielder Forest. In the upheaval of building Kielder Water the farmers on the dam site were tenants of the Forestry Commission and many water supplies to farms and other householders were disturbed. New springs of water were to be found and I spent many days dowsing on foot, and many times from the passenger seat of a Land Rover where longer distances were to be travelled.

Chapter IV

Dowsing on the Island of Lismore

O N 2 AUGUST 1984 I received a telephone call from Ian Thornber with a request to find water for several drillings on the island of Lismore, an island ten miles long and two to three miles wide in places. I agreed to consider and speak to Mr Thornber within a week.

Mr Thornber telephoned on 11 September with the ferry times from Oban to Lismore and in that conversation we fixed a date to meet – 9.50 a.m. on 17 September on the pier for the Oban crossing. Miss Stewart of the Rural Development Council for Lismore was to join us and would I contact her on a Lismore number which was done on the following day. There was much concern at my home prior to this appointment, which meant a journey of 524 miles to Oban and return.

The date to do the dowsing was now agreed and when hearing the national weather forecast for that week it was mainly for rain and gale force winds – not good news for a crossing from Oban to Lismore. For better or worse I decided I should take the risk and do the journey with my wife and two friends Mr & Mrs Christopher.

From the north-east of England to Oban there are many different ways to travel, but on this occasion I chose Carlisle – Erskine Bridge – Glasgow – Torbet – by Loch Lomand – Lochgilphead – Oban. I will say that on the journey the weather was kind to us. We settled in for the night knowing the time of the ferry next morning and that there was not one to follow.

Next morning was fine, the sun was shining and all was as planned. The ladies would stay to shop in Oban at shops they had been to before on a different mission attending the October cattle sales which included the famous highland cattle from many of the outer Islands.

Eric Christopher and I walked to the ferry on a morning that was like summer. We were on time and all was well, but we still did not know if the weather man had something in store. We set sail and the sea was like a millpond – it was not possible to have expected such favourable conditions and we were very grateful.

On the crossing Mr Christopher asked me if I had ever tried my divining rod on water, not meaning the water we were sailing on. I had not done this before and I was pleased the question had been put. Many times over my years of dowsing I have done dowsing while travelling in a Land Rover or a car and I was most interested to find what the reaction would be in a boat. The boat was not travelling at a high speed and I found it quite simple to make a comparison to what I had been doing out of a vehicle on land. To my surprise I found we crossed underground veins of water under the sea as if water was not there. This must be an interesting piece of information to other dowsers.

We arrived at the Lismore pier on time and were met by the promised delegation of Mr Ian Thornber who had made the request, Miss Stewart representing the Rural Community Council for Lismore and a person driving a Land Rover.

The plan as to where I would begin had been thought out by Mr Thornber and we drove to the south of the island to Mid Farm, farmer Mr McCall. On entering the farm I was stopped by an American lady who was writing a book on the Island of Lismore and was I the dowser who had come to mark out a number of wells and would I mind if she took photographs of my dowsing. I was pleased to say yes to that request.

Travelling down from the pier to Mid Farm I was beginning to get the real reason for me being on the Island of Lismore to find water for so many farmers and householders. Ian Thornber, whose invitation had brought me there, is a director in a company which was opening a roadstone quarry at Glensanda in sight of the people of Lismore looking across Loch Linnhe to the west. The gift of drilling to find water supplies for the farmers and others living on the Island was a kind gesture and would hopefully sweeten any opposition that might come in the way of the Glensanda Quarry project. I was sure this would be a welcome gift to the islanders who would know the value of water.

It was to be a long day and time was limited by the ferry so I made a good start by finding a vein of water 12m wide and 78ft deep. It was near to the farm and a site was marked providing a good access for the drilling.

The number of sites to dowse was given to me as eight but as I progressed the postman who was on the list for the drillings put into motion his bush telegraph system and before we boarded the boat for the return journey another six sites had been added to the list. If I had stayed overnight I am sure the number would have doubled.

The very fine weather stayed with us to the last minute. The veins in all directions were outstanding with the hills of the mainland in the distance a sight to see. It was so unbelievable for us to be so fortunate when Sunday's weather forecast for the week had been so atrocious. Now when I look back on the telephone call I made to Miss Stewart on the island two days later I was told on the following day to our visit the gales were so severe the ferry was cancelled. Within a week I sent the following letter to Ian Thornber:

On 19 October 1992 I telephoned Miss Stewart, who was at the time of my dowsing representing the Rural Community Council, to say I had never heard the result of my dowsing on Lismore. I asked in her opinion how she would rate the end result and she said very satisfactory.

Chapter V

By Word-of-Mouth Recommendation

Y FAMILY TREE reveals details of six generations before me and two after. All have been deeply involved in the world of agriculture and still are today in dairy, beef cattle, sheep and a cereal acreage of over 2,000 acres, being very conscious of the well-being of the countryside such as a planting of trees, both hard woods and conifers. In this chapter I would like to centre my thoughts and reference to the latter part of my early life, when I was introduced to water dowsing.

I could not enter that field as a business, because my commitments were too great in an established farming enterprise. The great interest I developed in dowsing became my main hobby, where weekends, holidays and evenings were the times I entered into and developed into a word-of-mouth experience which has given great joy to my wife, Anne, and myself. The places it has taken us to, the people of all walks of life over the length and breadth of the British Isles over a period of forty-nine years, and the challenge of dowsing for water on a site for cottage or factory – the interest is as strong today as at the beginning.

The pattern of contact is quite interesting. On the Hexham and Haltwhistle and surrounding area Ordnance Survey Landranger No. 87 there are 151 sites dowsed and distinctly show up as groups where one client has told his neighbour. The word-of-mouth contact applies also with well drillers in that area.

If the success rate was not very high my dowsing ability would have failed a long time ago. Even today in my seventy-eighth year of life every dowsing adventure has all the differences where, like the face of man, there are never two alike. It is not surprising when you think of the odds against. I have forty-two different kinds of client who can be living in any point of the British Isles, their needs are all different in quantity required. Ninety-five per cent of those who need the services of a water dowser will be experiencing a once-in-a-lifetime experience. If one could call it a profession, no other business could have such variation in clientele from one to the next.

If I had not been committed to agriculture, a life in well drilling would have been a likely alternative. Having a gift of the ability to locate underground water by dowsing and knowing the depth and quantity available would have given me an advantage in giving quotations to clients.

Dumfries and Galloway
area of South-West Scotland

There are changing trends in the demand for the skills of a water dowser. To demonstrate this trend I have chosen the area of Dumfries and Galloway in South-West Scotland, with its beautiful unspoilt countryside, and enjoying the lovely warm air of the Gulf Stream. One of my farming clients living on the Stranraer peninsula has a son twenty-one years of age who has never seen snow lying on their farm in the span of his life.

I have chosen this delightful area to illustrate the demand from dairy farmers who use a considerable amount of water and in the mid-1980s when water charges were rising, this section of farmers realized it would be worthwhile going into the costs of sinking a borehole, and that it would be advisable to engage a water dowser to see how much water was available.

Now in the 1990s and looking back ten years it has proved a worthwhile exercise.

I would like to refer to a paragraph from a book published in 1983 by Dick A. Richardson, *Water, Thank God – Adventures of a Dowser.*

Dick A. Richardson was born in 1913 in County Durham in the North of England. His father was Welsh and his mother Scottish. He says he took a ship for Canada in February 1928, where he logged in the winter and farmed in the summer, and settled in Loudoun County, Virginia.

In his book he makes reference as follows:

I must make an effort and write these fellows. P. B. Smith, (Secretary, British Society of Dowsers) wrote me a nice letter and sent some literature. I remember an article by Edwin Taylor, Esq. of Northumberland and County Durham. My home area. I had occasion to visit his farm and see some of his grand cattle. I notice he is now a member of the Council of the British Society of Dowsers.

Dick Richardson being a local man from my own county, I can only give him high praise for the contents of his book. He is in the same style of dowsing as myself over many years. Practical thinking with a good end result.

The Budding Dowser

It was on 6 September 1996 that I attended the British Society of Dowsers Annual Congress at Glasgow, where I was taking a workshop on water dowsing on the Saturday afternoon at 2.00 p.m. There is always a great interest from people in all stages of their learning, trying to add to their knowledge from one who has 'trodden the road before' – forty-eight years of it.

On this occasion in the hall where the water dowsers had gathered there was one person stood out from the others. I could see enthusiasm in her actions, sat with pencil and paper at the ready while the remainder of the class sat relaxed.

The will to get on in this young lady reminded me of my approach to things in my life where I wanted to achieve and brought back to me the source of my thinking which was when, as a Young Farmer, the club leader gave me the advice: 'If you want to succeed, get enthusiastic about it.' That advice has stayed with me, and I notice it in others, as on this occasion. It makes one want to help.

After my address, and the many questions, we proceeded to the practical dowsing on the lawns of the university. I found an underground vein of water to see how many of the BSD members were able to pick up what I was finding with my whalebone V rod. The V rod is the rod most suitable for water dowsing – when it begins to pull you can resist it going down until you get to the edge of the vein if you use a pendulum. As angle rods they would respond too soon giving a wrong reading.

The workshop went on to 4.30 p.m. half an hour longer than planned, but it proved the interest was strong. At this final stage of the workshop, Dr Pauline Roberts, the enthusiastic lady I referred to earlier, asked if I knew of a dowser who could do a survey for a water supply on the farm where she lived. I said, yes, my second grandson, Elliot James Taylor, who was in his second year at Wye College, in Kent, and travelled home to Northumberland via the A10 in Hertfordshire where Dr Roberts lived. The plan worked out that Elliot did the survey and marked the point to drill for water. Like myself, dowsing came naturally to Elliot. He travelled with me to dowse on farms and factories, one in particular, a leather factory, in Leeds where he and I dowsed the site, and found two veins, both good! We marked the point where they crossed with great success, test pumping yielding 288,000 gallons per day.

After the B.S.D. Congress was over Elliot dowsed the site at Heath Farm, through Dr Pauline Roberts. Also while at Glasgow I talked to Pauline of my link with the Agricultural Training Board in Northumberland, and Cumbria, by taking a small group of interested dowsers.

I agreed to give a day's training at the advanced level to assess what I thought the prospects would be. I knew of Pauline's willingness to try, and I could see at Glasgow she was a natural. A day was fixed for 5 December 1996 at 10.00 a.m. at Mosswood Farm, in South Northumberland. The basic aim of the training was to stress the important of being able to use the V rod – until that is mastered there can be no progress.

I confirmed my thinking that Pauline was a natural in the top 8 per cent by the way she mastered using the V rod, which allowed me to make progress on the days of the initial lessons. Homework in my view was an important part of the teaching: locate veins of water, make notes of the veins you find – they are all different in width and depth. It is these measurements that give potential of yield and cost, and help to build a picture in your mind so that it becomes more interesting.

To sum up Pauline's first lesson: I was very content progress was made, and hopefully there would be further success. I felt there would be.

The second lesson for Dr Pauline took place at Mosswood and some neighbouring farms farmed by my family on Friday, 26 March 1997. I asked Pauline to find a vein of water to do some measurements. She scanned the area and picked up the one I wanted. She walked towards it, the rod went down on the edge and she walked across counting her steps. She now got out her notebook and wrote in it: 9yds wide. She continued walking still counting, starting at one until she came to the depthing point at 33yds, again put in the notebook. Next was to find the direction of flow by standing at mid-stream on the vein and beginning to walk – there are two different responses. If you are facing into the flow of water, the rod dips instantly, whereas if you walk with the flow the rod dips after two steps. Make a little plan in the notebook – pulling direction of flow. Where the vein was running it was quite steep downhill giving an opportunity to see the difference of the depthing as you went down the hill. This part of the exercise was for experience.

Finding an old well was next on the list. It was at Wallish Walls Farm. I remember the old pump which was hand-operated and, like so many now, filled in and out of date. These old wells were nearly always found at the back door of the farmhouse, because the well was found before the house was built. To find an old well, find the vein of water generally six to eight yards wide, and walk along mid-stream if the rod goes down. If the rod goes down and then goes down again after three steps you could be in with a chance.

Dowsers have been called into measure the contents of a gravel deposit either on a river bed or from glacial drift. The method was practised by Pauline and myself on a riverside field at Allensford. The method used: from standing still, count your steps as you walk forward. If the rod goes down an eighth you can do a sum and calculate the value per acre $4840 \times 8 \times £25.00$ and you're in business.

We were going to do two farm sites as they approached me as a practical dowser – quite a test for any dowser and more so to a dowser who is not acquainted with agricultural needs.

Highfield Farm was just over 700 acres, a mixed farm with sheep, cattle and mainly under the plough. The sheep flock of over 700 breeding ewes was housed in winter to early April for lambing.

What the dowser needs to know about the water storage area is where the power point is to lift the water from the borehole to the storage. If a farm has some high ground where a storage tank can be built and then can gravitate to any part of the farm, the dowser is well advised to be as near to the power point as possible to sink a borehole. Having studied the above facts, Pauline and I together began the survey near to the power point and very soon we both picked up a vein of water on site and proceeded to measure its value. We were fortunate to find one so good and near to the farm, 60m wide and 83m deep. While doing the survey we got an audience. A police car stood on the roadside; after a while curiosity got the better of the police officer who drove onto the site. I do not think he understood the meaning of the word dowsing.

Fairley May Farm is much less being 180 acres but still needed the same procedure of beginning with a scan of the near 200 yards to see what was available. Both Pauline and I picked up the same two veins at this stage, not knowing their value, but we would soon find out. I was so impressed at the conclusion of this site dowse that I said to Pauline, 'I think you are there now.' I could now see the confidence was shining through. I could also see my reward in guiding Pauline along the road I had followed in my own dowsing career.

On 21 April 1997 I received a letter from Brian Jellyman whose business is based in Bath, Avon and on two previous occasions I have successfully dowsed water for his clients. He asked if I could dowse for water on five sites in the North Yorkshire area: a golf club and a dye works at Huddersfield, a transport company in Brighouse, a glass factory in Doncaster and another factory in Chesterfield.

When I was planning out the journey and the order of work to be done, I thought this would be the ideal occasion to invite Dr Pauline Roberts to join me on the survey to round off her training doing some real dowsing with a real end result. So I called Dr Roberts with my suggestion, she was very excited with the prospect and was willing to come along. But she was only able to be free on the Monday when I had arranged with Mr Jellyman to dowse three sites. I felt that would be sufficient. Pauline and I agreed to meet at Sunday lunchtime in the North Yorkshire area with a view to having a trial dowse before Monday to brush up on past training. This venture was still part of the training course for Dr Roberts which was nearing its final stage. I would now like to write a report on the progress to the end of April 1997.

Pauline, like myself, had the advantage of being a born dowser, where the dowsing instrument responds without great effort. I would say she is one of the top 8 per cent of dowsers, where the instruction is guiding the pupil in the right direction. My job as the tutor, and a successful dowser for so many years, is to get the pupil to follow my methods. I have also discovered so many short cuts which have saved a lot of time on any site I dowse, probably the most important of those being the ability to find veins of water from a distance, a further advantage being that you meet the vein at right angles.

Fortunately Pauline has the same ability. I had been dowsing many years before I discovered that valuable advantage.

On Sunday, 27 April 1997 Pauline and I drove into the Yorkshire countryside in search of a dowsing site to do a practice run. Pauline was the driver and being in a strange area took the wrong turn, which turned out to be a case of fate playing its part. We found the most beautiful site. It was Roche Abbey, largely in ruin, but the setting was second to none – it had been landscaped by Capability Brown.

The sun shone and it was a model site for our purpose of dowsing. After parking the car we entered the grounds of the Abbey and walked towards the entrance building with its large arches. At about forty metres from the entrance arches we both began to dowse by standing and doing a scan of the area of the arches, and both Pauline and I got a strong pull of our rods pointing to the arch. After walking about ten feet through the first arch, the rod went down which was the first edge of a water vein; when we reached the other edge of the water vein it was to an inch in line with the east wall of the building dating back to AD 1100.

We were so excited by the find, it seemed too good to be true that a water diviner had marked the site to build the arches. This was confirmed when we got to the main structure of the Abbey – a water vein was exactly under the outside wall as at the entrance. We also did some archaeological dowsing over the old foundations. I think we may have uncovered a piece of history linking dowsing with holy places.

On this trial run exercise Pauline's dowsing was equally as good as mine and put her in good stead for the site dowsing on Monday. There was a great deal of experience to be gained from all three sites dowsed on the day.

1. Harrison Gardner – dowsed by me two years before and yielding 60,000 gallons per day of beautiful clear water, where Pauline was able to trace my steps in picking it up as I did when I marked the point to drill. The purpose of this visit was to locate a second site for drilling. Pauline and I carried out the survey and found a vein

of water running parallel to the one drilled; it was 10yds wider and 50yds between the two. And the new site was marked for drilling.

2. Lightcliffe Golf Club, near Huddersfield, where the needs were 12,000 gallons per day. Standing on the car park facing the course we both scanned the area and both picked up a vein running E and W. Then picked up a second one running N and S. We each made notes in our separate notebooks as follows: No. 1 30yds wide and 78m deep, marked on two places (one where they cross). No. 2 28yds wide and 69m deep. The choice where to drill would have to be made by the club officials.

3. Marshalls Transport – when I dowsed this site two years before there had been a drilling done but it was of little value. I found two good veins on site, and marked both. On one the yield was good. On the other the drilling had been done in the wrong place, not near to my marking. We marked a point to drill with paint and made notes in our record book. The driller had not realized the importance of drilling where the dowser marks a site!

Chapter VI

The Healing Art and Dowsing

N MY EARLY teens I remember a farmer in the Tyne Valley, Northumberland who was the water diviner for the area, and in his later life he found he had the ability to heal among his friends and neighbours.

When I look back on my dowsing life as I write these lines it adds up to forty-eight years and in that time water dowsing has absorbed all the time I could spare other than my life in agriculture.

At times I wonder whether the 'Born Dowser' if given the time with his unique sensitivity could have been equally as successful as a healer. Why this comes to my mind was partly because of the farmer dowser in the Tyne Valley. When I look back to the years before my dowsing, maybe just one year before, a very interesting event took place which has remained unnoticed, and could now be interesting reading.

A very common infection in farming life where cattle were part of the daily way of life was a ringworm passed so easily from one to another, and also passed to the herdsman who looked after them. Cattle breeding and the existence of ringworm has gone on for hundreds of years and there were some farmers who possessed a magic cure, which was naturally held as a secret, and could only be passed on from male to female, the words to be passed on too. The reference to the operation was the 'Charming of Ringworm'.

Ringworm if caught by the human begins as a spot and grows in the form of a ring which grows by the day, reaches two inches across and spreads rapidly over the body where clothes are rubbing, such as on the neck or the wrist.

Doctors have not in the past found ringworm easy to cure. There were people in country districts that could 'charm' ringworm. My Uncle Robert Anderson, who lived at Mosswood Farm where I live at present, was one. This ability to charm or cure ringworm has been handed down for generations – Uncle Robert got it from his mother and it could only be passed down from female to male, or from male to female.

In the time of Uncle Robert's later years, when getting near to ninety years, his cattle man was smitten by a bad attack of ringworm. He at the time was bedridden and could not charm the ringworm. His wife, my Aunty Marney, was too frail to help. Because the sick man would have to bare his body he would prefer the charming be done by a male, and I was the person that he wanted the ability to charm ringworm to be passed on to. He being male, and I the same, looked to be an obstacle where the rule was to pass to the other sex, but with all the years of life and experience it was no problem. He would pass it on to my wife Anne, and she had to pass the secret to her husband. This was before I found that I could dowse for water and at that time there was no reason for me to think the two could be linked.

I got in detail my instructions on how to 'charm' the ringworm. And because of the urgency that it appeared to be according to the patient, for as yet I had not seen the extent of the sores; it was on the Saturday that I fixed our meeting for 4.00 p.m. on the Monday. We met at the given time on Monday when I asked Joseph to let me see the ringworm and he took off his shirt. I had never seen a person with so many rings on his back. The full area of his back from his neck down there must have been near to fifty, all different sizes.

I applied the treatment, doing it carefully over one and when I was satisfied that all had the treatment he put on his shirt and I asked him to come back at the same time on Wednesday, also saying to him, 'On no account wet the area that has been treated.' Wednesday soon came. I had no idea what to expect and off came the shirt. I looked with great care at each sore and was amazed to see that every one had begun to die, and it proved one hundred per cent successful. No more treatment was needed.

News spread locally about my success with the cure of ringworm and many people came to me for treatment, including children. One particular boy about eighteen years old with a large ring on his left cheek was having treatment from his doctor to no avail. I used my method of 'charming' with immediate response.

The medical profession of today, of course, are much more able to control the spread of ringworm, compared to fifty years ago.

Chapter VII

Hitting the National Press 1972

HAD PRESENTED a paper to the 1972 British Society of Dowsers Annual Congress at Cambridge and while at the Congress had talked at length with a fellow farmer dowser, W. G. Youngs, who lived in Norfolk. His dowsing ability included finding missing people, animals and lost property. So it was strange after talking to Mr Youngs that when I arrived home in Northumberland a letter was waiting for me asking me to assist in finding a lost wedding ring.

Fate has a habit of preparing one for situations like this. I had been by chance convinced by Mr Youngs at the Congress that it was possible to achieve such challenges; and on opening the letter with the request I could not refuse.

To look further into the personal side of our line with the Rowells, my wife Anne and I were godparents of Susan, the first child of Gordon and Sandra Rowell; we also travelled to Oban together to the Autumn Cattle Sales. It was at one of these sales that I purchased the West Highland cattle that I talk about in this book.

I telephoned Sandra Rowell to say I would look for her missing wedding ring and fixed a day to visit her that week. In preparation for my visit to take on a new challenge to find a lost object, my thoughts returned to the Cambridge Congress just days before, when I talked at length with W. G. Youngs on his success in finding missing people, lost objects and at times to help the police in searching for people who had gone missing in his area.

Armed with the knowledge that it could be done by Mr Youngs I set out for Birkenside Farm, two miles along the road. I began my dowse for the wedding ring in the lounge of the farmhouse and as an aid I asked Sandra for a small personal piece of something she wore, like an earring, to put in my hand while I dowsed.

My method was to rotate clockwise in a full circle and pick up a direction. I got a strong pull of my whalebone rod as I passed the window which looked out into the garden. No other direction was picked up in the full circle. The next move was into the garden and scan for direction, which I picked up immediately. I walked across the lawn in the direction the rod took me and came to a pile of garden refuse, on top of which were three sacks of garden weeds and rubbish. My rod pulled strongly down over the refuse heap.

Present at the scene were Sandra, Gordon, her husband, and two others of the farm staff to help if needed. The three sacks were emptied one by one and searched to no avail. I rechecked the remaining pile which had been under the sacks – my rod was still pulling down. Gordon was on his knees, carefully scratching his way through in search of such a small piece of gold. Suddenly Sandra shouted, 'It's there!' Gordon picked it up and the tears were running down Sandra's cheeks, tears of joy!

This story hit the National Press and I was inundated with requests to find missing gold rings from all parts. My time given to dowsing could not cope with an extra load of this size, and unfortunately I had to give up my search for gold.

Chapter VIII

The Pig Killing

N EIGHTEEN months' cycle is the lead-up to 'The Pig Killing Day', beginning at the birth of the baby piglet in the month of April or May. In this instance it was May.

The stages in its life are many, and so too are its keepers. Mainly farmers. I being a farmer will relate the story as I remember it in the mid-1920s before the days of fridge-freezers and modern techniques that have changed the pattern of life from placid, to the high-speed life of today with all the pressures brought about by the scientific methods of today, sixty-five years later.

The first change of life to the little baby piglet is when it is twelve weeks old and weaned from its mother from a litter of about eleven young pigs, ten of which will be sold as weaners for farm income, one gilt being selected to carry on the process from year to year.

It is now August and the gilt is fed on farmhouse scraps, buttermilk and meal ground from the grain on the farm up to the next stage in January when she is old enough to be mated to provide her contribution to the system. At this time we watch for signs of the gilt being in season with a view to walking the pig to the bore pig within the parish, maybe a distance of two miles, by tying a plough cord to its hind leg and guiding it on its journey. My father tells a tale when he was doing the journey in such an instance, when he met a male person returning from the local a little the worse of sense. When father was guiding the gilt past him he put his stick in the air, the gilt panicked, and the cord on the pig wrapped around his legs. Father being little more than a schoolboy at the time had never forgotten such an experience, and often related the event to me.

What was happening was part of country life and accepted as such. In the farming calendar there are many such instances that could be related to the way of life at the time.

We are now leading up to the period at the end of the month of April, sixteen weeks after the mating, which is the gestation period of the pig. All events of this kind on a farm are important and when a gilt is having her first litter then the risks are many. For example, if a baby pig squeals, the mother jumps up and when she lies down it could be on her baby piglets. And because of that risk when her due date comes, and a little before, it is worthwhile to sit with her over the birth.

There are signs when it becomes imminent, such as milk can be squeezed from the teats a few hours before. When she begins to give birth, keep a light burning. When the first piglet is born, you should have a helper to carry each one as they are born, put it in a little basket lined with a warm cloth, take it to the farmhouse kitchen, where the poss tub will be in front of the fire ready to receive them. The reason for taking away the piglet is to cut out any noise until the last piglet is born whereupon they should be returned to their mother to feed from the teats. After the last piglet is born the cleansings all come away and should match the number of piglets.

I recall an incident a year before when the sow got up and then lay down again quickly after, the result being she lay on three or four piglets which were dead and were buried in the stable midden. I was walking past the midden two or three hours later and found two little piglets running around – the heat of the horse manure had revived the piglets. Maybe there was a lesson to learn from such an experience!

Twelve weeks later the weaners are sent to market except the chosen one to play next year's part in the cycle. This day is also when the sow begins to be fed for that day in October called 'The Pig Killing Day'.

It is now late October and preparations are being made to fix a day with the local country butcher. And that same day is reserved by the family on the farm to share the various tasks, which is important in the farming family's calendar year. Events such as this register strongly in the young mind seeing all the hustle of the family. Boiling water is made ready with lines of pans, and kettles on the kitchen range for the butcher to shave off the hair. Black pudding is the first of the food items to be made by adding oatmeal, salt, seasoning and using old recipes handed down in farming families. About half of the black pudding is put in skins, like sausage, the remainder into dishes to cook in the oven, generally eaten with the sausage.

The Pig Killing

When the carcase has been shaved and washed it is hung up by the hind legs. It is now opened by the butcher to take out the liver, heart, bladder and small intestines to scrape for the sausage skins. After which it is left overnight to cool.

On the second day the carcase is cut up, beginning by cutting out the chain which is the backbone, including the tail, from tail end to the back of the head. The ribcage is now cut out from both sides and is ready to use as spare rib. The chain is also cut into joints, or the flesh is cut off to make into sausage meat.

Potted meat when home made has many advantages over that bought over a counter at a shop. There is not that desire to make it spin out into a larger quantity. The parts that go into potted meat are the trimming off the sides of bacon, a trimming off the hams, and by boiling the legs and any spare bones, spare meat from the chain, and meat and bones off the cheeks. When boiled and poured into bowls or dishes and it sets into a firm jelly.

Another interesting part of this little feast that is taking place is the rendering down of the fat from the inside of the ribcage of the pig. It is cut into slices or chunks of fat, placed in a roasting tin, put in the oven and at intervals poured into a container. There are some farmers who use the bladder of the pig to store the lard. As boys on the farm we used the bladder as a football. I once remember playing a prank on Old James. He was watching a cow very carefully that was over her due date. I played the prank by tying the pig's bladder to the top of the cow's tail and recall Old James hurrying into the farmhouse, shouting to Father, 'Boss, that cow's calving!' I sat very quiet for a while.

I will now come to the main purpose of the exercise that is to supply the farmhouse with bacon and ham for the span of one year. We are now reaching that final stage to salt the meat of the pig in a way to preserve it for that length of time.

It was a general rule in the countryside that only men's hands touched the ham or bacon to be pickled. Saltpetre was put into the bone joints, while coarse salt was mixed with about 20 per cent of brown sugar and rubbed in vigorously all over the flesh and the skin of all six pieces in the salt, two hams, two sides of bacon and two pig cheeks, which were then placed in a lead container once used for taking cream off milk.

There was a half inch of salt put in the bottom and two bacon sides placed on the bottom. On the bacon was laid the two hams and two pig cheeks laid at the side of the hams. Sugar and salt was sprinkled over, to remain untouched for a month. The pig cheeks are now ready to use and have a taste which is very pleasing.

The ham and sides of bacon will stay another two weeks and then be hung up in the kitchen to dry for four weeks before being put in the bacon box, taking out a week's supply to cut into slices with a sharp knife as needed. The taste of home-fed bacon is a treat with a taste of its own.

Sow and Her Litter

As a schoolboy of twelve or thirteen I was not always playing pranks on Old James. It was early in the month of May, the sow was due to give birth and traditionally a paraffin lamp was put in with her so that she could see her young and not tread on them, and at that final stage Old James had a look for any signs in the night – the real acid test as to what to look for is to squeeze a teat of the sow, and if milk is there the birth is within hours and not days.

On this night of the expected birth Old James took up position on night shift plus a noggin to keep him warm. The sow made it last a long time. I was anxious to see how the night had gone and made straight for the maternity ward, and to tell Old James his breakfast was ready if he was free to leave.

James had suffered a long night and breakfast would be a welcome change, so I volunteered to take over for breakfast time, which was willingly accepted. On his departure I suddenly became the midwife. I knew what to do, with a pair of scissors to cut the cord and steer the newborn round to a teat. I was in my glory, sadly at Old James's expense.

Fortunately it went like nature meant it to be. There was no noise, no complications, and it got to piglet eleven, which was the final one proved by the fact that the afterbirth followed. Whoever is there at the time counts the number of afterbirths to see if they match the number of piglets born.

I was so engrossed in my achievement on the day, I should have felt sorry for not remembering the feelings of Old James – and the way fate had played its part.

The Pig Killing Day

The pig killing day was not confined to farmers alone. It included cottagers, farm workers and allotment holders in an era of large families with a lot of household scraps, enough to feed a little pig.

On the farm, as I recall, it was an eighteen months' procedure, when a gilt was kept from a litter of about eleven baby piglets, which were sold at twelve weeks old, with the sow from that day being carried on for the ideal bacon pig having had one litter only and killed at eighteen months old in September or October, and having a good supply of bacon for the winter.

In the farming calendar of each year, during the 1920s and 1930s, and before that, generally in the month of October in readiness for winter, there was the pig killing day, and lots of tasty bites from the offal.

It was a time of plenty for a few days, all home-made from farmhouse recipes beginning with black pudding and not made up with biscuit meal; mince pies with fruit and minced pork; spare rib and crackling from rendering down the fat for lard which was poured into the bladder. There was the full length of the chain running from tail to head to cut into joints, and the making of potted meat which would keep longer.

The third day was to cut the pig up into sides of bacon, ham and pig's cheek, then rub in the salt on both sides of each and leave them for five weeks. The pig's cheek was ready to eat first at about three weeks. When it came out of the pickle it was hung up to dry in the kitchen for a month or six weeks, ready to use when it came out of the salt. Its final stage was into the bacon box and would last through to a repeat the following year.

Chapter IX

Tracing the Cause of Pollution, Darlington Factory

I RECEIVED the following letter:

Phoenix Tubeman Ltd.
Stephenson Works
Darlington, Co. Durham
21st May 1974

Dear Mr. Taylor,

For some time we have been endeavouring to contact a Dowser whose skill may assist us to trace some springs on our ground which are causing us trouble in low level sumps associated with our machinery. We wrote to the British Society of Dowsers asking if they could put us in touch with a local man with this peculiar skill, and they gave us your name.

We would be very pleased if you would for your fee and travelling expenses help us to trace the source and direction of this running water, and will be pleased if you will contact the writer by letter or telephone, or if he is not immediately available, Mrs. Jenkins, his Secretary.

Yours sincerely,
Phoenix Tubeman Limited.
J. E. M. Livingstone.

Wednesday 29th May.

I visited the above factory and found oil polluting the river Scern at the same part of the river as the place where the two veins passed

72

under the factory. I also saw a soakaway which could be the main cause of the trouble. The measurements of the veins of water were: No. 1: 12ft wide and 12ft deep; No. 2: 9ft wide and 12ft deep, just about river depth. I marked two places to dig outside the factory at a point before it was polluted, and also told them to stop putting waste in the soakaway.

On 20 June 1974 I received the following message from Phoenix Tubeman Limited: 'Down 15 ft. in clay and it is bone dry.' I responded by going to Stephenson Works the following day. On my arrival they were down a further 5ft and into water which was running in about 4ft of sand. They then continued with previous advice.

Chapter X

My Map Dowsing Experience

I HAD AN invitation to join a team of five dowsers at a map dowse of a room in a house where it was thought that there was an old well. The request was from Bill Cooper, President of the British Society of Dowsers. The task was to look for the well or any other thing of interest. My map of the room was filled in as my dowsing found it, and I posted it back to Bill Cooper, saying that my findings were very distinct. On 12 March 1996 I sent the following letter to Bill Cooper:

Dear Bill Cooper,

In response to your letter 8th March re the results of your experiment, and the facts you are building up. Because of your strong interest it would be very unfair on my part if I did not give you details of my method in finding the distinct measurements which I sent to you about the well and water vein.

My dowsing over the years has been 98% with a divining rod, which is understandable where my confidence lies trying to do the best on the occasion.

I know my subconscious mind cuts out to eliminate unneeded influences (a budding dowser in his or her early days is in a mine field, and it is only 'end result' that will build confidence). This is borne out as an example in the Bishop's rule when you pass by the depthing influence which only comes after you find the water. I find the lesser, and unimportant influences do not appear.

On receiving your request, my immediate thought was of my method to adopt. My dowsing career with success was with the rod, and that I must trust and does not complicate the dowsing.

My Map Dowsing Experience

I then carried out my plan, armed with a number of garden canes at the centre of the lawn at the rear of my house at Mosswood. I marked out in detail, and to scale, with the cans showing fireplace and door.

My method was as follows:

1. Stand 30 ft. from the long side of the room measurement.

2. Still standing at that point, point the rod at the room beginning at the left hand corner to scan the site, moving slowly to the right, with rod steady. When I have covered the full length of the room with the scan, return to any influence found and recheck to confirm.

3. Stepping out to see what I have found. There was only one time the rod went down. I now walk to that point and see what reviles. I walked the full 30 ft. to the room and stepped in and about half way across the room the rod went down. I walked on and still in the room a distance of 8 ft. the rod went down again. It had the hallmark of a vein of water with both sides within the room. I continued to walk on to the depthing point, counting my steps as I go. At just over five of my steps the rod went down for the depth, making it 16 ft. deep.

It is now very clear that there could be a well in the room and now is the time to look. I began at the west end of the room to walk mid stream to the east. I walked three steps and the rod went down. I walked on another 2½ steps and the rod went down again.

I trust you found my method very interesting.
Yours sincerely,
Edwin Taylor

Chapter XI

Black Streams and Health

VER THE years of my dowsing there have been many times I have been called to check on dwelling houses where the occupants have been concerned of such influences being present in their home.

My interpretation would be that any vein of water running under a dwelling house could be termed a black stream, where a very sensitive person could be subject to the dowsing influence given off by the vein for many hours of every day. In Germany, for example, doctors take a close watch on sick people where they cannot diagnose the cause of an illness.

On 9 January 1983 I received a letter from a doctor in practice near Hanover in Germany, who had patients in the South of England. I, as a dowser, received a letter asking me if I would be kind enough to dowse their home for such influences. Their home was in Ipswich, and their doctor was Dr H. Neiper, Krankenhaus an Silbersee, Langenhagen, near Hanover. His patients were Mr and Mrs Lingwood.

Mr Lingwood called me by telephone and asked me if I would do the survey. I said that it would be a journey of over 600 miles. I could tell by his concern it was important and agreed to and fixed a day to meet at his home in Stone Lodge Lane.

The business they were in was in London and they had decided that they could do it from their home, which meant living twenty-four hours per day in the house. Mrs Lingwood was now sick and in bed.

It was on 5 January 1983 that I made the journey from Northumberland to Ipswich, a journey of over 300 miles. I met Mr Lingwood at Copdack as arranged and followed him to his home, where he gave me a history of the sickness and how it had worsened since they spent the full twenty-four hours a day in their home.

The house was detached and south facing. I began my survey about 15ft from the house, on the south side and picked up a strong influence. I walked to the house without coming to the edge of the vein, moved to the west gable end and within one foot of the south edge I found the edge of the vein. I walked over it and it measured 18ft wide, wider than the house and was 30ft deep. It was in an exact line of the house, showing less than one foot of floor space the length of the house free from an extreme influence throughout. I talked to Mr Lingwood of the seriousness of living in it and advised him to get out at once, and I wrote to Dr Neiper in Hanover to tell him of my findings.

9th January 1983
Dr H. Neiper
Krankenhaus an Silbersee
Langenhagen
Hanover.

Dear Dr. Neiper

I have now been to Ipswich to the home of Mr. and Mrs. Lingwood of Tudor House, Stone Lodge Lane, and have checked their house for any harmful rays or radiations from underground streams.

This I have found to be the worst case of its kind that I have seen, in over thirty years of dowsing, and have advised them of the importance of vacating the house at once. While inside the house, it gave me a strange feeling of discomfort.

The Lingwoods were in agreement that I write to you and explain my findings and advice given.

Yours sincerely,
Edwin Taylor.

Chapter XII

Another Side of Dowsing –
British Gas Pipe Lines

WAS ENGAGED in a lot of very interesting work with British Gas in the late 1970s and early 1980s when North Sea Oil and Gas pipelines were being established. As the gas pipelines came south, crossing the river Tyne was very restricted because of the geology in the Tyne Valley.

What I was able to do in the sudden growth of the gas industry was relatively small, although important. Digging trenches about twelve feet deep through the countryside was putting at great risk rural water supplies to many farmers and country estates. It was in this sphere that I was called in by British Gas on some occasions, and sometimes by worried farmers. It was soon realized by British Gas it was in their interests to take serious notice of this danger because of the cost of replacing a rural water supply.

My diary entry for 6 November 1979 reads:

Surveying area of the Lake at Woodlands Hall, Knitsley, Co. Durham. Three springs supplied the Lake and measurements were as follows:

Spring No. 1: Is nine yards wide, and six feet deep at the point of issue. At the first fence line it is an estimated 20 feet deep. At the point of passing under the proposed British Gas line an estimated 100 ft.

Spring No. 2: Is again nine yards wide, and six feet deep at point of issue. At the turnip field fence it is an estimated 25 feet deep and where it passes under the proposed British Gas line, an estimated 93 feet deep.

Spring No. 3: 8 yards wide, depth not taken at spring, at fence line estimated 27 feet and where it passes under British Gas line 81 feet.

In my experience this pipeline at a depth of twelve feet or thereabouts will not affect the water supply at any of the three springs.

Pipelines with Northumbria Water

On this same hilltop in County Durham, and on the same British Gas pipeline I have helped other farmers. At White Hall Farm, Rowley, the underground vein of water on the line of the proposed gas line was just 12ft below ground. I asked British Gas if they would make the line 29yds along the vein where it was 25ft deep, which they did and rectified the risk:

I checked three veins of water crossing the line on Sheepwalks Farm — all three were deeper than the British Gas proposed line.

Little White Farm, Branspeth was my next call, where the supply did pass under the pipeline area but all was well in this instance.

At Peipy Farm, Stocksfield, in the Tyne Valley, I arranged a meeting on 5 February 1980. I surveyed the area near to British Gas proposed pipeline and found the water feeding the farm supply running at a depth of 6ft. If this pipeline had gone ahead as planned it would destroy the spring and would never be the same again. I advised British Gas to save the valuable spring by moving across the field to a point where the depth was 25ft deep at the crossing. They were very co-operative and the supply was saved.

8 August 1980. Mr. Hall, British Gas. Request to check springs at Shildon Hill, Corbridge.

Shildon Hill Spring. Underground water vein 3 yards wide coming to surface at trough and coming out of the hillside from a depth of 50 feet where the Gas pipe line goes through. Advise — will not affect water trough supply.

30 August 1984. Arranged to meet Mr. Hindmarch of British Gas at Site Office, Penrith, Cumbria 10.00 a.m.

With a long period of dry weather it is not clear if the British

Gas pipeline work is responsible for water supply failure on farms and the day was spent advising and trying to find out if British Gas or the weather were responsible.

Six properties were surveyed beginning at Bracken Rigg.

No. 1. A vein of water 5 yards wide and 7ft. deep at spring. A strong chance of pipeline damage!

No. 2. A vein of water 8 yards wide and 12 feet deep. As the pipe line depth goes to 12 feet there is risk!

No. 2A. A vein of water 10 yards wide and 12 feet deep.

No. 3. Garden 3 yards wide and 6 feet deep.

No. 4. Cheese Farm. 10 yards wide and 5 ft. deep. 5 yards wide and 4 ft. deep.

No. 5 Farm supply. 10 yards wide and 6 ft. deep. Collecting chamber not in mid stream and losing water from the side of the chamber. These shallow springs are all at risk from pipe line workings.

13 October 1984. Dowsing for water at Burmoor Farm, Wark, for Mr. Robinson.

Found 2 veins of Water No. 1 8yds. wide and 50 ft. deep.

No. 2 3yds. wide and 0 ft. deep.

Drilled 22nd April 1985. Yield 13,000 gallons per day.

Saturday 26th February 1988. I received a message from Mr. Robinson, Burmoor Farm, Wark, saying that water had reduced considerably from the borehole. It never changed in yield over the first three years of use. In the Autumn of 1987 a Government Department were doing a survey for oil in the area of Burmoor Farm, and also on the farm road to the farm steading, crossing the course of the water vein three times. It was from that time that the reduction was noticed.

The apparatus used for the oil survey by Spectrum Geophysical Services were bouncing shock waves in the process of their search. Because of the failing supply at No. 1 and No. 2, I marked site No. 3 to replace the loss. On 12 March 1988 I heard that Site No. 3 had been drilled and was yielding 11,500 gallons per day – very satisfactory in regard to yield.

With all the facts at my disposal in my mind it looked as if some plate of rock had been disturbed and let the water through to a lower level. I put my views to the farmer, Mr Robinson, the National Farmers' Union, the driller and put the facts to Spectrum Services, who did contribute a four-figure sum to the farmer for the loss he had suffered.

The strength of this case was the ability to show where the vein of water was by dowsing and where the apparatus was used. It also proved the importance of details kept in my diaries from 1984.

Chapter XIII

My Early Days Before Dowsing

Y FATHER was George William Taylor, born at Durhamfield Farm on 12 March 1891 and lived there until his marriage to Violet Winifred Hepton in 1917. He then took over the farming of Summerfield Farm where, during the First World War, like myself, he was a keen stockman.

The peak of his year was to compete in the Christmas show at the local auction mart at Blackhill in County Durham, where he would exhibit both cattle and sheep and, because of his ability in presentation, and success rate, he was many times asked to judge at agricultural shows and sales over the span of his farming life. He died in 1953 in his sixty-third year.

At the same auction mart, after I was fourteen years old, I drove cattle or sheep on most Mondays in the year, with the help of a border collie bitch, to walk the distance of three miles to the mart. The bitch knew off by heart every turn, every open gate, every street corner. That is the value of a good border collie.

When I look back I have inherited the same leaning towards livestock. The cattle that father was presenting at the Christmas show had to be single-purpose breed. They were a cross between the Galloway cow with black hair grazing on the hills of Galloway, in South-West Scotland and mated to the white Shorthorn bull, bred white over generations; the result being the cross called the Blue Grey. Father, like many more farmers had great pleasure from this special cross, which he purchased at Haltwhistle at the same sale in May each year. They were summered on good grass and housed for eight weeks in time for the Christmas show.

My attraction to livestock on the farm began for me at an early age. I remember one April morning at daybreak, before I was five years old, sitting on the window sill of my bedroom with my clothes on and listening for sounds of the shepherd who lived in the farmhouse and began his day's work at 5.30 a.m. His first call would be the lambing shed and I could not wait – I just wanted to see any new lambs that had been born through the night.

I recall one other April morning about two years later again at the lambing time, and my enthusiasm not yet waned, if anything more excited. The occasion was the Scripture examination at school and on that day it was half-day holiday, which allowed me to return to the sheep and lambs. The particular day had been a very historic event, which I remember to this day. The Rural Dean of Corbridge took the class, and on his arrival the first question he asked was, 'What happy event has taken place this morning?' And he said, 'A baby princess had been born to the Duke and Duchess of York.' The little princess is now our Queen. I say each year on her birthday, 'I remember the day she was born.'

When I was eleven years old I became a member of the Shotley Branch of the Young Farmers' Club, which was formed about 1932 and is still a very important part of farming life today. In the early days the members took on rearing a calf, keeping a record of food costs and at the end of the year the calves of members were sold by public auction at Hexham Auction mart in October each year, and the new baby calves were purchased for the next year.

In September of 1930 I entered my calf in the YFC class at Edmondbyers Agricultural Show. I also entered a hand-milking competition. My calf failed in lifting the honour but I was proud to get the red rosette for the hand-milking.

The way of life was different. A large number of farmers' sons did not get a wage. I was one. At seventeen years of age my pocket money was 2s 6d old money – today twelve and a half pence.

In the period of seven years leading up to the outbreak of the Second World War on 3 September 1939, money was very hard to find, and to leave out life in the 1930s would give a false image. The main form of transport for young people was a bicycle, or to walk, going to Young Farmers' Club events, meetings, and stock judging competitions. The cinema was at its peak with queues the length of the street; village dances were within walking and cycling distance. I passed my driving test (my first attempt) in 1938, in the second year since its introduction.

The day war broke out made the greatest changes this country had ever experienced. The day of the horse as a beast of burden ended overnight. Farmers were instructed to plough large areas of land which had never been ploughed for more than sixty years. It had to come into food production. The horse could no longer fulfil the need.

Tractors came on to nearly every farm in Britain and the walking speed of the horse in farming had gone from our country. No time now to save the nests of the lapwing. They no longer nest on the ploughed fields. Life in the countryside had to readjust to the needs of the time.

Chapter XIV

The Day She Changed Her Life

T WAS IN the spring of the year 1977 when a knock came on the door of the farmhouse at Mosswood Farm. It was a young girl of sixteen years of age, her size small. She had a great ambition to work with animals and said her first choice was to try for some work in a veterinary surgery, but to no avail. She was now hoping there was some vacancy on a farm.

Her apparent disadvantage was that she was a town girl and also I had never filled such a post with a female before. I could see the desire to achieve which was on the lines of my own thinking. There was a vacancy at Mosswood for calf feeding and young stock in general. The dairy herd was at Durhamfield, but there was quite a number of sheep to look after.

Her name was Pierette Elder. For me it was a new venture and I would give it a try (they say good stuff comes in little bundles). I asked her to come back Monday morning at 8.00 a.m.

After the first few weeks of Pierette's employment I could see she deserved some encouragement and there was a scheme where she could attend Kirkley Hall College of Agriculture in Northumberland on Monday of each week, for which I put her forward to take part, which she did. I could soon see it was an asset to her and she was making full use of it. Now I could also see the application of her knowledge was being used on the farm. One thing was very prominent: if she finished a task on the farm she always found work for herself. Such things I had not seen in the past in many young male helpers.

Pierette's mother was a sister at a local hospital and noticed when Pierette was feeding calves or lambs she was very conscious of the need to keep bottles for lambs on pails. It was a common thing at lambing time for a ewe to stand on her lamb's leg and break it. Pierette

Pierette Elder – shepherdess at Mosswood for eleven years

Pierette Elder at work at Mosswood Farm

Pierette Elder feeding the sheep on Mosswood farm

Pierette Elder at work at Mosswood Farm

took that in her stride and put on a plaster, to her quite simple. She dehorned all the calves and castrated the bull calves with a knife. At lambing time when lambs were presented wrong for birth, with her small size of hand and her ability to know how to correct it I could advise her very well. I was doing the same thing as a schoolboy with a small hand.

My liking for sheep had been passed on to Pierette in a big way, her ability to dress them for the sale ring, or the show field was soon recognized by other breeders and made the day when a red rosette came her way – a lamb she was caring for and feeding – at the October sale of blue-faced Leicester ram lambs made the sum of £1,800 in the sale ring, and was sold to a top breeder at Ayr on the west coast of Scotland.

With this help I was enjoying a new lease of life in having someone to handle the sheep as I would do, it came natural to her and she stood her ground amongst sheep handlers all over.

After a few years of going to major shows and sales she was now, through experience, able to go two days in advance of the judging day when the sheep needed to settle in and to keep an eye open for sickness or lameness. We exhibited at the Royal Show, Stoneleigh, the Great Yorkshire at Harrogate, County Show at Corbridge and local shows where competition was strong. At the autumn sales of rams and ram lambs we sold at Builth Wells in South Wales, Thornhill, south-west Scotland and at the largest ram sale in Britain held at Kelso, north of the Tweed in Scotland, where seventeen sale rings are selling at the same time. The starting bell rings at 10.00 a.m.

Besides 100 blue-faced Leicester registered sheep there was a commercial flock of ewes of around 400 for fat lamb production and there was a lot of work throughout the year – the feeding and housing up to lambing in March and April, marking, tailing and castrating of all male lambs. In June all adults are clipped and wool is wrapped for sale. In July the lambs get their first worm drench and all go through the bath for dipping for fly infestation. In the autumn the lambs are weaned, some being fat enough for sale, which will now be a weekly event. In October the year begins again when the rams go off with the ewes.

You can now see Pierette has a full-time task at peak times. She does get some help. She also gives help in return, driving a tractor and trailer to lead grain from the combine.

Now having been at Mosswood eight years and looking to the period at Kirkley Hall College she met up with Simon Fenwick, a farmer's son from Brinkburn near Rothbury who was employed on the machinery side of our enterprise.

It was one morning in the autumn of 1988 and now eleven years from that day her life changed. It was about 8.15. She said, 'Can I have a word with you after breakfast?' The tears were running down both cheeks. She returned after about twenty minutes, myself thinking all things possible. She said, 'Simon and I have got a farm.' I said, 'I will be sorry to lose you, but I knew this day would come, and I am very pleased for you. You will be a great loss at Mosswood.'

And now another eight years later, lambing her own sheep now, man and wife with a two-year old boy. And fate has again played its part. I wish them well.

Chapter XV

Kiloes

ARMING is a way of life where schemes of pleasure can be introduced without being expensive. You already know of my love for animals and the things I have learned from them. One such flair began from my interest in the West Highland breed of cattle belonging to the Western Islands of Scotland, off the outer and inner Hebrides and Argyllshire. These cattle were known locally as 'Kiloes'.

I have attended the autumn cattle sales at Oban in Argyllshire, where cattle from the Western Isles come off the boats in Oban and are driven to the auction mart in the town – a great sight to see. It was on one of my previous visits to Oban, and at the same time of my visit a demonstration of a new breed of cattle was being held on the Island of Luing where the farmer had purchased the island some twenty years previously, and in that time he built up this new breed by crossing the beef shorthorn and the West Highland and by selection had fixed the breed of Luing cattle, now registered as a breed – a very hardy animal, ideal for the high ground in Scotland. It is now a much sought after beast for beef production. There were two things which drew my attention on that afternoon of the visit of Anne and I to the Island of Luing. One was so noticeable 'that the cattle could not escape from the island'. The other thought that entered my mind was that at Mosswood there was an area of woodland of one hundred acres well fenced on three sides and bordered on the south by the river Derwent.

My thinking turned to reality the next day. Monday was the first day of the sale of cattle at the auction mart. I purchased seven West Highland steers about eighteen months old. They had come to Oban by boat from South Uist, part of the Outer Hebrides. The steers (male castrated cattle) arrived home to Durhamfield in early October 1973 and after the necessary dozing for worms and observation for any lameness, after a week they were introduced to their new home in the woods at Mosswood Farm. There was a lot of shelter under the large conifer trees, also areas of grass which had not been grazed by farm stock, only by deer, rabbits and hares.

The temperament of the 'Kiloes' (so called in Scotland) was good and as I had not had the breed on the farm before, I made it a rule to see them regularly. I did make some rules to stick to. For example, other cattle that winter out were given hay once a day and if snow was on the ground it would be twice a day. When fed this way they returned to the feeding point and at the same time in the day. My plans with the Highland cattle were to be quite different. I wanted them to live naturally and to forage for themselves and spread over the whole of the area of the woodland for even in winter time there is plenty of roughage. To feed them with hay would be a great disadvantage; it would stop them from roaming the full area with a wide choice of food.

On the first snowfall of their first year at Mosswood I made time to go to the woodland and observe. I was greatly surprised to see nature playing its part and saw something I had never seen before, and likely I would never have seen it without the Kiloe cattle. They were under

West Highland cattle at Mosswood

West Highland cattle at Mosswood

a stand of very tall spruce trees where the lower branches were weighted down by the snow, and the seven steers were happily having breakfast by nature putting it within reach, feeding on the lower branches. You can see plainly when animals are happy. I have seen them playing, doing a stampede through the trees and with their long horns getting longer they turned their heads sideways to miss hitting trees as they galloped by.

I was now getting my reward from my venture into West Highland cattle – two years later now they had become very friendly with their long hair waving in the wind. All seven were different in colour, ranging from a dark brindle, to golden and a very deep red. Others vary in between. They were maturing into large, good-quality cattle, having done very well in the woodland, which is south-facing sloping down to the river Derwent with a good share of the sunshine. I have had great pleasure taking photos and colour slides of them in the wild.

In the latest surprise they have sprung upon me, was when the river Derwent was in full flood. I was standing by the riverside. The Kiloes walked down the slope to the river edge, walked into the water, swam over the river with only their heads above water, walked out at the other side, all seven of them, shook themselves vigorously and walked on unperturbed. West Highland cattle down through the years have swum from isle to isle and take to water very easily.

I had the pleasure of their company for four years and I felt so much wiser in many ways because of their presence at Mosswood. It would have been too much of a luxury for me, or my seven friends the Kiloes, to carry them on to old age. Sadly that time had come. The only option available was to offer them at public auction at a store cattle sale at Hexham Auction Mart, on any Friday throughout the year.

In June of 1977 that day came at the time of the year when such cattle were in demand, and also the time had come for us to part. It has been an experience I will not forget, and sentiment cannot be allowed to control common sense!

Chapter XVI

1949 to 24 February 1953
Bolton by Bowland

T WAS IN August 1949 that Joseph Anderson, a farmer from the Mid-West of Canada, was visiting his brother at Mosswood Farm, where I now live. His brother was married to Father's sister, hence the reason for him calling at my home at that time, Durhamfield Farm. After a short time the conversation got round to water and divining which is used by the farmers in Canada and he said he would like to show me where water was under the farm.

I knew nothing about divining for water and watched Joe Anderson use a piece of fencing wire shaped in the form of a V. He did not show me how to use it, nor was I bursting with enthusiasm. But when he had finished his short demonstration he threw down the piece of wire and then went to visit his brother. Some feeling began to stir in me to try that piece of wire. I picked it up and returned to where he said there was water. When I walked over it the rod dipped. That was the moment I found it worked for me.

From that day I knew of a new dimension. It was not just what was on the surface of the earth. I began to know of veins of underground water, how deep they were, and the quantity to expect if they came to the surface. For the next twelve months I passed through a stage of learning, getting the feel of the rod, finding the best kind of rod for me. At that time it was the hazel, V-shaped, which was sensitive and springy. It was not until 29 November 1950 that I was able to make progress when I received the following letter:

York House, Portugal Street
London WC2
29–11–50

Dear Sir,

I am pleased to inform you that your application for membership of this Society was approved by the Council on November 23rd. I enclose a copy of the rules.

Yours faithfully,
E. H. Lampson
Ass/Sec. British Society of Dowsers.

The above letter opened the way to a new field of possibilities, and they began to unfold by me making use of the Society's library and selecting the books written by others about the masters of water divining and their methods. I was also to receive the quarterly journal which has a worldwide circulation.

When I began to read into the methods of others and finding it worked for me I put these new ways to practise and finding new ways of my own; finding a surface spring and tracking it back underground, checking it for depth and width; finding old wells on farms that have all been found by dowsers in the past, and seeing how neatly they were placed midstream on a vein of water. Through joining the Society I could purchase various kinds of divining rods and many other things about dowsing.

I soon found that I could use my improved knowledge of dowsing on the farm, finding field drains and water pipes, also building up confidence which is vital if you are to become a dowser.

Probably the most important milestone in the life of a dowser is the one I had arrived at, getting a request to find a water supply for a village using 4,000 gallons of water a day. The following letter put the wheels into motion.

Richard Turner and Son
Bentham.
18th September 1952.

E. Taylor Esq.

Dear Sir,

Further to our telephone conversation today we would like to confirm that our Mr. Swinglehirst will be waiting for you at the above office at lunch time on Thursday next, September 25th, and will then take you to Bolton by Bowland to the site where we hope to find water.

Yours faithfully,
pp. Richard Turner and Son
Swinglehirst.

In a dowser's life of finding water this is the crossroads of make or break. I had prepared myself in my study of dowsers' methods but I think my greatest teacher has been my observations of wells found by dowsers in the past and without fail these wells are sited midstream over a vein of water. There are two types of failure which I have found in my study. The first is where a small amount of water is in the well, because the well was sunk on the edge where the dowser marked the point where the rod goes down. He may not have known to find the other side of the vein, the point to drill being between the two edges of the vein. Not all dowsers in the past knew of the method of depthing as done by myself and other water dowsers today. They were very accurate in finding the vein. Most wells were sunk to about 30ft and there would be failures when water was below that maximum. In my years of dowsing I have found very good supplies by drilling on veins where there was a dry well, because they were not down to water level.

On Thursday, 25 September 1952, I arrived at the appointed time to meet Mr. Swinglehirst at his office in Bentham and travelled with him to Bolton by Bowland. It was the wettest day that one could be out in, and I thought then that I was on a mission to find water.

We arrived at Bolton by Bowland and were taken to the land where it was hoped water would be found by the land agent for the Bolton Hall Estate. The area of three small fields by the roadside was the site chosen, for its convenience. The land agent said the level of water consumption for the village was 4,000 gallons per day so it was now in my hands. I was at the point of no return. We began to walk up the field and the agent asked me if I would check that particular place in the field. The ground was wet. I then realized that a local dowser had advised them to dig at this point. I checked and found there was a small vein of no value for what we are looking for.

The land we were on was on a steep slope and I thought the water would need to be on higher ground to run to the village, so I checked as we climbed the hill and found no water worth recording. The top of the field levelled out and I came to a vein running north to south with a reasonable amount of water. I put in a marker to return to later. I then found a vein running east to west, being better than No. 1. I depthed the latest one and estimated 85ft deep. I felt satisfied that what I had found would supply the village. It so happened that two veins of water at different depths crossed at a very level site at the top of the hill and at that point I knocked in my first real water well.

I said to the land agent to drill to 100ft to make sure that water would stand in the borehole. That water would be found at two levels and the yield would be above the requirement at 6,000 gallons per day. I asked Mr Swinglehirst if he would send me a log of the drilling and the result.

I knew it would take time before I received the result of the well at Bolton by Bowland, but on 26 February 1953 a letter arrived, five months after that very wet day in September. I looked at the postmark which was Bentham. What news did it contain? There were no past dowsing events to my credit to give me confidence to open the letter, nor that the news would be good news when it was opened. I hesitated no longer and opened the envelope, which revealed the result of my first dowsing survey, marking the point where to drill, and now the result of the drilling.

The report contained facts which were beyond my wildest dreams, the end result being a great success and proved to me that the method I had used was correct – now after many hundreds of similar results I still use the same approach for a survey to this day, forty years later.

During the many years of dowsing I have discovered a number of short cuts that have shortened the time taken for a survey. Experience being the greatest teacher has also been a contributory factor in shortening the time for a survey.

Nearly twenty years had passed in my dowsing career when I discovered that I could find the underground water veins from a distance. This time-saving advantage can be illustrated by relating to a particular dowsing survey when I was asked to find a large supply of water, 20,000 gallons per day, for a felt factory in West Cumbria in 1991. The area available from which to find the water was about five acres, which limited the chance of much selection of good underground supplies.

On arrival at the factory it was a cold wet day. I was taken into the office to meet the owner, who told me the daily consumption was considerable, washing the hides and skins and preparing them for the leather industry. Standing in the office and seeing the rain pouring down I thought it was the ideal occasion to see what direction water was in before going out in the rain. I took out of my inside jacket pocket my divining rod, slowly scanned the whole area of the factory and picked up the influence of three veins of water. I then went out of the office knowing where to go outside. There was a larger grass area to the east of the factory site. I then proceeded to the Number 1 vein that I had found from the office. It measured 36yds wide and 120ft deep.

Number 2 vein was 67yds wide and 183ft deep. When I went to mark the third influence found from the office it was outside the boundary of the factory, so I recommended No. 2 to drill.

Chapter XVII

Basalt, Dalerite and Camptonite

HAT IS that something which makes the dowsing rod go down, or the pendulum swing? There have been very many views given as to why it does take place, and there is one sure thing: they cannot all be correct.

So many dowsers have given their theory over the years which should qualify me not to be out of order by giving my views on how it works. When I walk over the field in search of underground water, there is a place where you come to it, where the rod dips strongly. This is on the edge of a water vein. What is that something at the edge of a water vein that makes the rod go down? The question is that so many people in the past have applied their theories, which are many, and they cannot all be correct. There is also that something that makes the pendulum swing, which comes under the heading of dowsing. In my experience as a dowser, with a divining rod in search of water, the rod reacts on the dowser's body in a way causing the rod to dip. If water is not there, nothing happens. The rod does not rise up to say no.

While watching a pendulum dowser he gets a yes answer from the clockwise swing. If the answer is no, it is anti-clockwise. You would get a 'don't know' answer when the pendulum swings. If you ask the question wrongly the pendulum will remain stationary, until it is replaced.

This brings me now to the main question of my theory of the mysterious 'something'. I could always see mystery in the methods of many other dowsers. There were things in my practical thinking that did not fit. Things that would not be part of my water dowsing. Suddenly, while thinking of the contrast between the pendulum dowser, and myself, I thought that the division between the two is the mind, including the subconscious applying to the pendulum dowser. My

The Author in 1990 – Mosswood Farm House in the background

method is physical where the reactions are coming from muscular reflex. The way I carry out a survey to locate underground water is deliberate and straightforward. It is of use, or no use. I am not asking the rod to tell me, or show me where water is. I pick up the influence from a distance and the rod takes me to the water.

It is a natural assumption for dowsers and others to believe that water is the cause of the rod dipping down. In my early days of dowsing, I thought that to be the 'Something'. People have asked me to show them how it works and could I go to the kitchen tap or would I walk over a bridge. I soon found that it did not work for me.

In my long experience of regular dowsing I have found water is not that substance that dips the rod. A few years ago I was travelling by boat from Oban on Scotland's west coast to the Island of Lismore to mark out sites for water supplies on the island. On that journey I used my divining rod to check the effect of surface water, being the sea, which had no effect on me, although I was able to locate veins of water under the seabed. If I am dowsing on a very wet day, and water was the attraction, drawing the dowsing rod down, it would be impossible to dowse when the ground is wet.

The only explanation I can think of for the cause of the rod dipping

The Author

on the two edges of a water vein is a very small amount of radiation which will escape where the earth crust is broken by earth faults. It is also true that earth faults are the hidden veins and arteries where the water dowser locates some very good yields of water. I have had many high yielding wells, the best being just under half a million gallons of water per day for irrigation. The effect of that minute amount of radiation could tighten the muscles in the dowser's arms and caused the rod to dip.

The same cannot be said for the pendulum dowser because I am convinced we are dealing with two separate kinds of people. In this case it is the mind, conscious or sub-conscious, which directs the pendulum on its course to give a positive answer.

In the wider field of dowsing, there are water dowsers who have a mixture of both mental and physical. There are times I feel a sensation of being led, or guided, by another force.

If I am in the passenger seat of a vehicle it is common for me to use my divining rod. On one occasion I recognized a different kind of reaction from my divining rod: instead of going down as for water, it just wanted to bob up and down all the time without going fully down or up. The rod was telling me something I did not understand at that time.

Some time after finding this new rod movement I was dowsing at Mosswood and when I moved round in a circle scanning the area for other springs, I noticed there was one particular direction where I picked up my new-found action of the rod. It was not possible to locate the cause of the strange new action on my rod. My curiosity overruled me and I planned to spend some time and make the 'unknown to where' journey. My plan was to travel in the direction of the influence stopping the car at intervals to check if I was still on track. When I reached the town of Hexham I had travelled over twelve miles and still going and getting the same direction as before. Another six miles and I felt the pull of the rod stronger and I was soon to the edge of whatever. By then I was just before entering the village of Gunnerton, about midway between Hexham and Bellingham in the North Tyne Valley.

At this stage I had no idea what it was to be. Could it be oil or some kind of mineral? I did not know. But I now felt committed to find the answer. On returning to my home at Mosswood I stood in the morning room with my dowsing rod and again checked what I had proved a distance of twenty miles away, opening up a new chapter of my dowsing by knowing that I could detect an influence at what seemed a long distance away.

While the divining rod was in my hand I thought there could be other things that I did not know of. I could, from the same stand in the morning room, pick up directions for two very good veins of water, which I often practised on, and the one I had just traced. I moved round very slowly with my rod set very tensely to check for others of this new feeling. My window faces north. The newly discovered influence was at ten to the hour as I faced north. To my great surprise I found the direction of another three. No. 2 at ten past the hour. No. 3 at twenty past the hour. Continuing to rotate clockwise I found No. 4 at twenty to the hour. All four caused the rod to bob up and down, distinctly different to the reaction for water.

A look at the ordnance map gave me no clue. I then took out the Geological Survey map for the area and it stood out in front of me as plain as daylight that at these four points was a very high concentration of hard igneous rocks of Basalt, Dalerite and Camptonite.

Chapter XVIII

Watercolour Painting

FTER I had written in longhand the bones of my proposed book *Walking on Water* my hands were in need of something else to do. I still had several interests, none of which could fill the void left by completing my book.

A local professional artist had chosen the driveway into the farm at Mosswood as the material for a watercolour painting. When he had finished the painting I was attracted to it so much that I bought it and it is now hanging with pride of place in the lounge at the farmhouse at Mosswood.

At this stage I never thought of myself as an artist, but I will say if anything tipped the scales with me towards watercolour painting it seemed that fate again had played a part pointing me in a direction.

In the early stage of my interest in painting I was heartened by the fact that Winston Churchill at seventy-three years of age took to painting – in 1993, I began at the same age of seventy-three.

My painting has given me the greatest of pleasure. It is a relaxation and in my three years to date I have completed nearly a hundred. My late wife, Anne, used to say to me, 'What are you going to do with them?' my answer being, 'I haven't really thought about that.' There was one thought that was fixed in my mind that if I did show any promise, I would not part with any until it appeared that a style was forming. I have been quite flattered by the remarks of others who paint watercolours.

I have a near neighbour who has had quite a long interest in watercolour paintings. She was calling on other business and I asked her if she would like to look at my paintings: she was remarkably impressed. I said to her (Mrs Cookson) that I had never had any lessons or instruction and she remarked: 'Never do so.'

Mosswood Farm House

Front view of Mosswood Farm House

Part of the collection of stone troughs at Mosswood

Anne Taylor with the working sheepdogs at Mosswood

Farm animals add great interest and seem to bring the picture to life. I like to put a wide variation in the landscape pictures, also a wide difference in sky and cloud formation. I am attracted to yellow in general through my painting. Swans help a painting either in flight or swimming on quiet water.

There is too some enjoyment and challenge in the framing of paintings, selecting the frame, its colour. The surround too can play a large part in the end result of framing a picture, both in depth and colour.

Chapter XIX

Robert Anderson

osswood Farm has been steeped in history for a long, long time, which includes and is surrounded by some of the most romantic scenery on the beautiful water of Derwent. This place is asserted to be that referred to by Sir Walter Scott in his poem on Rokeby in the lines beginning:

> And when he taxed thy breach of word
> To you fair Rose of Allenford,
> I saw thee crouch like chastened hound
> Whose back the huntsman's lash hath found.

I think I should pay tribute to my late uncle, Robert Anderson, and my late aunt, Mary Sarah, who was my father's sister, who placed me in a position to inherit this beautiful part of the Derwent Valley, which joins land owned by me upstream in the same valley. I feel very proud to live in what is classified as an area of outstanding natural beauty.

My Uncle Robert was a self-made man. Through life he set up challenges for himself to achieve and would then accomplish them. He was a very able ploughman and set his sights high. He was sought after for and acted as a judge at ploughing matches and he took on the challenge in 1908 in the Regional Ploughing Competition held on the north-east coast at Hipsburn between Alnwick and Alnmouth.

Many times he told me how he prepared for that day, which meant taking two horses and the plough to the nearest station, changing at Newcastle on the Edinburgh line, heading for Hipsburn. His most dangerous opponent liked a drink, and Uncle Robert felt he would not fall foul to that danger. His horse when walking in the furrow had small feet, was light bred and if anything a little sharp. So to take off a little steam he would get on its back and have a gallop into Allenmouth and back to slow it down in the competition. If I had to put words to that, 'He was doing his homework.'

Robert Anderson was ninety-one years old when he died in 1959 and when that day came round to his very end he lived through every minute of the ploughing day, because he had won the title of champion of swing-plough handlers, which was the highest honour of the day.

In 1922 when I was three years old, Robert Anderson purchased Allensford Mill, Mosswood Farm, Wallish Walls Farm and seven cottages, which gave him a new freedom – the difference between landlord and tenant which opened up new opportunities, such as felling and planting of timber and not having to purchase fencing materials. Mature timber could be sold as an addition to annual income, and he had the ability to make his own decisions.

In the 1936 issue of *Who's Who in Northumberland*, the entry is as follows:

Anderson, Robert C.A. J.P. Farmer, Mosswood Farm near Consett, Northumberland. Born 1868 at Allensford. Eldest son of the late Robert Anderson. Educated at Castleside. Married 1908 Mary Sarah, daughter of the late George Taylor of Durhamfield. Member of Hexham R.D.C. since 1919. (Vice-Chairman 1928). Northumberland C.C. since 1927. Alderman 1935; Chairman, County Agricultural Committee since 1932. Chairman Agricultural Education Sub-Committee since 1932. Chairman County Federation of Young Farmers Clubs since formation in 1932; Vice-Chairman, County Experimental State Cockle Park, since 1932; Won Championship Best Swing Ploughman in Northumberland and Durham 1908.

Robert Anderson led a very active life in farming and his many interests until well into his eighties. I remember two examples in his eightieth year. He had sheep going to the fat market in December at 7.30 a.m. He saddled the horse, loosed the dog and gathered the sheep. In that same year the Royal Show was at Lincoln and he took my brothers and I. There was no stop between Northumberland and Lincoln, where Uncle Robert parked his car and remarked, 'One of you lads can drive home.

In later years of one's life we can become aware how fortunate we have been to have had the loan of such beautiful things around us in a lifetime and to pass on to the next generation, and I now see my grandsons taking part in the pattern of life as nature meant it to be.

I am sure if Uncle Robert and Aunt Marney, as she was known – they never had children of their own – could look down today they would be very proud to see life going on as they had known it a hundred years ago.

Chapter XX

Bishop's Rule

‘ISHOP'S RULE’ as applied to all my water findings is as follows. It would be fair to say at this stage that I have found many short cuts during my years of dowsing; this paragraph is for the beginner. And as I discovered it!

As a beginner you are walking out over a field in search of a water supply for a client (at this stage you know your rod, and what it means). You arrive at where the rod goes down and you mark the spot with a garden can or whatever. You are not sure if you have met the influence at right angles, so you step back and approach the influence about ten metres from your first mark. The result is again marked revealing the direction of the line of flow. You are now able to walk across the influence and record the width which is the guide to the yield. Then you continue in the same direction until you again reach a wave band causing the rod to go down. This you again mark and record the direction from the width, this being the equal distance down to the water.

Quantity is based on width of influence, for example a four-metre width could yield 4,000 gallons per day, sufficient for a country cottage. Depth is as measured, except when drilling through clay, which for some reason has an influence. Where clay is present you must expect to drill deeper to the water. Having read of my explanation of Bishop's Rule will allow you to return to my basics to trace a spring under ground as far as you wish to go, noticing generally as you climb the hill behind the spring the depth increases, and width does not change. You can be deceived by instinct of yield of a surface spring if you measure the flow. If it is being forced up to surface under pressure from deep down it can go dry in a drought period, and if you dig down there is sufficient, hence the value of estimating yield.

When in a dry period the pressure falls and the spring goes dry, the main stream continues on its way to where it comes to the surface along the line.

Much of my self-training time was spent on this particular item, which included tracing water out to the surface, a distinct confidence builder, when you master the technique of following the line of flow. If you get mixed with another supply it is very rare to meet two alike, so stick to your first width measurements, which do not change.

At nearly every farm or country house of a previous era there is a well found by a dowser and nearly always sited perfectly midstream on underground water. A few are sited on the edge of the influence band, the result of a budding dowser.

Chapter XXI

The British Society of Dowsers and its Origins

Y PERSONAL link with the British Society of Dowsers began on 23 November 1950 and my membership has been unbroken from that day to this, now into my forty-third year as a member. In my early days of membership I was content to absorb the contents of the Society's library books which concentrated on dowsing for water; the other great source of information was the quarterly journal of the Society. I think to this day I still have the first quarterly journal of my membership.

As I became more known as a water dowser, in 1971 I addressed the BSD National Congress at Cambridge which was the forerunner of presenting a paper at 12 BSD Congress and also at the International Congress at Oxford in 1983.

In 1974 I was elected on to the Council of the Society and it was a pleasure to take an active part in the affairs of management. In 1978 I became a Vice-President and remained on the Council. In 1983 I became an Honorary Life Vice-President of the BSD – the only one at the time of writing.

During all these years of close links with the management I have been an advocate of applying a common sense attitude to the art of dowsing; and very much opposed to adding unnecessary frills to it in the form of showmanship.

There are so many things that I find complicated – some people cannot dowse in Wellington boots, some cannot dowse on wet days. I do not like to dowse in rain, but if you travel 200 miles to a survey you cannot chase the rain away. If you add conditions to your dowsing, you have got to add others. It is like telling a lie – if you tell one lie, it takes another ten to cover your first, so do not begin.

In the British Society of Dowsers origins presented to the 1983 International Congress I read with great interest the days of Portugal Street and Colonel Bell, whom I met in his office and corresponded with him in my very early membership days, now a long time ago, and it is good to recall the man who did so much for British dowsing.

When I became a member of the British Society of Dowsers over forty years ago little did I think of the strong links that started that day. In those early days of membership I was attending Council meetings of the National Cattle Breeder Association in London, on which I represented a Cattle Breed Society. On one of those meetings I called at York House, Portugal Street and met Colonel Bell, the then Secretary of the BSD. My very strong desire to be successful as a practical dowser was kindled stronger after that meeting with a personal contact which has remained to this day in that other part of my life as a countryman.

In 1969 I was invited to give a paper to the BSD Annual Congress held at the Caley Palace Hotel, Gatehouse of Fleet, Kirkudbright, Scotland, although sadly it was not to be because of a family bereavement. The following year the National Annual Congress was held at Cambridge which was the forerunner of fifteen occasions at their congress where I presented a paper emphasizing the importance of the practical approach to dowsing in the search for water. I hold no place for showmanship or the many diversions that are displayed by amateur dowsers which only do harm to the dowsing image.

The British Society of Dowsers is made up of about 1,300 members of which 300 are overseas. It has a very active Council, of which I was a member for a number of years. I found it a great disadvantage living in Northumberland and most BSD Council meetings being held in London. I am quite proud of being the only Hon. Life Vice-President of the Society.

To benefit the members the annual Congress moves around England and Scotland, which guarantees a well-supported occasion from Friday to Sunday each year.

Talks Given to the Annual Congress of the British Society of Dowsers		
Vol. 22	Practical Dowsing in Relation to Agriculture	
No. 151	A talk given at Cambridge by Edwin Taylor 1971	7p
Vol. 24	Twenty-five Years of Practical Dowsing	
No. 165	A talk given at York on 3.5.74 by Edwin Taylor	7p
Vol. 25	Drainage	
No. 176	A talk given at Peebles on 18.9.76 by Edwin Taylor	6.75p
Vol. 26	Water and Wells	
No. 179	A talk given by Edwin Taylor at Harrogate on 2.4.77	10p
Vol. 26	Many Years of Dowsing	
No. 183	A talk given by Edwin Taylor at Harrogate on 15.4.78	7p
Vol. 27	The Cost of Well Drilling	
No. 187	A talk given by Edwin Taylor at Harrogate on 5.5.79	8p
Vol. 28	The Place of Dowsing in the Eighties	4p
No. 191	A talk given by Edwin Taylor on 24.10.80 at Carlisle	
Vol. 30	Dowsing for Water	
No. 202	A talk given by Edwin Taylor at the Golden Jubilee Conference held in Oxford in July 1983	7p
Vol. 31	A Gift Appreciated	
No. 214	A talk given by Edwin Taylor at Harrogate8p Conference in November 1984	8p
Vol. 33	Water Dowsing for Irrigation	
No. 224	A talk given by Edwin Taylor at the Conference in Carlisle in October 1986	5.75p

The above talks have all been published in a Quarterly Junction of the British Society of Dowsers. The above papers are the joint property of the contributors and the Society. The contributor has the full rights to reproduce. The Journals that contain the talks are now available.

Chapter XXII

British Geology

O WRITE about the art of water divining would not be complete without at least one chapter on the subject of British Geology, which is a vital part of the scene whenever the dowser goes in search of water.

One has to realize the extent the dowser depends on the valuable source of information provided by the Institute of Geological Sciences in their publication, *British Regional Geology*. If a dowser, or water diviner, is searching for water without making use of this essential advice he is missing out on something of great interest.

I have studied British Geology since 1946, which was for Northern England, with the price printed on the front cover *Price 25 6d net*. My dowsing began in 1949, and the two subjects became one immediately, each being complementary to the other, both in interest and value. As my boundaries widened in search for water I purchased the appropriate Regional Geology information for the new areas I was being called to search for underground water. I can think of some dowsers who have not made use of, or do not know about, the underground picture as I see it, for example the limestone outcrop at the top of the Yorkshire Dales or Scotland's East Lothian with its lovely red sandstone. Without this knowledge I would feel like a blind man walking over a field to where the rod goes down, and deciding where to knock in the peg.

The highest concentration of my dowsing lies in the valleys of the North and South Tyne and their tributaries. Well sites marked in this area in south Northumberland now total 130 up to September 1992; the average depth of wells in the area is about 55m. It is an area rising up to 1,500 ft. and very exposed along the line of the Roman Wall, which is one of Britain's largest tourist attractions. If you stop for a drink of water at the Housesteads Roman Site it will be water found by my divining rod.

The geology of this area is interesting. There is a covering over all the higher ground of 6 to 9 metres of boulder clay which came in with the ice flow. Cutting through the area is the Whin Sill which stretches to the sea north of Blythe. It is intrusive igneous rock. To the south is a blanket of millstone grit series and under that, covering the whole area, is the carboniferous limestone which shows up in many of the river beds in the area. One particular site I marked was on the Whin Sill. It was a very hard drilling and a good supply of water was found on entering the limestone under one hundred feet of the whinstone. Whinstone is a popular road-making rock, very widely used.

For my next group of sites surveyed for underground water I will travel across the Scottish border at Carter Bar, on the A68 scenic road stretching from Darlington in south Durham to Princess Street in Edinburgh, a distance of about 150 miles. The views that meet you as you cross the Border at Carter Bar, if you get the right day, are magnificent. Looking to the right are the Cheviot Hills spanning the border between England and Scotland. In front are the Eildon Hills near Melrose, the centre of my next group of site markings. In the distance to the left are the hills as far as you can see.

The town of Melrose is a place where character shines through. Its ancient abbey is a feature of the locality. The people of Melrose and the adjoining towns are great rugby enthusiasts. Ettrick and Lauderdale District is famed for its textile industry, with the woollen towns of Galashiels, Hawick and Selkirk. It was near the town of Selkirk that I marked my first site for a borehole. It was like so many others being average in depth, quantity and little else to say. A few weeks later I enquired if all went well with the drilling and was shocked to hear that there was no water. My reaction was to arrange a site meeting to establish the reason for my failure, for it was very much in my interest to have a satisfied customer, so a date and time was fixed, and within days we met on site. My first check was to make sure he had drilled at the point marked, which was correct. I next referred to my notes from the previous visit, which were the same, and correct. I carry a length of cord with me to check the depth of the bore by putting a weight on the end and lowering down to the bottom, then laying it out on the surface and stepping out the predicted depth. The drilling was not down to the water. I advised him to return with the drill and take it a little beyond my given depth. The owner of the farm turned out to be the owner of the drill also. He never told me the result of that drilling but the drilling company have recommended my name to twenty-five farms in the Melrose area that have all been drilled with a satisfactory result.

Even in that small area of fifteen miles across there is great variation. The Eildon Hills near to Melrose can be seen for miles with their three peaks standing out on the skyline, all within a distance of one and a half miles. The hills are the denuded remains of a campsite where Caccolith of trachytic rocks intruded into the Upper Old Red Sandstone in Carboniferous times. Where the river Tweed passes under the A68 road two miles east of Melrose it is plain to see the outcrop of the rich colour of the Red Sandstone which is a good water-bearing rock for borehole drilling; if a fault can be found in the rock by dowsing a much greater amount will be available.

Chapter XXIII

Mid-Northumberland

OUTH of a line of the Southern Upland Fault running from Stranraer to Dunbar the rocks are mainly Greywakes, a form of sandstone with a variety of mineral and rock fragments and a paste-like matrix of the same material, and finer-grained silt stones and shales. The majority of the twenty-five sites marked out for drilling have been drilled into Greywakes which is a dominant feature around Melrose; one of the drillings at Midlem was artesian.

My journey now takes me to mid-Northumberland, forming a triangle with the towns of Alnwick, Rothbury and Morpeth, the two river valleys being the Wansbeck running out to sea, two miles north of Blyth, and the Coquet reaching the sea at Amble. I have been dowsing for water in this area for forty years by 'word of mouth' recommendation only. To date I have surveyed and marked out points to drill for fifty-one clients in the region of these two rivers.

The scenery of this unspoiled area of rolling countryside is a treasure, fast disappearing in most of England today. The two valleys are noted for the quality of their livestock, both cattle and sheep, which are now being exported for the food markets of Europe.

Geology has several interesting features, the most prominent being the Whin Sill which passes through the area, in places standing very prominent and giving rise to bold escarpments such as may be seen north of the Roman Wall, and in the Belford area. It forms sea cliffs in the Farne Islands, Bamburgh and Dunstanburgh Castles are built upon it, and it is responsible for many waterfalls including High Force. In an Economic Geology report the rock of the Whin Sill can be crushed for road stone or concrete aggregate. Quarries on the line of the Whin Sill are producing thousands of tons every day for road-making in the north of England.

119

This is the rock which I can detect with my divining rod at a distance of twenty miles or more away. It has a movement entirely similar to that which I get searching for water when the rod goes firmly down at the edge of a vein. The reaction to Whinstone is as if the rod was alive, bobbing up and down.

Limestone is uppermost in the Coquet and Wansbeck Valleys, in this area as thick as 70 to 100 metres. At Berwick-on-Tweed it reaches 200m.

Chapter XXIV

The Retirement Cottage,
the Barn, Swaledale

I N NOVEMBER 1991 I received a request to locate water on a property in Swaledale in North Yorkshire. The call came from a Dr and Mrs Butler who were living in the university town of Oxford and were professionally linked with the colleges. We made a date to meet which was Friday, 29 November at 2.00 p.m. at the small hamlet of Marske, a delightful place on the Marske Burn which joins the river Swale a quarter of a mile away. The beauty of the narrow upper valley of the river Swale is known throughout the country; characteristic are the 'field houses' which are soundly built of stone. Their use is to house the Dales cattle during the long winters of the North of England. The hay to feed the cattle was stored in the upper floor of the building and fed to the cattle two or three times a day.

Our meeting was as planned and after the introductions we proceeded to the site in question, a distance of four miles which in late November can be a bleak and difficult journey, rising up to a height of 1,150ft above sea level. The site, which was on the market, consisted of a quarter of one acre of land walled round with a drystone wall. On it stood a well-built stone barn which in its past had housed cattle. In the For Sale notice it was without water, electricity or any modern convenience. In the area of the site it was doubtful whether water was within its boundaries. The next few minutes were going to reveal the answer to what meant so much to two people who had travelled the long distance from Oxford.

I began the dowse and picked up the signs of water. I did full circle to see what else there was, without avail, so I walked towards the influence that was in the distance hoping it would be within the boundary wall. I came to the edge of the stream just within, then stepped across it a distance of eight and a half yards, running at an angle which was their good fortune for it to be within the boundary at one small place only. When I depthed it the measurement was 156ft. Dr and Mrs Butler were relieved to see how near they were to a disappointment. Their plan was to convert the barn into a dwelling for their retirement within a few years' time and in their words 'get away from the bustle of modern time city life as it is today'.

During the last twenty years I have dowsed for many people wanting to do the very same exercise. The remote areas are all beyond the reach of a mains water supply. I have located water in the foothills of the Cheviot Hills on both sides of the border, several along the Roman Wall in Northumberland, in the Pennine Hills and Yorkshire Dales.

Chapter XXV

Roddam Hall, by Alnwick 1992

RODDAM HALL is agreeably situated a little distance west of the Coldstream road, on a bold eminence, which to the south forms the banks of a deep dell. The house is a modern building probably on the site of an older hall; it commands a very pleasant view towards the valley of the river Till which flows into the Tweed.

It is very obvious by the stately trees and shrubs around the present Hall that it had been originally developed as the country residence of a prominent family whose name is mentioned in the history of Scotland and Northumberland for several hundreds of years.

The present owner of Roddam Hall is a businessman with many interests, but he does devote a large amount of his time to agriculture, both in his interests generally and the commitment he has to the land he farms extensively on his estates at Roddam Hall and ten miles to the north, his Hetton and Holburn estates.

The manner which news is spread is sometimes very strong. It can be by chance, or by intention. In this instance the story began from the 'Pink Palace', headquarters of Radio Newcastle.

I was asked by a young lady who was a reporter for the BBC if I would demonstrate the art of dowsing, which I had now been doing for forty years, locating water principally for farmers and landowners. I accepted the invitation to demonstrate and a meeting was arranged for us to meet at the Pink Palace on the edge of Newcastle Town Moor, where cattle are grazed within the city boundary and it was ideal to be on grass where it resembled the real thing.

My method was to make the demonstration similar to that of any client needing a water supply. The site was unknown, as is the case in all my dowsing over the years. I found the reporter to be very talkative, which was good for my purpose of giving a commentary as we proceeded with what was to be a replica of all my dowsing.

I began in the usual way by scanning the area for a lead which I quickly found and proceeded towards it giving a commentary at the same time, which was being recorded on tape to go out on BBC Radio 2 during that week. Lord Vinson of Roddam Hall in Northumberland, listening to his car radio, heard the programme on my dowsing and contacted Mrs Catherine Busby of BBC Radio Newcastle for my address. A meeting was arranged to do a survey for underground water at Roddam Hall, also at his Hetton and Holburn estates to find out the potential water situation – for Tuesday, 16 June 1992 at 10.30 a.m.

I arrived on time and discussed the quantity needed, and where; also some basics regarding the siting of water storage and power to drive water delivery by pumping. It was not possible to make a timetable for the day so it was agreed to spend the morning at Roddam Hall, with lunch en route to the agricultural estate at Hetton and Holburn estates, a journey of about fifteen miles.

Lord Vinson had not seen a dowser at work, so I demonstrated the procedure by finding a vein of underground water on the lawn south of the Hall, which I found by dowsing, explaining each process in turn. By scanning I found the direction, then walking towards the influence and coming to its edge, I marked it, walked across the influence counting the steps in metres and made a note of the width in my notebook. Then I continued to walk from the edge until the divining rod went down again, still counting my steps as I went. The number of steps in metres would be equal to the depth of the water. This wave band throws off at the 45° mark. The measurements of the vein under the lawn were 16m wide and in my mental thinking 135ft deep. The site was not marked for drilling because I felt there would be better. Also it was not in a convenient place to harness the existing layout of tanks and power.

We now proceeded to where water storage tanks were in present use. I surveyed this south-sloping field and found what would be a suitable supply to back up the present spring supply. The vein influence was 30m wide and 135ft deep. As there were two tanks in the field I marked a point to drill at the nearest point to each, as on the plan, giving a choice.

We then proceeded to site a spring one mile west of the Hall and, travelling by Land Rover, we climbed up onto high ground and looked to the north-west on that summer day – a magnificent view of the Cheviot Hills with the sounds of lark, curlew and lapwing, a real bonus to the day.

The spring came to the surface at three places, each one coming from the same vein of water which was 52m wide and 18ft deep. Much more water could be tapped by digging with a JCB at a point where I marked. A very high iron content was present in this spring. Because of this and the mile of pipe maintenance, it would be worth reconsidering the borehole at the Hall.

The afternoon was to consist of a much more extensive survey over the whole of the Hetton and Holburn estates, the plan being to find where water was available and in what quantity. It was very difficult at this early stage to make any plans other than to consider the needs. This opportunity arose when we stopped for lunch on the journey to the afternoon session, when we were joined by Lord Vinson's estate manager who remained with us throughout the survey.

Hutton and Holburn estates are a very fertile area of well-managed farms on a ridge between the Northumberland coast at Bamburgh to the east and the Till valley to the west. It is mainly arable, with a large dairy unit with its young stock, beef cattle and a large sheep flock making it among the larger farming units in Britain.

The ideal situation for a water supply would be to find it on the higher ground to gravitate to the various farms. If not found on the high ground it could be pumped there. We began the survey at Holburn Village which is on the highest ground. I quickly picked up a vein of water running under a crop of standing corn and so I walked into the crop to establish if it was what we were looking for. It measured 41m wide. I was pleased to have this as a starter measuring at the better end of what I was hoping to find. To save walking through the crop of ripe barley I moved out of the field to get the depthing correct. As the vein ran under the highway it was much easier to step out the measurements. The water was 255ft at this point. A discussion between Lord Vinson, his estate manager and myself then took place to report my findings and to mark the site to drill if this site is chosen.

Veins of underground water are generally in straight or nearly straight lines. The drilling has to be done at the midstream point, but can be moved along the line of flow for convenience. It is also important to consider the operator, when selecting that the site is accessible for the driller. This site was marked just through the gate into the cornfield off the road, very convenient if chosen.

Site No. 2 at Holburn Mill was to be next on the list. Before leaving Holburn Village our next survey site was pointed out and it stood out in my mind that the vein just marked seemed to be going in the direction of Holburn Mill. At the No. 2 site we quickly found my thoughts to be correct. The vein was found near to the farm and measured 41m revealing its identity, but the depth had changed to 210ft. As there was no other vein to compare, the site was marked and a grass sod taken off at the point to drill.

Site No. 3 was Hetton Steads and it was unbelievable that the same vein passed under the farmsteading, width being the same, the depth now 207ft. The point to drill was marked in the stock yard.

Site No. 4 was Hetton Law, and when nearing the farm we were again going to cross our No. 1 vein. Travelling in the Land Rover I took out my divining rod to say when it was crossed. We stopped where the rod went down and sure enough it was the same for the fourth time, the depth now 231ft. When I drew the plan of the day's dowsing it is quite remarkable to find a vein marked in four places.

Site No. 5. Stopping at the farmstead at Hetton Law I was very pleased to find a change, a vein running very near to the farm. When I stepped it out I found it to be 61m wide and was very pleased to report my find with such potential – even the depth was different at 159ft, no doubt in a different strata.

Site No. 6 was Hetton Hall. I found a vein of water passing very near to the Hall, running in a different direction than previously, it measured 40m wide and 243ft deep, a very easy access for the driller. The drilling site was marked as on plan. We moved on to site No. 7 at North Hazelrigg, which proved to be in my judgement the poorest of the afternoon survey, but the survey had to be done and on this instance, as so many times before, reported my findings. The best available was a vein 30m wide and 126ft deep. A convenient site was marked.

Now to our final survey of the day, No. 8 at Holburn Grange, home of the dairy herd, and hopefully favourable! As luck would have it a vein of water was within the boundary of the farmstead. My fingers were crossed at the stepping out of the width which was 52m wide and 312ft deep, a very pleasurable conclusion to a long day.

We now returned to the Estate Office at Hetton Steads, looked at the farm maps and I left a copy of my various notes. Lord Vinson and I returned to Roddam Hall where I collected my car and we said our farewells. His parting words were, 'Mr Taylor, I am amazed at your confidence.'

A letter received 20 July 1992.

Roddam Hall
By Alnwick

Dear Mr. Taylor,

I thought you would be pleased to know that we have now drilled on two of the sites that you dowsed. At Hetton Hall we have hit a substantial quantity of water at about 120 ft. At Holburn Grange Farm, likewise but about 200 ft.

I am very grateful for your help in this matter. You might like to zero your internal depth measurement gauge – it seems to be running slightly deeper than it should.

Thanks to you it looks as if we are going to have a water supply of better quantity and quality than we could have believed – and are most grateful to you.

Lord Vinson.

Lord Vinson of Roddam Dene LVO DL

House of Lords

As from: Roddam Hall
Alnwick
Northumberland
NE66 4XY

I wish to record that I used the services of Mr. Edwin Taylor to dowse for water for me on my Roddam and Hetton Estate Farms during the summer of 1993. We subsequently drilled two holes with great success in both cases hitting a substantial quantity of water slightly prior to the depth that he had indicated.

I could not recommend more strongly the services of Mr. Edwin Taylor whom I believe to be a dowser of the highest competence and integrity apart from being very pleasant to deal with.

3rd January, 1994

Chapter XXVI

Ewieside Woodland –
Ethel M. Houston

ON 29 JUNE 1990 I received the following letter:

58 Frederick Street
Edinburgh
Edwin Taylor Esq.

Dear Mr. Taylor,

Professor and Mrs. Fowler of Old Easter Housebyres, near Melrose, are clients of mine and recommended you to me. I have a small woodland investment of just under 100 acres at Ewieside, which is about 3 miles south of Cockburnspath on the A1. I enclose a plan of the woodland which already indicates water supply from a spring which used to service the farm house. There is also reference to a spring at the far end of the wood, but I am quite keen to discover the possibility of water elsewhere. I would like to have access to an adequate water supply as I think we may face droughts in the future and it does help to know just exactly what potential water supply is available.

I shall be most grateful if you will let me know when you might be able to come up and inspect the wood.

Yours sincerely,
E. M. Houston.

I am primarily interested in locating other 'springs' or adequate additional water supply.

I responded to E. M. Houston's letter and agreed to meet on site on Saturday, 7 July 1990. On a survey of this size and the fact that it was a woodland area where the grass was tall made it very difficult to get through in places. One cannot order a fine day, but on this occasion the weather favoured fortunately us.

It had been explained in Ethel Houston's letter what was required. We met as arranged and after the introductions boarded my client's vehicle which was a four-wheel drive and set out to find the unknown. Having a driver allows me to dowse from the passenger seat and when we cross over a vein of water I ask the driver to stop, get out and measure width and depth and I know immediately whether it is suitable to mark or discard.

I began the survey at the east end of the Ewieside woodland which was long, very irregular and sloping into a ravine. As we were travelling through a side in the first section I felt that we were above water and asked if we could stop. I stepped back about twenty metres to be in a position far enough from the vein to check the line of flow, which I will now explain. I had been dowsing for water nearly twenty years when I became aware that the influence of a vein of underground water could be picked up by a dowser from a distance. This discovery has saved me many long hours on a site where several places are to mark. The great advantage of this ability is when you arrive on a site and scan the surrounding area by turning full circle and can pick the influence of a vein of water at a distance of 150 metres or less. In that full circle you may find more than one in some other direction. If the first is to be the one of your choice you now walk towards it. When you get to the edge of the influence and the rod goes firmly down you know that you have met the vein at right angles, and you are on the edge. Going in the same direction count your steps to the other side of that vein. Make notes of all measurements, which are the basis of estimated yield when the time comes to bore.

To continue, I was looking along the ride holding my divining rod and doing a half scan, which proved in this instance the vein crossed the ride which allowed me to do the measuring by stepping out in metres, making No. 1 quite easy walking; the width was 34m, depth 147ft. These figures are listed and a plan drawn of the survey.

No. 2 was much more difficult – none of the measurements were on any track or ride. The width was 30m, depth 120ft.

No. 3, like No. 1 was easy and allowed me to stay on the ride; to get to No. 3 was a very steep climb for the vehicle. Width 25m, depth 99ft. This one would be on a different strata because we had travelled up a very steep incline. No. 4 was like a twin to No. 3 crossing the same ride about 200 metres to the west. The width was 40m, depth 150ft.

No. 5 was in a grass field and also ran into the wood. The calculations were done on the grass area being width 60m and depth 126ft.

No. 6 was again crossing a ride, but very near to a pasture field where the measurements were taken as width 45m, depth 156ft. The point to drill was marked on the side of the ride as the pasture field had a different owner.

No. 7. obliged again by being able to walk on the ride and do my measuring. Width 40m, depth 144ft.

Any of the seven sites (marked at places where a drilling machine could get to) in my experience had the signs of yielding a considerable amount of water. The choice one was No. 5 and it was at the lowest point, which would mean costly pumping if used. Seven well sites marked:

No. 1	Width 34 metres	Depth 147 feet
No. 2	Width 30 metres	Depth 120 feet
No. 3	Width 25 metres	Depth 99 feet
No. 4	Width 40 metres	Depth 150 feet
No. 5	Width 60 metres	Depth 126 feet
No. 6	Width 45 metres	Depth 156 feet
No. 7	Width 40 metres	Depth 144 feet

58 Frederick Street
Edinburgh
10th July 1990
Mr. Edwin Taylor.

Dear Mr. Taylor,

Ewieside Woodland

Many thanks for your letter of yesterday with the Plan of the Woodland, showing the seven places you have marked as potential sources of underground water and showing the drilling points and the red lines showing the direction of flow.

I was very glad to meet you and your wife and grandson. I shall have great pleasure in recommending you to any of my clients who might require your services.

Yours sincerely,
Ethel M. Houston.

Chapter XXVII

Country Cottage – Tod Le Moor

N THE outlying areas of Northumberland there is a great demand for second homes. Many are very remote and in places where a mains water supply will never reach because of the long distance of piping that would be needed and cost would overrule the need.

I am called in to many dwellings which fall into this category and supplies of water are generally there insufficient quantity to supply the need of such a cottage or small house. Many of these older houses had a well at the door. It was not there by chance. The well was found by a dowser before the house was built, which makes sense.

Mr Mackay was a plumber by trade, with a business in the country market town of Rothbury, a large agricultural area of the south foothills of the Cheviot Hills on the Scottish Border. I have spent many dowsing days with Mr Mackay on agricultural estates in that area where he was recognized as knowing the country way of life. He was not to tell where the water tank was because he had put it in when it was new.

I received the following letter dated 4 June 1973:

38 Cheval Place
London SW7
4 June 1973
E. Taylor Esq.

Mosswood Farm
Consett
Co. Durham.

Dear Mr. Taylor,

Thank you for your letter of the 1st June advising me that you found a good supply of water about 150 ft. below ground inside the boundary of Tod le Moor. This is excellent news and I have asked Mr. Mackay to obtain authority from the River Board and then to arrange for the drilling to take place.

Thank you very much for dealing with this job so quickly and I enclose my cheque in settlement of the work you carried out. Yours truly,

Bill Hastings.

My notes at the time read: Found supply seven yards wide and one hundred and fifty feet deep. Result. A good supply found.

Chapter XXVIII

Mr Hindmarch, Longhorsley

N THE early days of my dowsing I received a telephone call on a Saturday afternoon – Could I help? Mr Hindmarch had a drilling machine in his farmyard to redrill a borehole that had been drilled two years previously. Mr Hindmarch was in a predicament and I could hear anxiety in his voice. I promptly said, 'I will come immediately,' a great relief to him. He did say to me in that conversation that the drilling site of two years before had been chosen on the advice of the Geological Department as a likely place to find water and the resulting bore had a very intermittent poor supply from seepage water only. The intention of the drilling company was to redrill the two-year-old bore in the hope of success. Mr Hindmarch was shocked when I said it would be a complete waste of their time and his money.

I then set out on my journey of thirty miles to the farm on a cold and very foggy afternoon with visibility about thirty yards, a journey not to be taken for pleasure. When I arrived at the farm my first thought was to check the site of the borehole to see if it was worthwhile drilling deeper. The immediate survey showed it was without water which put it in the category of being a failure.

Now to find the site for borehole number two. I very soon picked up the signs of what I was looking for, a vein of underground water. I walked towards the influence and my divining rod went down; this marked the edge of water. I stepped across it and after twelve of my steps the rod again went down giving on the other edge. At this moment I knew I had found my site for borehole number two, less than thirty yards from the failure (but yet to be proved). I then continued to walk away from the vein to check the depth, and came to that point where the rod again went down at a distance of 44 steps or 132ft to the water.

I then marked the point to drill, saying to Mr Hindmarch, 'On no account move the place to drill.' I wished him well and I set out on my journey home, Mr Hindmarch saying, 'I will let you know.' Within twenty-three hours of leaving, at 3.00 p.m. the following day, the telephone rang and it was Mr Hindmarch. He said, 'We have found the water and it is running down the field.' The new bore was test-pumped for yield and it was producing 10,000 gallons a day.

A few months later I was passing the Hindmarch farm and Mrs Hindmarch answered the door. I enquired about the new water supply. She said, 'It's lovely. I can now bath the children one at a time!'

When I look at Map 81 of the Ordnance Survey in the near vicinity of Longhorsley I see a pocket of twenty-one sites that I have surveyed and marked for well drilling, nearly all for farm supplies, except one which is a very successful garden centre.

The fact that I never advertise my dowsing ability seems to be revealed in the pockets showing up in various parts of the British Isles by word-of-mouth contact only, which has suited my way of life as a farmer, but which can be very demanding at times during the year.

An interesting report could be written on nearly every survey I carry out. There are no two farms alike. No two farmers alike. Their needs are different. There is great variation within the wide extremes of the agricultural industry and all the hundreds of surveys I have done and the people for whom the survey was done have covered every walk of life, all in search of that little ability of an ancient art I humbly possess.

Fenrother Lane Farm is near to Longhorsley and farmed by Mr Storey who had the misfortune to lose his spring water supply at the same time as a gas pipeline passed through his farm. Mr Storey approached the gas company who liked to keep a good relationship with the farming community and were willing to drill for water. On 7 September 1983 I received a telephone call from Colin Jeffries, a local field draininage contractor living at Longhorsley and representing Mr Storey. He asked if we could fix a day to survey for a water supply at Fenrother Lane and the day was fixed to meet on site, 24 September 1983.

I first checked the old well south of the farmhouse, which was a vein 5yds wide and 30ft deep – no use for the present demand. The vein of water I found next passed under the farmsteading and measured 10yds wide and 93ft deep, being very conveniently placed. I marked a choice of three places to drill, two on the west side and one on the east side; measurements for all three were the same. The reason for marking three was that it was not known on the day where the storage tank was to be sited. All arrangements were then made for drilling, storage tanks, pipes and cable for power. Only one thing had been forgotten — there was no provision made to drain away surplus water. The well proved to be artesian with water flowing out of the bore.

Chapter XXIX

Blackhills Farm, Rattray, Perthshire

T WAS 1 May 1988 that I received a telephone call from Mr. C. K. K. Frampton, who farmed 800 acres of rich farmland growing mainly fruit, and wanted extra water for irrigation. He had already sunk two boreholes which he was using. They had been surveyed by Ballantine, a well-known water dowser from St Andrews, Fifeshire who I met many times; sadly he died a few years ago and he has been very much missed for his dowsing ability.

I fixed the day of 19 May at 10.30 a.m., to meet at his farm just a short distance east of Blairgowrie. The plan would be to travel north the day before, a distance of about 165 miles. Blackhills survey looked as if it would take some time to select the best choice of veins.

The day of the 19th arrived and I arrived on site as planned. Mr Frampton took me to his office and began to mark out a plan for the survey. He told me about Mr Ballantine's visit and I asked if he minded if I tried where the previous drilling was done. He did not mind. I asked what form of power he intended to use to which he replied it would be a portable generator, which was quite a relief to me. When power from the farm is relied upon it restricts the area you have to survey because there is a greater loss of power the further distance you get away from its source. Having looked at the plan of the farm we were now ready to begin the survey. Mr Ballantine's drilling site was near to the farm and I made that my first start. I found he and I thought alike which I was pleased to find. As there was quite a lot of travelling to do Mr Frampton took his Range Rover. I noticed when looking at the farm plan that the highway ran across the farm in the form of a cross which meant that all the better quantities of water would have to pass under the highway and I could find most of what was there from the passenger seat in the Range Rover. We travelled north-east on the road from the farm travelling at a speed of about

15 m.p.h. When we had travelled the length of two fields I felt the pull on my divining rod and that was the sign to stop and take stock. I got out of the vehicle and began as if I had walked to that point where I was getting the first signs that a vein of water was near to me. When the rod dipped I rotated. I knew that was the direction to walk and I would soon come to the edge of a vein of water. I had my notebook and pen ready to take down details of what I found. Its width would tell me if it was suitable for irrigation. I now came to the edge of the water vein. The rod went firmly down. I counted my steps as I walked over the vein. The rod would go down at the other edge. It had now gone down and I called this in my notes: Site No. 1, 28yds wide. I stepped out from the other edge walking in the same direction until the rod went down again. I had counted 52yds which was the depth so I filled in my notes: Depth of No. 1, 166ft. When you look on the farm plan you will see direct direction of flow which was found on the road. I moved into the field to get space to measure and then marked the site where to drill at midstream.

Site No. 2 was also found from the passenger seat of the Range Rover. It crossed the road at Cluanie Cottage and it was 40yds wide and 60ft deep. The drilling point was marked in field number 43 on the other side of the road from the cottage.

Site No. 3 was on a vein of water which ran north-south over a large pasture field on the highest ground on the farm, which would be an ideal place to find water to gravitate to the other parts. It was 50yds wide and 138ft deep, the best so far. With the site being so favourable I looked for a vein that crossed No. 3 and was very pleased to find one which I called Site No. 4, which was 56yds wide and 120ft deep. I marked the site to drill No. 3 where 3 and 4 crossed. I also marked a point to drill on No. 4 alone as it is likely to be the best single vein. The crossing place of 3 and 4 will rank as one of the best I have marked over all my years of dowsing.

Site No. 5. Again found out of the Range Rover crossing the road at the field gate entering field numbers 30 and 31. I measured 40yds wide and 210ft deep. Another good potential supply.

Site No. 6 was found in field number 41, to the south of the farm. It was 42yds wide and 66ft deep, not well sited on the farm for access, but could prove valuable for other reasons. The point to mark was made near to the hedgerow to minimise inconvenience.

At the end of the survey we returned to the farm office and put the details on to the farm plan showing points to drill and direction of flow. To sum up on the day's survey, I was pleased with what I had found and where they were placed on the farm. The crossing place of 3 and 4 was the highlight to me. The fertility and the climate in that area of Perthshire must be very good seeing field after field of raspberry, black and red currants, loganberry and many others that would contribute to the jam-making factories in Dundee and other large towns.

Mr Frampton told me how long the fruit growing had been going on in the area. On this farm alone there was an annual encampment for pickers who came out to the country from Dundee for the few weeks in the year when the fruit was ripe. Many of the families have now been coming for three generations.

One thing was very noticeable to me. The beech trees in that fertile area were so tall and healthy for it is on the road from Perth to Blairgowrie where the famous beech is on that roadside. Foresters and horticulturists travel from all over the British Isles to see that well-kept beech hedge.

Site No.	Width	Depth	Notes
1	28 yards	156 ft.	Field 5
2	40 yards	60 ft.	Field 43
3	50 yards	138 ft.	Field 35
4	56 yards	120 ft.	Field 35
5	40 yards	210 ft.	Field gate 30 & 31
6	42 yards	60 ft.	Field 41

Chapter XXX

Sandyford, Haydon Bridge

N 20 FEBRUARY 1973 I received a letter from Smiths Gore, Land Agents, of Corbridge on Tyne, requesting my services as a dowser to locate a water supply for a client at Sandyford, situated on high ground near to the Roman Wall. It is a stock-rearing farm, carrying both cattle and sheep. The existing supply is inadequate to maintain the number of livestock.

I replied to the letter saying I would be pleased to do the survey and if convenient I would like to meet Mr Mackay, the plumber, at 10.30 a.m. on Tuesday, 27 February on site at Sandyford.

At that time in 1973 I was Chairman of the Rural Water Supplies Sub-Committee of the Rural District of Hexham. I met regularly with G. Gourley Esq., engineer and surveyor with the Council. He knew of my dowsing because of the number of wells I had found in the area. I asked Mr Gourley if he would like to join me on the survey and see the process through at the various stages, he as the professional man and I the diviner. He agreed to come to the survey and I was pleased.

The day of the 27th came and we met as planned. I knew that the quantity needed for this size of unit was in the region of 10,000 gallons per day. The next important thing was to find the water as near to where it was going to be used, also near to a power line. I found the first vein of water at the entrance to the farm. Mr Mackay from Rothbury had been with me many times before and knew my procedure, but with Mr Gourley I wanted him to see how it was done. The vein I found was 7yds wide and 120ft deep. It was ideally placed for drilling, power and water storage.

Whenever I do a survey like this it is better if possible to have an alternative to compare and select the better of two or more. In this instance there was not another to compare without putting it to disadvantage by moving away from the farmstead area, so I consulted with Mr Mackay who was arranging the drilling and installation, and the siting was important to him. Where I marked where the two veins crossed I only had a square foot to put in the point to drill, although the mark being put there could be moved along the vein, but had to be marked midstream. The seven-yard width in my view would be capable of yielding over the 10,000 gallons per day which was the aim. Another survey was complete and I was just waiting the result of the drilling which should be soon.

Sheet 87 of the Ordnance Survey landranger map refers to 'Sandyford' as 'Seldom Seen'.

Later I received the result of the drilling at Sandyford. The borehole was test-pumped for yield and the result was 20,000 gallons of water per day. Water was found at 128ft and found its level in the borehole 30ft from the surface, meaning there was 98ft of water standing in the bore. Another very satisfactory result.

Chapter XXXI

Brundeanlaws

IN SEPTEMBER 1987 I received a request to find a water supply for the Hon. Lady Julie Arbuthnot of Brundeanlaws, Jedburgh, Roxburghshire. There was a new house to be built and I was sure time would be important, so the request was dealt with as urgent.

The date of the survey was arranged for Saturday, 5 October. It was one of the many fine sunny days in the autumn of that year when it was a pleasure to be out, and very much more so on reaching Brundeanlaws.

The A68 road is the scenic road to Scotland and as my home at Mosswood is on the side of that road, the journey to Scotland was A68 all the way. When you cross the border at Carter Bar the views of Scotland are of scenery which is second to none. It was just three more miles after crossing the Border that I left the A68 road, turning right into the foothills of the Cheviot Range. About three more miles on this, the Morebattle road, I was to turn right again, now facing south to Brundeanlaws, which was at the end of the road, and out of sight until the last quarter of a mile of the journey. We met as arranged, made our introductions, and went into the farmhouse for a cup of tea and to talk about the water supply, and also about her farming which interested me as much as looking for water.

To help see the picture more clearly I will explain as it was related to me over that cup of tea. Lady Arbuthnot was getting a great deal of pleasure from this farm in the hills where her shepherd was resident in the farmhouse. Her husband was a doctor. She also farmed in France and was trying to get a balance of time with her life and her farming. She was in Scotland for the lambing time and sales, and in France most of the winter period living about six months in each. The dwelling that was to be her Scottish home was to be situated just after leaving the Morebattle road, leading to the farm at Brundeanlaws.

We now travelled up the half mile to the site of the proposed house, where foundations were marked out. My objective now was to find water near to the house. I took my divining rod from my inside coat pocket and scanned the surrounding area to find the nearest vein of water. I felt the pull of one on the south side of the proposed dwelling and walked to it with a view to building the picture of its worth. I came to its edge, then walked over it, counting my steps, each one being one yard. The width was ten yards. The good thing was that it was inside the boundary. To depth it I moved on to the road to get a measure of the depth without interruption. When I was on site there was a hedge in my way. I stepped it out on the road and it was 93ft deep. It seemed ideal for what was needed and a stake was knocked into the ground midstream as marked on the plan being the point to drill.

I received the following note on 10–11–1988:

Brundeanlaws
Jedburgh
Roxburghshire
10 November

Edwin Taylor
Mosswood Farm
Allensford
Consett.

Sorry not to have written and thanked you before for finding our water for us. You were quite right about the depth 95 feet where there was a spring of water. We have had a super supply ever since.

There has been plenty to make an ornamental pond system. Do drop in when you are passing – wish you would come to France to find water there – our bill last year was £400. Hope your sheep have done well.

Yours
Julie Arbuthnot.

Chapter XXXII

A First Time Instance – Martin Bergins

O N 21 NOVEMBER 1992 I travelled into Scotland to keep an appointment with Martin Bergins, a dairy farmer at Over Langshaw, five miles to the north of the historic town of Melrose. Like many other dairy farmers who are finding water charges high and likely to go higher, he wanted to sink a borehole on his own farm. The reason for my visit was to survey for the water by dowsing near to the farm.

It is now over twenty years since I discovered my ability to find water veins from a distance, and it has been a great advantage, by not needing to walk long distances on a survey for underground water.

There has up to now been no disadvantage, but recently while writing about dowsing, it occurred to me that a situation could arise by beginning a search to find a vein of water at a distance, while by chance, standing upon one. Within days of thinking about this situation and how to deal with it, something very strange happened as if fate had played a part to be prepared.

When I stood at the point nearest to where Martin Bergins would have liked to find the water I began to scan the area and see what was in the vicinity when there was a strong pull on my rod to the west. I thought the signs were good. I continued to turn clockwise, there was another strong pull on my rod, and suddenly I knew there was something different. It was too exact. For the first time in twenty years I had that experience.

It was now going to be interesting for me to see how it was going to unfold, to confirm that what I was thinking was correct, that I was standing on a vein of water and the two influences I had picked up were in fact the two edges of a vein of water. My method to prove that would be to begin again by scanning and when the rod dipped walk in that direction to where it firmly went down, put in a cane marker, then continue in the same direction for five strides; while facing in that direction scan the area in front, which should be blank, turn around to retrace my steps, but before doing so scan the area towards the cane. The rod should dip. I now walked to the cane where the rod firmly went down. I was now on the edge of the vein, and would now walk over the vein counting my strides until I reached the other side, which measured 42m. This vein of water was very good, an ideal situation for where Mr Bergins wanted it. All I had to do now was the depthing.

I stood on the edge of the vein facing away from it, and walked away from the vein counting my strides as I went. When I reached the depth wave band the rod went firmly down. On this occasion it was 71m of 210ft.

Chapter XXXIII

The Old Well, Tantobie

O N 28 MAY 1980 I received a request to find an old well at the Oak Tree Inn at Tantobie, a few miles north of Durham City, in the land of the Prince Bishops. The property had recently changed hands and the purchaser was a Mrs Hurst, who while looking at the deeds of the inn saw that a well was marked. She thought it would create a feature and add to the character of the old property that she had acquired.

Tantobie is only a few miles from my home and having become interested myself in finding the well, I called Mrs Hurst to say I would telephone soon and let her know in advance before I came.

I thought out my method to solve the mystery of the missing well which I would hope to find in the following way:

Most farms I go to in search for water have old wells near to the back door of the house, always perfectly lined out by stone and sited midstream on a vein of water and no doubt found by a dowser. If you are quick-thinking you will realize the well was found before the house was built, which makes sense, so it was also likely this old well was in place before the inn was built.

It was in the evening of the last day of May that I did the survey to find the well. I began at the rear of the inn and found the vein of water that some previous dowser had found some hundreds of years before. The vein was 4yds wide and 15ft deep. By finding the vein I had reduced the area of my search down to four yards wide. I now walked along the line of the vein and the rod went down. I walked on in the same direction and after three yards it went down again. To confirm that I turned around and walked back over it again. The rod dipped at both places. A report in the press dated 4 June 1980 read: Old Well found at the Oak Tree Inn, Tantobie, as forecast by a dowser on 30th May.

The Author Dowsing

Chapter XXXIV

Portpatrick

ON 11 AUGUST 1992 I made the journey to an area beyond the town of Stranraer, the main port when travelling to Northern Ireland from Northern England or Scotland. The purpose of my going there was to locate underground water for farms on the peninsular west of Luce Bay, a very fertile part of the south-west of Scotland enjoying the warm moist air of the Gulf Stream which was very noticeable by the presence of palm trees and other trees and shrubs of a warmer climate. The Botanical Gardens at Logan Tower, halfway down the peninsular, are outstanding in their particular field, attracting visitors from all parts of the world.

My dowser friend in Scotland, Michael Cranfield, warned me of the area around Stranraer to be difficult for a dowser to gain success, for which I thanked him. In my way of thinking, to move away from the dangers of failure is not getting an answer to the difficulty, and my feeling was to find out myself and see if my years of experience could give some light to the reason for failure. If true it would be very important to know and would add considerably to the knowledge for dowsers of the future. I knew also from Michael that he had dowsed for water and marked a site to drill at the Portpatrick Golf Course. Unfortunately for him and the Club Committee, the drilling proved a failure without any sign of water.

Before I made the journey to Portpatrick I asked Michael if he would mind if I checked the site of the dry borehole. He had no objections. I thanked him and said I would let him know what I found. My contact by telephone was Mr Irving at Holly Holme Farm who kindly made arrangements with my other clients for the day of dowsing.

I kept my appointment with Mr Irving to meet at 11.00 a.m. and began with his survey. I asked what was the daily consumption of water on the farm, which I could see carried a dairy herd. The amount required was about 5,000 gallons per day, which gave me a guide to what I was looking for. I scanned the area to see what was near to the farm and I could feel two veins within reasonable distance. I checked the vein near to the farm buildings which was 10yds wide and 120ft deep. In my opinion this vein was in the right place to serve the farm, and also had a good potential for yield. I now marked my first site for drilling in this area where confidence had been damaged by a number of dry boreholes.

My second site marking was for Mr Torrens at Auchabreck, another dairy farm needing a much larger quantity of water than Mr Irving. I found a good vein 29yds wide and 201ft deep.

We broke for lunch at the end of survey two. Mr Torrens and Mr Irving joined me for lunch, and at the same time gave us a chance to discuss the next survey. Mr. Torrens had another farm one mile from where we had lunch at Port Logan, a small fishing village of just a few houses and the hotel which was popular with the local people and a great attraction for the tourist, where the sea lapped up to within fifteen metres of the hotel door, which faced west and looked across the sea to Ireland. On a clear day on the higher ground of that coastline can clearly be seen the Mountains of Mourne. I was there on a clear day and enjoyed having seen those hills standing up on the skyline.

Back now to Mr Torrens and his site number two which was Mullhill Farm, Port Logan, on a flat plateau about 150 feet above sea level and very exposed to a west wind. I stood in the farmyard to scan the area to pick up the strongest influence from the pull of a water vein, which I found to be in the direction of the sea (it was not the sea water that caused the pull). I walked in the direction of where my divining rod was taking me towards the sea, which was a distance of two fields or about 600 metres, and was very surprised to find myself going so far. Did it mean that it was something above average? I began to feel much more life in the dowsing rod which meant I was now within the depth distance of a vein; then the rod went firmly down. I stopped and paused, then walked and counted my steps to the other side of the vein, making a note of the width, which was 51yds. I then stepped out to the depth wave band which was 210ft deep. At a distance of 200 metres from the farm, I marked two points on the line of the vein to drill.

Site No. 4 of the day was for John McFadzean of Barhill Farm,

Ardwell, a young man and wife team setting up in farming with a dairy herd of British Friesian cattle, and in the difficult times of 1992 in the farming business any saving would be a contribution to stay in the industry. In this instance if water was under the farm and could be tapped the saving could be considerable, hence the reason of my visit. I found a vein of water running under the length of the farm buildings which could be drawn from at a convenient point to suit the farm. Two places were marked on the same vein for Mr McFadzean to make the choice of which would be most convenient. The width of the vein was 25yds which seemed like having a good potential for yield, the estimated depth being 150ft.

Chapter XXXV

Barhill Farm, Ardwell, Stranraer

IT WAS NOW March 1993 and I had received word from John Banks, who had done the drilling of the above well in February. He had given me the good news that the well was test-pumped and was yielding 24,000 gallons per day. He also on the same visit to the area put down the bore at Holyholme for Mr Irving which was a successful result, yielding over 12,000 gallons per day, far beyond the needs of the farming system. The drilling at Auchabreck was not so good at this stage. I predicted water to be at 201ft, but the bore was down to 240ft and then stopped drilling.

There were some important factors which I hoped to discuss with the driller which could mean the difference between success and failure. I had already talked to John Banks, the driller, asking him what the drill was going through at the time it was stopped. He said hard rock! I asked if clay had been present at the drilling. He said the drill had gone through 100ft of clay. I had warned all through my dowsing experience that depthing is upset by the presence of clay and the more clay there is, the deeper the drill should go to find the water. My third question to John Banks was what was the drill into when water was found at the previous two successful drillings at Barhill and Hollyholme. One was through the rock and into shale, and the other through the rock and into gravel. Adding these facts together with the past experience I have had with the presence of clay, and to be through the rock into water-bearing strata, all led me to believe that there was still time to turn this drilling into success and not failure.

There are no truer words than 'Experience is the greatest teacher'. It is true throughout life. But at no time more true than in the field of dowsing for water. There is an experience at every turning and the good dowser will record every one, mentally or otherwise, for the day when he needs to refer to that example and be sure that day will come.

My journey to Stranraer from the beginning seemed to be shaping into a challenge which it has proved to be and I am very much wiser having been there. It looks now that new calls are coming through for a further visit to the area.

Chapter XXXVI

Kennetsideheads

T WAS THE first day of March 1993 when I received a telephone call from John Banks of Osprey Well Drilling, Dunfermline, in Scotland. He asked me if I would dowse for water at a farm near Kelso in the Tweed Valley. His machine was working in the area and he also asked how soon I could do the survey, because he was moving to another area. The farmer, James Mitchell, was also anxious to have the drilling done as soon as possible.

We agreed a site meeting for the survey at 11.00 a.m. on the third of March, including the farmer. I said weather permitting because there was a considerable amount of snow lying on the hills over Carter Bar and if it got worse I would telephone the night before.

On the morning of the meeting it was fine with dry roads to make the journey into Scotland, although snow lay like a blanket away from the roads. When I approached Kennetsideheads Farm it was away from the snow area and showing the green fields of a very fertile farm. James Mitchell met me at the farm office door and to my great surprise I knew him well through his being a member of a Sheep Breed Society, the same as myself. John Banks made all the arrangements but had not given the name of the farmer to me, hence my great surprise.

After the preliminaries of what quantity of water was needed and where the power was for the purpose of driving the pump to lift the water, I scanned the area with my divining rod to get a direction, which took me on to the close-cut lawn of the farmhouse. I indicated to Jim Mitchell that water was under the lawn, to which he said, 'I don't want it there.' John Banks and I said together, obviously thinking alike, 'You can only get it where it is.' I then said that as it was in a vein, we could move along the line of it. So we left the lawn, crossed the entrance road into a small field and marked a site to drill by taking off a grass sod. I said that if we found no other this one would do. The measurements were 20yds wide (a guide to yield) and 120ft deep; also it was very near to a power point. Jim Mitchell, the farmer, then said that the mains supply came in at the other side of the farm buildings and would I check that area with a view to using the supply pipe from the mains to the farm.

We walked around to the other side to the point where the mains entered and I found a vein quite near to the mains pipe. It was much better than No. 1 measuring 38yds wide and 160ft deep. The site was marked in the usual way in readiness for the arrival of the drilling machine.

Before I left the farm John Banks sped away to catch his man with the drilling machine to begin the borehole. He said on parting, 'I will let you know the result.'

It was now time for me to leave the farm with the job done and Jim Mitchell asked if I would like to see his livestock. I replied, 'I never tire of looking at good stock.'

The Kennetsideheads herd of pedigree Holsteins is a very noted strain of dairy cattle, being Scotland's highest yielding herd of 203 cows, being milked three times a day. The management of all the stock from cows, bulls, young stock and calves was superb; their contentment and comfort was a pleasure to see. This top management is reflected in Jim Mitchell's prices for cows at sales, where three pedigree cows recently sold added up to over £10,000. I hoped the result of my dowsing could match the quality of stock and their care that I had witnessed on my visit to Kennetsideheads.

On Saturday, 6 March I received a telephone call from John Banks giving the result of the borehole drilling at Kennetsideheads. He said, 'Your estimated depth of No. 2 site was given to be 160 feet. We found some water at 155 feet. At 165 feet the yield was test-pumped and was producing 24,000 gallons of water per day.'

I was very pleased to get a result to match the most outstanding farming unit that I remember seeing in Scotland.

Chapter XXXVII

Tarnside Farm, Farlam, Brampton

O N 22 AUGUST 1990 I received a telephone call from Mr Reed to help in finding a water supply. We agreed a date within a week. I prefer to know as little as possible about any scheme before my visit as it is so much better to begin with a clean sheet. When I arrived at the farm on 25 August the picture soon began to unfold. The farm had livestock with sheep and cattle running out onto the hill.

Where farm animals are kept, water plays a very important part during their whole life on the farm. In August 1990 the drought was causing hardship on this particular type of unit.

It was natural that Mr Reed wanted to try and avoid the costly method of getting water by borehole which at that time the drilling and installation would have been in the region of £3,500 and is not practical at the present time because of the uncertainty of the future of agriculture, and also where such a farmer is a tenant farmer he has the choice of asking his landlord, who would be reluctant, or spending his own money mainly to the landlord's advantage.

The water, which was drying up, was coming to the surface on the hill ground; in times of plenty it would be directed by pipes to the farm and several other fields. So how could I help a man in this predicament?

My first assessment was to know that cost in this instance had to be affordable, so the digging would need to be done by his own farm machine with a front or rear digger. If he could do this I could help him.

I began my survey by checking the present supply to see if all the water was coming to the surface. Spring No. 1 was 4yds wide and 12ft deep, and was not going to get the water he needed.

In the field above the spring there was water coming out of the hillside, which I checked and made the following notes:

Spring No. 1	4yds wide	Guide to quantity	12ft deep
Spring No. 2	6yds wide		10ft deep
Spring No. 3	3yds wide		9ft deep
Spring No. 4	6.5yds wide		10ft deep
Spring No. 5	10yds wide		10ft deep

I was heartened by the findings and came to the conclusion that a clay band, or a shelf of rock, was the cause of each weep of water out of the hillside, obviously all coming from the same source. Water filtrates down to the non-porous strata and comes out to the surface.

The advice given to Mr Reed was as follows:

First of all dig in at No. 1 to 12 feet and if sufficient use until a more permanent scheme which I recommend as follows and as on plan above.

The five springs are all running water, and are all in a position to run to the collecting tank, at this I think 4 and 5 should have ample. Dig to ten feet deep at 4 and 5 first and measure the flow for quantity. If sufficient build the collecting tank as on the plan and lead it down to the tank near to the farm where it joins No. 1. Then under the road to the farm. If other fields are to water from the collecting and more water is needed there is in reserve spring No. 2 and No. 3.

The above scheme is in no way costly and could be done by the farm's labour.

Chapter XXXVIII

G. A. Watson, Hamsterley, Bishop Auckland

T WAS A Sunday afternoon at the end of November 1991 when I received a telephone call from a Mr Watson of East Kays Lea. His call sounded urgent. He had just purchased this small farm with, like so many, a very poor supply of water from a spring. He had a drilling machine at the farm which was down to a depth of 280 feet and it was as dry as dust. Could I come and advise. I had no choice in a case of urgency and agreed to meet at his farm in about one hour.

All kinds of things passed through my mind on that short journey, such as whether some advice had gone wrong? A short time later I had my questions answered. I arrived at the farm East Kays Lea and met Mr Watson who I had not met before. I felt truly sorry for him. He told me without asking that the driller had said he would find water at any point on the farm at 40ft. But this could not be true because the land was on a sloping hill side.

The purpose of my journey was to get Mr Watson out of the situation he was in. I checked the borehole for water and there was none in my view. I then checked the spring which had supplied the farm. It was not dependable, showing signs of drying up.

There was not much choice of water near to the farmstead and the best vein I could find proved to pass within two feet of the dry bore. I immediately thought, am I putting myself in a corner? I could not get out of using the vein which I thought was the best and yet it was within two feet of a dry bore. I have never been faced with this problem before.

I was confident in the methods of my dowsing and I told Mr Watson that if the dry bore was not drilled my mark to drill would be on the vein of water that passed by the dry bore missing it by 2ft. The influence of the vein was 11m wide and 252ft deep, not as deep as the drilling that had been sunk.

Mr Watson said to me that the driller was going to pull out the next day, or consider drilling another bore. I advised Mr Watson as follows. As he was already committed to the expense of the dry bore my first advice would be to get someone with explosive and to ignite it in the dry bore at 252 feet. If my predictions were going to be correct, shattering the rock would let the water into the dry bore and save the cost of further drilling. But he could not get explosive for this method and the drilling operator could not wait, so it was decided to drill where I put in the peg.

On the Wednesday of that week I received a telephone call from Mr Watson to say, 'We have found the water, depth as stated 250ft. Test pumping has given the yield of the borehole as 14,400 gallons of water per day.' It was a well with a lot of challenge and concern for Mr Watson, who now is very content.

Chapter XXXIX

Durhamfield, Shotley, Northumberland

VER THE many years of my dowsing for water, mainly for farmers and landowners, several of my clients have put the question to me 'Have you ever practised your dowsing skills on your own farms?'

I have always been conscious of this fact whenever I get to that point in a survey when I mark the point to drill. That is the moment when you are telling someone to spend a considerable amount of their money without any other evidence than your word. At this stage I always explain how I have arrived at the decision to mark the most suitable vein to do what it has to do – points to consider, quantity needed, power point to drive a water pump, water storage area. I also find if I take a friend who understands the water dowsing technique the client is anxious to talk to my friend about my success rate, or anything to reassure him he is doing the right thing. To almost all people who sink a borehole it is a once-in-a-lifetime experience.

I make these points because in this exercise I suffer the same anxiety as a client; in fact maybe a little more. Should the dowse on home ground be a failure I am not sure how I would feel.

Durhamfield Farm was my home since my marriage in 1943 to 1972 when my son married, and he still farms there. During 1989 with water charges rising, our water charge for Durhamfield with a dairy herd of 200 milking cows came to £2,190 for the year.

I contacted Malcolm Bell, our local drilling operator to give a price for sinking a borehole. He was not able to give a price because of drilling through the unknown, but he said in the region of £3,500 and it was agreed to proceed when arrangements had been made to get consent from the National Rivers Authority or Northumbria Water, in whose area the drilling would be done.

Durhamfield, Shotley, Northumberland

Anyone contemplating a similar scheme should take note there is a procedure to the one we were about to go through. I wanted on that occasion to follow the rule book to be able to advise others doing a similar exercise. Over the border in Scotland, where I do quite a number of surveys for water, the law has not yet got the many restrictions that we have in England. Most people who own land in Scotland can bore for water and use it without consulting any government department.

The first step in the scheme to provide Durhamfield Farm with underground water from the farm itself was to get a date fixed with the drilling operator who knew of the proposed drilling. He gave us 18 June 1989 to commence the drilling.

Twenty years ago I dowsed a vein of water very close to the farm and it was my opinion at that time that if ever a time came to bore for water this should be the vein to tap. The influence showing the width was 52m, the prediction for the depth to drill being 150ft. First signs from the dowsing angle looked favourable. The next decision was where to select on the line of flow at midstream. Governing that decision was the power point and the situation of the supply tank built below ground level, capacity 40,000 gallons, sited 120m north of the farm. The drilling had to be between the farm and the tank. As the surface of the ground was sloping in places, a piece of level ground at midstream was selected and the peg was knocked in.

The 18th came and drilling began. The first 35ft was mixed sand and gravel; then 5ft gravels in soft grey-blue clays; entering into harder ground 15ft weathered sandstone with clay bands; small water entry; 21ft medium-hard sandstone, giving a water entry; then 51ft blue and grey fine shales, with hard bands of sill and stone, giving a water entry; 18ft very hard rock with many fractures, loosing 100 per cent air returns; 10ft medium hard-sandstone: a total of 155ft was the depth of the bore, which took three days. Casing had to be put down to 60ft because of the sand and gravel.

On the morning of the fourth day the water in the bore was measured and stood at 95ft of water, 60ft from ground level. It was now test pumped with a delivery of 600 gallons per hour that continued for four hours without lowering the water in the bore. On that pumping test the well was yielding over 14,400 gallons of water per day of clear, good-tasting water. At this stage I was very satisfied.

The next important thing to do was to get the local Public Health

Department at Hexham to take samples to do a full test, which was carried out by the Public Analysts for the city of Newcastle-upon-Tyne.

On 14 September I received the result of the analysis. The items I was most concerned about were nitrates, lead, aluminium, which were very low. Bacteriological results, nil. It had an iron and copper content which could be controlled. It was suitable for drinking as it stood, but would stain clothes. From my point of view a very satisfactory result! And now to the application for a licence to abstract the water.

The application for a licence (other than a licence of right) to abstract water from underground strata in this instance had to be made to Northumberland Water Authority, giving the:

Table 1: Full name and address of the applicant and Map ref. of point to drill. Underground strata, occupier or potential occupier.

Table 2: Map ref. of point – Description, Borehole. Depth 50 metres. Diameter 8″. Lining 20 metres.

Table 3: Map ref. NZ054509. Type – Submersible pump. Capacity in cubic metres 5 cu. metres per hour. Method of measuring or assessing quantities abstracted – Meter.

Table 4: Map ref. of point – NZ054509. Maximum quantity (in cu. metres) per year – 16,425. Per day – 45. Per hour – 4.5. Period of year 365 days. Purpose – agriculture.

Table 5: Crop. Period. Acreage. Maximum no. of ins. Per acre. Not applicable to this bore.

Table 6: Purpose, Agriculture. Point of discharge – slurry storage. Reason for the application – a spring supply has failed. Formal Application. Enclosed with the application copies of the newspaper dated 1 and 8 December 1989 of the *Hexham Courant* in which the notice to bore was advertised. The notice was also published in the *London Gazette* dated 1 December 1989. Also enclosed is the map of the farm showing the point of abstraction and the land on which it will be used.

It is now over nine years since the borehole was sunk. The yield of

The Bungalow
Lane Head
Coanwood
Haltwhistle
Northumberland
NE49 0NU

10 January 1994

Dear Sir,

I have been in the water well drilling business since
1957. Mr Taylor has devined each bore hole I have drilled
over the past twenty five years. I have found depth and
water quantity to be 99% accurate. In my opinion this is a
very good record. The only factor to upset the depth of
calculation is bolder clay.

Yours Faithfully

Malcolm Bell

Malcolm Bell

the well taken in August 1992 was just over 19,000 gallons per day, above the yield at the time of drilling. It is general for wells to improve with use.

The final cost for drilling, sleeving, electric cable and piping was £3,600. Two years of water charges more than covered the cost of the whole scheme.

It has been the experience of living through the Durhamfield scheme that has taught me many lessons and I will be much wiser when I come to advise others over their concerns in the early stages before any results are showing and the extra money they must find. The whole exercise has been satisfying and rewarding.

Chapter XL

Lt Col. D. N. Stewart

T COL D.N.STEWART of Midlemburn, Selkirk had a water supply problem which I think is worthy of mention. So many farms are supplied from a surface spring one or even two miles from the farm, and Midlemburn was one of these where water was piped nearly a mile. The old iron pipes were beginning to deteriorate in several places between the spring and the farm. Colonel Stewart needed a reliable supply of water for his farm and livestock; my survey would hopefully find the ideal scheme for this particular place.

I arranged to meet Colonel Stewart on 21 September 1990 at his home which was within the farm boundary 300 metres from the farmsteading. He gave me an outline of his need and where the water was to be used, which included his home, the farm buildings with a farmhouse, two cottages and several livestock watering troughs. I assessed needs to be in the region of 10,000 gallons per day.

I always try to begin my survey at the source of the present supply. In this case the present supply had sufficient but was being lost from the poor pipes on its journey to the farm. I measured what the spring was capable of yielding and will call this site No. 1. It was 9m wide and 15ft deep, ample to supply the need.

To get the alternative we must return to where the water was used. Colonel Stewart thought that as his house was on the higher ground it should be the place to look. I found a vein of water passing within three metres of his garden fence, ideally placed if its measurements were right. At Site No. 2, I stepped the width. It was 21m and 156ft deep. It looked good with plenty of water and I marked the site at the nearest point to power.

The next was to compare the two possible sites both able to do the job. No. 2 had clearly the most water, and would be pure, but would

Lilliesleaf (08357) 324

MIDLEMBURN,
BY SELKIRK,
SCOTLAND.
TD7 4QF

This to confirm that Mr
Edwin Taylor. has found two
sources of water on this property.
One (artesian) in May 91 and
the second in Sept 93.

They were both located at the
exact spot. A miracle to the
likes of me!
from Phoebe Stewart

cost about £3,000, but there should also be water to spare for other purposes. No. 1 would do, with none to spare. Its great downfall was the replacement of the pipeline, a great danger from pollution. Considering the two, No. 2 in my view was far superior, and would prove to be the cheapest in the end.

The conclusion and finer details of the scheme were discussed in the comfort of Colonel Stewart's and his wife's home. It was plain to see he had been a cavalryman, with a love for horses. In the spacious and sun-filled lounge were the many items that revealed where his heart lay, and the very stately showjumping horses which he had on the farm for a rest until the beginning of training for the Horse of the Year Show in London.

When I dowsed the No. 1 site there was a particular large grey horse that put his tooth mark about two inches long on the boot lid of my Mercedes. That large grey was the famous Murphy's Choice that is seen on our television screens at the time of the Horse of the Year Show.

The conversation led round to the Olympic Games held at Helsinki in the early 1980s when the British Equestrian team had been trained by Colonel Stewart. He was very proud to let us see his gold medal which the team brought home to Britain.

When I think back over the years and think of the wonderful people which dowsing has drawn into my life from all walks of life and the untold pleasure it had given me, even putting these words on paper reminds me of various incidents other than the dowsing for water.

There is a happy conclusion to this story. The well site marked was drilled, proved artesian and was rising to six feet in the air.

Chapter XLI

Whitfield Hall, Northumberland:
27 March 1990

HITFIELD HALL is finely seated on the West Allen, six miles south of Haydon Bridge. It is a large farming unit of its kind, ranging from the valley bottom of the West Allen, up to the heather hills of the Pennines. The farming unit is principally livestock, being cattle and sheep. The estate has some let farms and a number in hand forming the farming unit.

It was in early March I received a request to put a day to one side to survey some of the Whitefield Estate farms for water supplies, including checking some springs for yield.

A date was fixed to meet at the estate office on 27 March 1990, on which day the estate map was on the table to form a plan for the survey, including where to begin for the first one.

Site No. 1. It was agreed that we start the survey at Wolf Hills Farm, highest lying of the sites we would be on that day. It was predominantly a sheep farm with a flock of a better-class Swaledale sheep, and a herd of Galloway cattle, a very hardy hill breed. The mode of transport was to stand on the drawbar of a farm tractor over the moor for one mile. The tractor driver had to know every bump and turn, wet and dry, plus the knowledge of the hill to get to the survey point, which was in Dykerow Fell.

The water was coming to the surface and feeding into a large pond. The survey was to establish the quantity of water in the vein.

It was running west-east and measured 19m wide, which is a good supply, sufficient for a farm, and 30ft deep which, where it came to the surface, was coming up under pressure. A site was marked as on the plan to follow.

168

We travelled downhill to Site No. 2. On this occasion we travelled by Land Rover on the track to old lead mine workings travelling nearly half a mile on Agers Hill Fell. The thought in mind was to get a gravity-fed supply for Todds Burn Farm which was a mile to the east. There was a risk of mine shaft pollution, which I noted, and pointed it out to Mr Blackett-Ord. I marked a site away from lead workings 32m wide and 105ft deep. At this depth it would need to be a borehole, and there was no electricity on the site. I said it would be better to drill at the farm.

Site No. 3. Todds Burn Farm was the most needy for a new supply. As we travelled on the road to Todds Burn I picked up a vein and picked it up again behind the farm, which seemed very good. It was 42m wide and 162ft deep. I then marked at a suitable site for the farm and also for the driller.

We next travelled a few miles to Site No. 4, Morley Hill, on the other side of the valley to No. 1, again on high ground. A little humour came into the picture at this point. As we were travelling by Land Rover and climbing the hill on a fell track, a cock pheasant, when he heard the Land Rover, thought it was feed time and came running up the field on our right, caught up and ran alongside the Land Rover as we opened and closed gates. The driller man who was with us said, 'He has been here the last three years,' which brought the comment from Mr Blackett-Ord, 'He is a wise bird. He never takes to his wings, so he would never fall foul to a shooting day.'

When we got to the site at Morley Hall and measured up it was 18m wide and 40ft deep. Some water was coming to the surface but the depth put it out of reach in practical terms. It would be too far to take the power for pumping the water.

Site No. 5, Mains Rigg. Present supply was from a spring two fields away from the farm, pipes and collecting chamber were all intact. The weak link in this supply was in a dry year there was not sufficient water. I measured the width which was 10m which pointed to yielding much more than was coming to the surface. The depth was 12ft, quite within reach of a JCB digger.

As all things were in place other than the water I advised to dig to the depth stated, and if clay was found when digging they must expect the water to be deep.

The final site for that day was at Ninebanks, a small spring which measured 3m wide, which was a non-starter.

We then returned to the estate office to leave a copy of my notes made during the day.

Chapter XLII

Ballechin, Perthshire

IN JULY of 1983 I received the following letter from Miss E. M. Honeyman:

Ballechin
Ballinluig
Perthshire

Dear Mr. Taylor,

I saw you on television successfully finding water and it occurred to me that perhaps you could help me.

Foresting at the top of my farm results in the present supply drying up after a short dry spell and as I have a lot of cattle it is a great problem.

I wonder if you would consider coming and seeing if you could find a supply as I have a feeling there is a good chance of this.
I hope you receive this as I only got part of your address – I think you mentioned that you did it occasionally as a business.

Yours sincerely,
Elizabeth M. Honeyman.

It gave me great pleasure to respond to Miss Honeyman's letter because I knew of her as a prominent cattle breeder of beef Shorthorn cattle. She was also a breeder of pedigree Aberdeen Angus cattle, and a close farmer friend who was also a breeder of cattle of the Aberdeen Angus knew Miss Honeyman quite well having met her at the Perth bull sales. I was also a breeder of pedigree Shorthorn cattle and am still an Hon. Life Member of that breed society. If or when we meet we could have a lot to talk about.

We kept in touch by letter and telephone and finally fixed a date for me to do a survey on her estate on 16 August 1983. Miss Honeyman posted to me a map of her estate showing the various places she wished to explore which gave me a picture in my mind of the layout of the farms. I was committed to do a survey at a farm called Mungoes Wells Farm, near to North Berwick at 10 a.m. on the morning of 16 August and planned to meet Miss Honeyman after lunch.

It was a beautiful day with a bright blue sky when my friend Eric Christopher and I arrived at Ballechin Farm on the Strathtay Estate of Elizabeth Honeyman, which includes also Ballinluig, East and West Mains, Haughs of Ballechin, Derculich, extending to some 4,000 acres of land in the beautiful Strathtay Vale, and bordered on the south by the ample river Tay. The lands vary from the fertile haughs by the river to the steep hills some 800ft higher up.

I am always happy to arrive on time for a meeting of any kind, and this time after a journey of about 170 miles it was good timing to keep the appointment. We talked over the plan of action to begin at the meeting point and then see how the events of the afternoon might unfold. It is understandable that one cannot really make plans for a scheme like this until the whole survey is complete and even then alternatives show up where decision is needed. The size of the estate, where water is found and where it is to be taken have to be considered.

Site No. 1. The distillery supply was 15yds wide and 42ft deep marked near Ballechin Cottage gate. Should have a good yield.

Site No. 2. Still running in dry times but had no quantity and was just 3yds wide.

Site No. 3. Was worth exploring. It was 8yds wide and 6ft deep. Advised to dig with JCB and lower the well. At this stage of the survey we were fortunate to have good visibility and a cloudless blue sky showing up the hills surrounding us to the north up to 2,500 ft. We were now changing our transport from Land Rover to Agrocat, similar to the old Bren-gun carrier, an open-topped vehicle. Its present use was to take hay and feeding stuff to cattle, sheep and a herd of farmed red deer on the highest farmed land on the estate. So we got into the Agrocat, Miss Honeyman at the wheel. There was a bar to hold onto which we very much needed too, as we were travelling over ground that no other vehicle than a tank would cross.

When we reached the deer park which was well fenced, and drove to the deer, they were unconcerned because they knew the vehicle carried their food and Miss Honeyman's call was that of their feeder. It was interesting to see the stags lying away from the herd. In September they return for the mating season.

The views from this high vantage point of the Tay valley below and all round us were spectacular, seeing higher ranges of hills in the background.

Now back to the reason why we are up on this high ground. One of the springs of water supplying Ballechin rises in the deer park and that was the next on the list.

Site No. 4. Deer Park. An existing supply. It was not dependable being just 3yds wide and shallow.

Site No. 5. Dowsed and found a vein 12yds wide and 18ft deep beside a lime kiln. Recommended to dig and replace No. 4 and feed into existing pipes and tank. Yield could be 8,000 gallons per day.

Site No. 6. It was quite an experience getting up the hill and I thought while climbing that going down could be an even greater experience.

We now began descending the hill to Site 6 – a small surface spring which could have the water channelled into a cattle drinking trough. Spring to dig out and lower 3ft.

No. 7. Very poor. Not marked.

Site No. 8. The Agrocat had been left behind and we had now returned to the tranquil travel of the Land Rover to the Hall which had been the residence for the estate. No. 8 is the Garden Well. It was 8yds wide and 18ft deep. Advised to pump it out to empty each day and measure each day's yield.

Site No. 9 was at Home Farm. It was 8yds wide and 27ft deep. Marked point to dig.

Site No. 10 was a continuation of No. 9 going towards the old Hall. The width was the same, 8yds wide and 21ft deep. Marked.

Site No. 11 at West Ballechin. The spring of water had dropped down to a lower strata.

During the afternoon while travelling between dowsing sites we had the opportunity to talk about the cattle, sheep and deer farming in the

Highlands in contrast to what I was accustomed to in south Northumberland.

The time spent at Ballechin will be long remembered from a dowsing angle as the divining rod could reveal the true potential of a water spring making it possible to calculate its value.

From a scenic value it was a great bonus to see the beauty of Tayside; not forgetting the pleasure of meeting Elizabeth M. Honeyman, charming, hard-working and coming from a beautiful estate.

Chapter XLIII

J. I. Bell and Sons, Wotlas Moor Farm, Bedale, Yorkshire

O N 21 APRIL 1985 I received a call from Mr Bell, who told me they needed water for irrigation on land growing potatoes, and the quantity he needed would be 6,000 gallons of water per hour. The gallonage required was governed by the type of system that he wished to use. He then went on to say that he had called in advice from the Geological Department who advised he would find water at two points on the farm. Those two sites had now been drilled, one was totally dry, the other in the farmyard had some seepage water only – it too was a failure. Mr Bell had been given my name as a dowser and would be very grateful if I could help. I said to Mr Bell I would be very pleased to come to Bedale and see where things had gone wrong within the week.

The date fixed was Saturday, 27 April 1985. When we met I wanted to clean the slate by checking the two dry wells. The one in the farmyard was within three feet of water, hence the reason for seepage in the bore. At the other, it was as dry as dust, and no water near to it in any direction.

Now for the survey. There was a fair amount of challenge in what was to be done in this survey. The quantity needed was a challenge and would need extra time. The unfortunate result of the first two borings, which would be costly and off-putting to the farmer, now placed my position as a dowser in the public eye.

Survey No. 1 was to assess the vein of water that was close to the bore sunk in the farmyard. It was 29m wide and 120ft deep, which seemed promising. Before marking a place to drill on this vein I hoped to find another vein of water crossing no. 1. This I found on Survey

175

No. 2. No. 2 was 27m wide and 132ft deep, and marked at the point where the two veins crossed.

When a drilling site of this kind is marked out you have no choice other than one square foot of ground where the midstream line crosses. I have used this method several times when seeking water for irrigation. You are also doubling your chances of getting water.

Survey No. 3 was in the same field as the very dry bore. It was 24m wide and 80ft deep. This vein had disadvantages for it was the poorest one of the day for yield, had no other vein crossing it to supplement it, and there was the thought of the very dry bore.

Survey No. 4 was a vein 40m wide and 60ft deep. This site was marked at a point where it could deliver into a large natural pond, also having the advantage of filling the pond at out-of-season times for irrigation. Mr Bell would not be calling on the borehole to deliver 6,000 gallons per hour, but could draw that quantity from the pond and top it up at the same time. So in fact it was not urgent to find a high-yielding well. This vein was marked in two places.

Survey No. 5 was on the highest ground on the farm. It was a large field of about forty acres to grow potatoes that year. If water was found in this field it would gravitate to all parts of the farm, an important point when selecting which of the sites had the most advantage. With my divining rod I soon got the feel of a very good vein. It was 60m wide and 200ft deep, much deeper than the earlier ones, but we had climbed to the higher ground, which would have affected the depth.

Because of the prospect of number five and the direction it was running, which was right through the middle of this long field, Mr Bell wanted to mark it at three places. The width remained the same on all three markings but the depth changed to 270ft at 5B and 255 at 5C.

When we settled down in Mr Bell's office to compare the different sites, my advice was as follows. First choice No. 1 and No. 2 because of their proximity to the power point and being able to join the two veins together. My second choice was any one of the three marked sites in the potato field being No. 5.

No. 1	29m wide	120ft deep
No. 2	27m wide	132ft deep
No. 3	24m wide	80ft deep
No. 4	40m wide	60ft deep
No. 5A	60m wide	200ft deep
No. 5B	60m wide	270ft deep
No. 5C	60m wide	255ft deep

It was not very long after my visit to Watlas Moor Farm that Mr Bell called me on the telephone to give me the result of the drilling which had now been done. The Bell family had chosen No. 4 to drill first because of the storage in the pond, and its proximity to it. It was test pumped for yield and was delivering 16,500 gallons per hour or 396,000 gallons per day. A very good result after the concern about the two dry boreholes.

Chapter XLIV

Red Hills Spring Water

t is now three years ago since I was called to dowse a site on the fringe of lakeland's beauty at the village of Skelsmergh in Cumbria.

Being called out to locate underground water has many different reasons. This one was more of an exception, not following the rules of expectation. Red Hills is a well above the average sized dwelling, built on a hill rising about thirty feet above the surrounding farmland, and is itself covering an area of half an acre.

When I arrived on site I was given the details of Mrs Denise Read's concern about water leaking into the cellar. My first thoughts were so very puzzled. I could not understand why the contours did not match what I was seeing, a natural mound with a dwelling on top and water running into the cellar, at the highest point. There must be some strong force of pressure pushing the water in the vein up to the cellar.

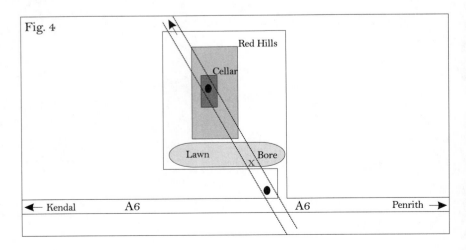

My curiousity was now demanding that I uncover some facts of the strange things that exist on this half acre of land in Cumbria.

I now began my search on the lawn at the east of the house. The date was Saturday, 16 November 1996. The following are notes in my diary of that date. Found a vein of water passing under the lawn at 30ft deep and going under the house and down to the cellar and found the water vein was passing under the cellar at just a few feet deep.

The picture was begining to build so I then walked down to the entrance which was a steep hill and on the level roadside I found the vein and took the depth at that point and found it to be 45ft deep at this point, proving it was rising very steeply from the rock below.

The findings on this dowse were so different to other dowses I do, its purpose was to get the water out of the cellar. The only way in my mind to remove the water from the cellar was to drill mid-stream at a point near where it passes under the lawn which would be costing thousands of pounds.

The now important question was, is there some means of recovering the expense, to save the annual water charges and see how many years it would take to cover the loss? Every dowse I do I am conscious of the means of recovery of costs.

On this same subject, on that day I walked down the steep hill from the lawn to the entrance of Red Hills to measure the depth of the vein at that point. It stood out a mile that this water is coming from a great depth, a very rare occasion in my years of dowsing.

I have dowsed for several people going into the "Spring Water" bottling business. I thought this rarity at Red Hills could have qualities that are different which looks as if that could be true.

Mrs Denise Read has now entered the field of "Spring Water" at Red Hills, Skelsmergh. The water now coming from the spring is crystal clear direct from the deep rock. Extract from certificate of analysis 04-02-99 (mg/litre) PH: 7.69; Calcium: 62.9; Sodium: 32.7; Magnesium: 18.5; Potassium: 14.4; Chlorides: 42.; Sulphates: 198; Nitrates: 0.376; Fluoride: 0.225.

This vein of quality water should yield 10,000 gallons of water per day.

Appendix I

A List of Professions Whose Members Have Asked for my Services as a Dowser

Agricultural Training Board

Architect

British Gas

Consulting Engineers

Cottage Owners

County Council

District Council

Dry Dock Constructor

Factory Proprietor

Farmers

Forestry Commission

Golf Courses

Independent Television

Land Agents

Landowners

My Services as a Dowser

Medical

Ministry of Defence

National Garden Festival

National Trust

Polo Green Proprietor

Racecourses

Appendix II

The Cost of Well Drilling

A talk given by Edwin Taylor at Harrogate on 5/5/79

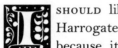 SHOULD like to begin by saying how pleased I am to be in Harrogate again. I accepted the invitation to speak to you because it is a very nice part of the country. I am not a Yorkshireman but I feel quite happy to come to Yorkshire and to Harrogate again. The Congress has its normal popularity, a nice crowd of people and new faces coming along each year.

When you think of the heading of my talk you may wonder how anyone can fill in the amount of time I have been allotted by discussing this subject and a few figures on pieces of paper. Figures themselves, I think, are a very uninteresting subject, so I will not dwell too heavily on them. It might be better to change the title of my talk to 'A Day in the Dowser's Life,' but I will include the figures, which are vital to the subject if you are to have a little idea of what the costs are in this modern age when you do such a thing as well drilling and water finding.

I should like to outline a complete operation from beginning to end. We have many times talked on the subject of water finding and discussed all the different aspects of dowsing, but today I should like to give you a drawn-out description of the operation from the very beginning up to its conclusion, including the price.

How does it all begin? Frequently in the form of a telephone call or a letter from some land agent, asking you to find water. Or perhaps from a private individual you get a little envelope addressed by hand and you immediately try to judge the person who had sent the letter. You get all kinds of ideas of what he may look like, and when the day comes to meet him you are completely taken aback, because he is nothing at all like what you imagined. I am sure it must be exactly the same the other way round. The clients send for you and they wonder what sort of old geezer will turn up. They have probably been wondering if they ought to send a taxi for you and then you drive up in your car.

Anyhow, that is probably how it starts – with a telephone call or a letter, and then you make arrangements to go to whatever place it is. Generally it is an urgent call, so, being a farmer and knowing that people only ask to see you when they need you, I try to respond by going as quickly as possible, because they may have a driller lined up and need you there fairly quickly. You get down to making a date; then they wonder what your expenses are, and naturally you quickly put that question on one side. Then you come to the day of the dowse. It is important if you are in this business of dowsing to know how to present yourself. It is no good riding up to a farm on a pushbike or something like that and giving the impression that you are a very inexperienced person.

One of the things that very often happens when you arrive at the farm or factory or whatever it may be is that they begin to look at you, because to them you are a mysterious person at this stage. They expect you to have straw growing out of your ears or something like that, and they start to say things like, 'Have you forgotten your bag, sir?' They are sort of dropping little hints. I just say, 'Now will you please show me what you want?' Then we proceed to the place and I put my hand into my pocket and bring out a divining rod and that eases the tension. 'At least, he has got something with him.'

The first operation I carry out is to scan the area. I used to cover a lot of ground, but instead of walking over half the countryside I now use the divining rod to find direction. I have fairly well perfected the technique. I ask the person where he would like the water to be and that obviously is the place to start. By scanning the area I can tell from quite a distance whereabouts we are likely to find the kind of supply we are looking for. It is important that you ask your client what quantity of water he wants, if it is 300, 400 or 10,000 gallons a day. When you know the kind of thing you are looking for your mind seems to react to it. If somebody says, for instance, 'Walk over the bridge and see how your whalebone reacts, nothing happens. I am not looking for water under a bridge, so it doesn't act on me. Similarly, if I am looking for a supply of 5/10,000 gallons a day I do not get immediate reactions to something that is only producing a minute quantity. This demonstrates that the mind is largely the controller of what we are doing.

An essential question is where the water is needed and whether it will be a gravity supply. You have to be fairly skilled in advising someone on these matters and to have a little knowledge of what the requirements will be. Now if you are not up to your job you are going to fail somewhere down the line, and I think if you are going in for dowsing you must be skilled enough to advise beyond the point of saying that you are going to find water here. You have to be able to advise someone where he should site his storage tank or you might end up by getting the blame for something that goes wrong. It is important to know that your power lines are accessible, and again don't forget that your client is a very inexperienced person on this subject and is depending on you, as the professional, to give him advice.

I wonder again does your client need an alternative scheme? I am sure he must do. If you are going a distance to do something give him the first choice and then give him a second choice. It is not difficult to say, 'If that one is not what you want there is a second supply here.' You can give him advice but try to leave the choice to him. What I try to do is to suggest two alternatives – one on the cheap and one which may be much more costly but probably more businesslike. If you offer something near the surface, which is going to entail probably an afternoon's work with a spade, or a couple of men and two spades, this will cost very little money at the end of the day and it costs very little to find it out. I have had many instances where this cheap alternative has come off and they have ended up with a good supply of water without spending very much money. The other way, the costs of which I will deal with in a moment, is far dearer than many of you imagine, because whatever you touch today in the form of labour is a very expensive item.

You need to know the depth because a lot hinges on this in regard to prices. My method of assessing quantity is always the width of the stream, and the depth is the distance between the stream and the third waveband. This gives me a rough idea of what the quantity is and whether it is suitable for the person's demands and whether it looks to be beyond his means. If you would have to drill about 300ft down and the person just has a cottage you have to assess the individual's financial position – I always treat everyone individually – as you cannot ask anyone to spend a lot of money if the job doesn't warrant it.

You have to have a licence to explore before you can drill. Oddly enough, it is called a Building Licence. You cannot order anyone to drill for water unless you have a licence and there are other costs for licences afterwards.

Coming now to the costs of well drilling, last week I obtained the right up-to-date costs for each operation. When you ask a driller to come on to the site there is a charge to get there. It is £150 for a machine to come on to the site within 10 miles of the operator's base.

With regard to drilling, I am used to yards, feet and inches and can't get away from them, but for you who are modern thinkers it is £15 per metre, which would be roughly £5 per foot for a bore of 6″ to 8″.

In putting a drill down, for the seepage at the top it is usual to line the top 30ft and it costs £45 per metre. I cannot think this is correct, but it is the figure that was given to me for lining the top 30ft.

At times some drillers might need water laid on the site and stored ready for the work drilling to wash out. Some people use compressed air, which is the same thing, so you might have that cost but you might not.

Test pumping at the end of the operation is £26.50 per hour and that may be an 8-hour operation or it might be a 3-day operation, according to what you need to do.

Around the top of the drilling is the cement casing to seal off any seepage that would get in. This, of course, would be an extra cost and would be taken on a sort of time spent and cost of material plus 20 per cent basis.

That is basically the cost of getting the job done, which is a fairly substantial amount and at the end of the day would run into four figures. So when you go as a dowser on to a site you are asking people to spend a lot of money, and when they have spent the money you have to be fairly dependable and see that they are getting value for it. You cannot just go along as a very junior amateur and say, 'Yes, I will find you water.' I think it is obvious that a reputation has to be built up, and if it is the right sort of reputation one person will tell another about you. If it is not you will disappear into the blue and that is it.

As a matter of interest I have the drilling prices of the year 1966 to show how prices have varied. This is for a job I did 12 to 13 years ago:

On to the site: £95
Casing totalled   £33 15 0d.
Cementing surface   £55
Boring 5⅞ in   £170
diameter 85ft at   £2
  (it is now £5 per foot)
Pumping test 80/- per hour
    Total: £398

 I think that over these 12/13 years the price has more than trebled.
 Dealing just a little further with costs I have a comparison here between a mains public water supply and a drilling, which I think is interesting. We know what the price of water is in this modern age. It is now going beyond 50p per 1,000 gallons and it varies in different regions. I know the Northumbria Water Authority charge at the moment is standing at 46p per 1,000. In Yorkshire it is over 50p and in the South-Western Water Authority area it is 59.4p, so there is not a standard charge throughout the country. This indicates to me one thing – water is becoming more and more valuable, it is becoming scarcer and scarcer and the price that we are going to pay for it is going up and up. This should drive anyone who is a consumer in any quantity to consider whether to pay this amount of money or to put a borehole down and have his own supply at around 4p per 1,000, but you first have to consider how much it will cost to abstract that water from the ground.

The cost of around 20 million gallons per year
at 50p per 1000 would amount to   £10,000

Against that the borehole drilling would cost   £7,500
You would have a grant on that of 20%,
  which would make it   £6,000
The pump in the borehole costs   £3,000
less 20% grant   £2,400
Storage tank for 12,000 gallons   £2,000
less 40% grant   £1,200
(You wouldn't get a grant against a tank larger
  than your scheme was, because the
  Government don't pay out money for

which they are not getting a return)

Total Capital Cost:	£12,500	
Less grants		£9,600

Annual costs: Depreciation of Capital Cost at 20% £1,920
Abstraction charge 20 million gallons at
4p per 1,000   800
Electricity and maintenance costs 200   £2,920

It would therefore be a very attractive business to consider well drilling in comparison with a public supply of water.

Here is a further point to consider in regard to cost: Imagine the difference between the value of a property which has a supply of water and one which has not. You will find the difference is tremendous.

I have mentioned that you need a licence to explore. You also need a licence to abstract, and there you come into the hands of officialdom. Quantities have to be mentioned and whether it is for private or business use. For a country cottage or private house you need a licence for your water but it won't cost you anything for the amount abstracted. The given figure of 20 million gallons per year is the sort of quantity that would normally be expected and I am sure they would never think of charging for the very small amount that a householder would use, at least in this present age. What will happen in the future I don't know. It could very well be the thin end of the wedge, like so many things that we see in officialdom.

The Public Health Department come into the matter, because they will want to know what the quality of the water is. They will allow water out of a borehole with a much higher bacterial count for public use than they will out of a mains supply, principally because there may be no alternative, but if it is not a very good count and there is a scheme passing your gate the Public Health Department have a very strong hand. They can say, 'We are sorry. Even though you have gone to this expense we think your water is not fit for human consumption.' In other words, there is a little twist in the tail. It might be all very well if you live on a hilltop 20 miles away from any other supply, but if there is a mains supply passing the gate it is possible that they might say your water was not fit for human consumption. I hope there are no Water Board officials in this room to hear me say so.

Those of you who are just beginners at water finding will discover that you have this awful waiting time between giving the advice and getting the end results, and it is very rarely a short time. It is generally a few weeks or maybe longer before you know what they have found, and it is a very anxious time for both you as the dowser, whose whole reputation is hanging on this piece of information, and for the client, who wonders whether he has been asked to spend his money wisely or unwisely. You need a reasonable constitution to stand up to this strain. How accurate are these first results likely to be? I think you are either spot on or you are not even in the race at all. When I made my very first find of water I couldn't believe I was so accurate both on depth and quantity. In other words, it works provided you get on to the right lines. I did my first drilling at two points and I was within 2ft in both predictions of the depth. That gave me great heart, to think I had set out on the right foot. I am not boasting but I believe that it works very accurately if you have the right technique in the first place.

Now that I have given you a rough outline have I put you off or do those of you who are budding dowsers feel like setting out on the whole operation of advising, dowsing and being confident of the end result? You have got to start somewhere but you can't go around willy nilly. You have got to go into it like a business and set about the job as if you mean it and realise its importance.

You probably wonder who your clients will be as you go down the line. The majority of my clients, I being in the farming world, are estate owners, golf clubs – they require water for sprinklers on the greens, so they need dowsers and generally try to get them on the cheap – farmers, Government Departments and country cottagers who need a small supply. The National Trust has been a regular client of mine and so has the Forestry Commission. They all typify the ways of country life. This is a cross section of my clientele other than the odd case, such as a dry dock with a leak, or, as I mentioned last year, a factory with a pollution problem.

I think it is important that you have a little knowledge of geology. You are much better equipped if you have some idea of the strata and what they consist of, which are water-bearing strata and which are not. Clay is a very tricky one. It is the only thing that sends me haywire when depthing. Keep a firm hold on the rod when you are dowsing, because clay could trip you up.

We had a question asked last night on how dowsing works and I am still no wiser. I have held many theories on how it works and my ideas have changed. I began by thinking it must be a reflex and all kinds of things, but I am now fairly convinced that it is the mind. It may be the subconscious, but it is in any case due to the mind rather than anything else, and I think I had better leave it at that.

We spoke here last year of the legal position of dowsers, of where the law might step in, of how far we are committed as users of the rod when we advise people as we do. I would not like to weigh too heavily on the dowser. I would like to put the responsibility on to the person who engages him. I think you should make it perfectly clear to your client that a dowser can only be expected to do what his little piece of stick is telling him. You are doing your best, like any other professional, but he must understand that there is no guarantee.

I have always tried to keep operations as simple as possible, it makes things so much easier. You wouldn't go from Harrogate to London if you wanted to get to Edinburgh! I would just like to point out to those who are setting out for the first time that you don't have to make the job bigger than it need be.

In conclusion I should like to mention four main points:

1. The dowser is invaluable. Nobody else can do what he does nor any instrument, at least, I haven't yet found one that can. You can find water without a dowser but it will probably cost twice the price. The value of the dowser is that he can pinpoint the water at probably a much lower cost than if you had to keep drilling until you reached water.

2. It is true that dowsing works. We are all sure of that. We are no longer just trying to prove that it works.

3. The heading of my talk is costs and we are all aware of the importance of costs. Remember, you are not playing with a client, you are asking him to spend a lot of money.

4. Look professional at all times. Never ride up on your pushbike. Remember to look professional and to set about it in a professional manner.

Appendix III

Water and Wells

A talk given by Edwin Taylor at Harrogate on 2/4/77

THE SUBJECT that has been given to me is Water and Wells. I will deal with the Water part first.

I should like to point out how important water is to our existence. In the early stage of life I believe we existed in water. We now consist of 60 per cent water during our life and if we don't have water we die after about ten days, so I think we should all realise how very vital and important water is in our lives.

We are now entering what I would call the era of the valuable minerals. I think we are finding out that water is a very vital thing to our nation, to our existence and to our industry. Food, I think, is becoming a scarce commodity and water is coming into a similar category.

The world mass of water, I am told, is constant. The water level on our planet does not vary. Now the amount may be constant but in form it is continually changing. The rain that falls is evaporated again and comes down as clean water, and it is in this process of coming down as clean water that we try to make use of it. I think that the whole picture of the water problem was probably magnified in last summer's drought. We were not prepared for the drought. We got wiser after it and we discovered many things during the drought that have made us realise better the value of water to us all as a nation, as workers, as tillers of the soil and as ordinary householders. I think there is no one here who has not been affected this year. We have in our audience tonight a prominent forester. No one knows better than he that the young trees this year are very scarce because of last year's drought. There are many other things affected, in the potato world, for example. And we are now in the eighth month of the downpours which have come since then and which we don't like so much of.

I think the drought has caused us to think more in terms of the value of water, in other words, to invest in water. An amount of 20 million gallons per annum is not too large for many factories and farms. Our island is covered with farms which are using an amount of water like this, and I feel it would be useful to think of that figure when considering an example. To speak in round figures, a few years ago when I spoke on this subject water was 30p per 1000 gallons. Today it is standing at 50p. I think I then made the prediction that it would not be many years before it was 100p. But standing at 50p means you now have a round figure of £10,000 per annum if you use water from a public supply. Now the comparison I should like to make is that if we invest in water we sink a borehole, and I think I would be on the outside by putting the figure at £7,000. I would spend £8,000 on a pump, so I should end up with a figure of £10,000, but against that there would be grants of about £2,000. Then there is the storage tank, which would bring the total figure spent up to rather less than £10,000. But this would be for a large number of years, and there is no shortage of water once you get down below the crust of the earth.

So making the comparison, after you put a price on your capital and on your other costs, the cost of 4p per 1,000 gallons for subtraction, and your electric power, I think you would end up in the region of £2,500 to £3,000 per year as compared with £10,000. In other words, it is a very worthwhile investment as against mains water which can only go up in price. If you do a very simple sum you can be better off at the end of the day.

By investing in water you can get several spin-offs. You could have your fishing pool, shooting – some people might like a shot at a wild duck – your boating, irrigation and probably encourage the tourist trade. But if I dare at this stage, Mr Chairman, I should like to indulge in a little story.

I mentioned fishing and this reminds me of an American specialist in medicine who came to Britain and met his Harley Street friend. They went off to fish in Scotland and while in the boat accompanied by the ghillie they were discussing various things in their profession of surgery, and the ghillie was sitting very quiet. After a while they turned to the ghillie and said, 'Has anything wonderful ever happened in your country?' The ghillie said, 'Oh yes. There was a case a little while ago where a local farmer had to have a serious operation. They took him in and got him on the table – I should explain that, as it was in Scotland this was the kitchen table – and discovered that he would have to have a complete new inside. They wondered how this could be done and all they could think of was to take one of the old ewes out of the field. So they got the old ewe and they laid them side by side and the operation was carried out.' The American specialist looked at the Harley Street man and then said to the ghillie, 'Well, what happened to the man? How is he? Was the operation a success?' and the ghillie said, 'Success? He produced two lambs in the spring.'

Now to get back to serious matters, the second part of my talk is on Wells. I think someone once coined the phrase, 'Score with a bore.' This is probably where we as dowsers come into the picture, as we can play a very useful part in finding the nation's water. We have proved that it can be found successfully. I have been saying this week, and I feel very strongly on this point, that I believe there is a place for someone from this Society somewhere on the National Water Strategy Council. I don't know who it should be, but when conditions were laid down for people who were to be on the Council it was said that they had to have a particular interest in the countryside and indeed in agriculture. As this Society represents the dowsing world, and as we can prove that we have been successful in dowsing for water, I think we should be entitled to some particular place, however small it might be. There is somewhere in there where we could play an important part.

Now to deal with the siting of wells: I think the probable reason why Bernard Smithett asked me to speak on this subject tonight is that he was interested more in terms of the wells. I think it is vital and important that as dowsers we know just what we are setting out to do. If you are called in by a client you have to know his needs. If it is for a golf course, for example – I have been asked to find water for a golf course before now – it is very important that you understand your countryside and therefore know whether or not the client is asking for the right thing. He might know his particular needs but I think you have also got to be able to say if necessary, 'Well, I think you are doing the wrong thing.' If you are sufficiently country-minded and educated on the subject of water you should be able to advise people.

The factors that come into it are knowing where the electric power is, knowing whether you should lead power to the water or the pipe from the water – which is the less expensive – the cost of carrying the cable or the cost of carrying water in the pipe. These are all fairly important items for the dowser to realise when he goes into the matter.

There is no doubt that there are anxieties from all angles for the people concerned. There are the anxieties of the dowser. When you are invited you are fully conscious that you are asking a man to spend a lot of money, and when you have spent the money for him and he is drilling the hole it may be 2–3 months before you get the result. I can assure those of you who have not gone through this process that it can be a very anxious time indeed. Again, it is an anxious time for your client. He has spent the money. He is wondering what you are worth, and if you have had no experience in dowsing he is a brave man to begin with. There have got to be some brave men along the line to be willing to have you in the first place. Then there is the driller. Again, he has his anxieties and he has his experience, too. I have seen the driller, when I have been on the site, turning his back and having his little joke, as if to say when we get the water, 'Well, there's bound to be water here, anyway.' That reminds me of a particular place where the land agent drove me and he said, 'Well, really you can find water anywhere here.' I said, 'I'm sorry then. I shouldn't be here.' That was one man's attitude. These are the little things you get if you are a dowser. You have to have a fairly thick skin.

Dowsers are not new to the sinking of wells. My experience over the years has suggested that the dowser has been a very accurate man in days gone by. Almost without exception the wells that I have gone to have been discovered by dowsers and they have all been very accurate indeed with the exception of one. I can only think of one failure from my own travels in looking at old wells. A particular village had an intermittent supply, probably three days all right and two days with no water at all. I looked at the old well and discovered that it was just off. There was about 2ft between the edge of the well and the edge of the stream and I am sure that this was the answer. It was not on. It was getting intermittent percolation of water through from the stream to the well. Generally these wells were near to the back door. Mrs Dalby was trying to ask me a question yesterday on this and I couldn't quite make out what she was meaning – which hand they would have the bucket in. But I think it was a fact that they did try to site the well at the back door, and I wonder if they didn't sometimes find the well first and then build the house. Probably that would have been the most sensible thing to do, if you look at it very carefully.

The art of building a well is bound to come into this. If you see the wells you will realise how accurately and carefully they are built. They are probably 4ft across. For the depth they generally went down to the level where they found they were getting too much water to work in. They may have gone down just far enough to get sufficient water for their requirements, because I have discovered in several wells that they never got down to the stream. If they had a stream at 30ft the diggers probably got down to 20ft and then found they had sufficient water. Lots of people have come to me and said: 'The old well has gone dry.' but it hasn't gone dry; they have merely begun to use more water than when the well was first dug. This is what I have generally found; they had never got down to the water in the first place. This thought could probably be a relief to some people who have a well that is going dry.

Someone else has raised a point tonight that I think is important, that is the returning of water under ground. It is a number of years since I raised this very point at the Cambridge Congress. We know that the water levels on the eastern plains of Britain have been lowered by 50ft in the last era. If this continues the eastern side is going to face a very great problem with water. This wet year is not going to replace water to that extent. I think the only way it could be replaced would be to redirect amounts of water into the substrata, and I am sure that this could be done in exactly the same way as you take water out. There is no shortage of water in this island. It is all running out to sea. Underground reservoirs could very well be supplied and replenished by returning water under ground.

Our present day digging has changed. It used to be the old spade and shovel, but the wells that I have done recently have been done with a mechanical digger. It has a reach normally of about 15ft, probably the depth of this room, and there are many wells that need not be any deeper for the smaller requirements. But I had one where they had to dig to 30ft, at least I predicted 30ft, but they did the wrong engineering on the subject. The digger did that on two levels. He got the first 12ft down in a double-sized hole and then he brought in the digger and went down the next stretch. I thought that this was very good and he reached the water about 30ft down with the digger. Once this is done you can form the well with 4ft concrete pipes standing on end and fill it back in. This is the easy way of doing it and you find out very quickly if the water is there.

There is such a thing as a licence to abstract water, and anyone who sets out to get water without this licence discovers that in this age he is breaking the law. A licence is not difficult to get. It might be harder on the eastern plains, but in this part of the world I don't think it is difficult at all. For a private dwelling you get your water for nothing. If you need it for a farm I think it costs 4p per 1,000 gallons — some nominal charge like that. But I know someone who forgot to send in for a licence. He got a very good water supply — I think it was about 70,000 gallons a day. When his drilling was all completed he came to me in a great panic and said, 'What shall I do? I never applied for a licence.' I thought the best thing would be for him to forget it.

Obviously we are living in an age when we have a certain amount of pollution and I don't think we could deal with this subject without saying something about the pollution of water. The water supplies of our country are becoming more and more polluted and the authorities are doing their best to rectify it, but one very interesting story comes out of it. The river authority had come down very heavily on one particular factory in Cleveland, and the factory asked me if I could find their pollution which was going into a certain river. What they thought I was going to do I don't know, and on the first invitation I wasn't very sure myself what I was going to do, but we looked at it and at the end of the day very successfully. What was happening was that on the riverbed there was continuous pollution coming from a chemical that was used in that particular factory. They knew what the chemical was, because it had been analysed, but how could they find it? Well, I discovered very quickly that there was an underground stream going under the factory from where their waste was, direct to the river at exactly the same depth as the bottom of the river. It was just sheer misfortune that it was there, but fortunate that we could trace it in that way. My advice was to get back to the factory yard, cut it off and pump it out, which was done. This was another case in favour of the dowser; something was discovered and done and turned out to be successful. It just shows that you can be used at more things than sinking wells.

I have spoken of polluted water. The extreme opposite to pollution is the spring. I don't think it would be right not to mention springs and the beautiful clean water that we can have if we are dwelling in the country and can get a spring supply. We have all seen the beautiful, crystal clear water that is coming out of springs, and when we compare it with the water that comes from the tap, that has been used over and over again, it should make us realise that this lovely clean water is a very valuable thing that anyone can possess. How different a cup of tea tastes when made with that kind of water instead of with the chlorinated water that we see coming out of our taps! I hope there are no Water Authority people in the room tonight to hear me make that comment.

As to the final details of the driller's charge – and again I think Bernard had this in mind when he asked me to speak on this subject – what are the costs involved? If you are inviting someone to sink you a well what does the driller charge and what are his costs? I am not fully up to date with the costs, which may have changed.

Firstly, there is transport to the site, which, as you can well imagine, is a fairly costly item, with all the material that has to be moved.

Lining the first 30ft of the drill hole. This used to be done by an iron pipe, or a metal pipe, but the recent ones I have seen done have been done much cheaper by plastic pipe, which would be about 6in to 8in.

The cement sealing and time of cement setting: You would think this a waste of money but you can't get by without it. The drillers have got to stop while the cement sets on the sealing of the pipe at the top, so you are paying for time when they won't be working.

There is the boring to the required depth after the casing. If it is over 100ft you have another 70ft to go.

Then there is the baling out. If it is a small cottage or small farm supply probably baling out would do the necessary calculation of what your spring is producing and would also do for the test pumping. I think that under the Act today you have to do so many hours test pumping and see the level to which the water falls during those hours of pumping.

You also pay for the time that you lose the water, if this happens. You should have a continuous supply of water going into the drill hole, and therefore you generally have 2–3,000 gallons of water standing for the driller to keep his tools supplied with water. Now if it happens that you get 20ft down and there is some cavity and all the water disappears, you have to pay the driller for the time wasted while you get a new supply of water.

You can therefore see that if you are setting out to drill it is a fairly costly business. The test pumping is generally a three day job, and, as I said before, the licence requires you to fill in details, and I think the people who are doing the drilling are also under an obligation to provide this information to the authorities concerned.

When you have finally got it done you have to get the water out. With modern methods of pumping there are several kinds of immersible pumps today that you put down. If you are fortunate enough to have the water coming well up, fair enough. The immersible pump seems to be the usual thing. You run an electric pump from your dwelling, farm or factory and it delivers the water to where you want it. Then again I would point out that if ever you go to find water for someone you must please remember that you want it to be somewhere near to where this power is. It is fairly vital that you do not just go there to advise a person where the water is. You have to consider the whole picture, because if you advise someone wrongly you are not going to be in business very long as a water diviner.

Our jobs vary from the cottage to the larger factory. On one particular occasion I worked at a cottage which someone had bought. It was a very small cottage with no water supply. He had hoped he would get his water from the neighbouring landlord, but the landlord turned this down. He said, 'No, sorry. We have no water to spare.' Whether he didn't give anything away I don't know, because there was lots of water there. The man who had bought the cottage then thought, 'Well, I have bought a pup here – a house with no water,' and he asked me to go over. On my first visit I found water within 2 yards of his perimeter but actually on the landlord's ground. He approached the landlord, who said, 'I'm sorry, you can't drill there.' He came over to me again in a panic and I went back to search very carefully for another supply. The whole area that we had to play with was no larger than this room. I found another, much smaller supply – not one that I would normally recommend but at the end of the day he got sufficient out of it – about 250 to 300 gallons per day, which for his purpose was ideal. so that was the cottager. I think that normally you would not recommend such a small amount unless you were put in a corner, as in this case.

Who are the clients for the dowser? The local landowners, trusts, sporting people, industry, farmers, cottagers are a fairly wide range of clients, but I don't think that such a thing as advertising can come into this, because you advertise yourself by your results. If someone has the feeling that he is going into business by cutting a stick from the hedgerow and notifying all the likely clients in the north of England, he is going about it the wrong way. I think the only way to do it is to build your reputation on your results. You have to put extra study into the subject to make sure you are right, because if you are not right you will soon be out of business.

There are variations in wells and I would like to mention the peculiarities of different wells that I have found, although their names may not mean a thing to you. There is one at Law Trewett. Two or three farmers drilled to 100ft and after hitting water it came up right over the top. If you are fortunate enough to have an artesian well of this kind you have something that is enough for whatever you want. I don't think those farmers ever expected to get what they got, coming up to the surface with all that force behind it.

Corn Hills is another example of a well going dry. With extra digging, another 20ft down, there was any amount of water.

There was an interesting one at a little village near to some former lead mining works. There were 6 small-holdings all in a row with about 300 yards between, each of them having a well at the back door. To my surprise I discovered on being called to one that all these 6 smallholdings had their wells sited on the same line. Obviously the dowser had been there and sited the wells, and the cottages were then all built on the same line. I doubt whether any other person in recent times realised why those cottages were built halfway down a field, and it came to me as quite a surprise to find that that must have been the reason.

Slaley Forest is worth mentioning here, because it is one of those very shallow wells which produced a great deal of water without any great expense. Whatever I do I am naturally trained to be cost conscious, and I think that if you are not cost conscious you are asking your client to spend money when he doesn't need to. This particular well is about 5ft deep. When they were down to about 4ft 6in they telephoned me to say 'We are down to 4ft 6in and not a sign of water.' The telephone message reached me about 2 hours later and I hastily went to the spot, but by then the water was flowing; there was an ocean of water. That was one of those instances where there was a lot of water very near to the surface, and again it shows the value of the dowser.

Edge House is an example of finding water at the top of a hill. I always say you find water at the top of a hill. At Edge House I was making up the hill and the farmer said, 'We don't want to be up there, we want to be down here.' I said, 'Well, it depends on where the water is,' but at the end of the day the drill was put down and there was a wonderful supply of water coming very near to the surface at the top of the hill. It is surprising, but if you have high hills in the background you very often get this head of water behind on some range of hills, bringing the water up to the same level.

There has been the occasional mistake in my experience of depthing. I think it would be fair to point out to those of you who are budding dowsers for water that the mistakes have not been in locating water, but there have been two or three occasions when the depthing was out. On the second visit I have made very sure, by holding the rod very, very firmly, that I didn't make the same mistake twice on the same site. On each occasion I was right the second time by holding it very, very firmly. In each case there was a band of clay at the precise depth where the water was predicted in the first place. I had been warned about this but had probably not taken sufficient notice. Now you can feel that you have been warned, too. If you are dowsing make sure that you take a fairly firm hold and don't let the stick just go down anywhere. You ought to be resisting the stick until it goes down and you can't stop it.

Looking on the lighter side, I had these two experiences. I was to give a demonstration to a party of farmers on a certain occasion, and postcards were sent out notifying all the farmers in the district that this demonstration would take place at a particular hall. They turned up and two farmers sat scratching their heads and I heard one say, 'Dowsing? I thought it said closing.' They expected to see little green bottles to pour down someone's neck. I was rather surprised.

What I thought very interesting was the case of the non-believer when he found that the rod moved in his hand. I had this experience with someone who just did not believe in the subject. It was at the Durham School of Agriculture. I was invited by the principal to demonstrate dowsing to the students. One of the lecturers very firmly disbelieved. I got him to hold the rod and walk over a particular place in the field, and the stick went down. You would have thought something had struck him, because he was shocked, and this was something that I didn't think could happen. He must have firmly disbelieved in the subject to be shocked when the stick did go down.

How does it work? Probably this is the fifty thousand dollar question. We have all gone through the process of wondering if it is the reflex action of the muscles or whether the rod is a medium or the contents of the rod or whatever it is, but you have heard that distance doesn't mean anything. I firmly believe it is in the mind, which had distinct abilities if channelled in the right direction. I am sure that we are all on the doorstep of something that will be very, very interesting in the coming era. But with respect to all those people who have the little gadgets please keep it as simple as possible. You don't need all those refinements. You don't need to have something attached to the end of your stick, and you need not be holding anything in your hand other than the rod, provided you have your mind tuned in to what you are looking for. If you are looking for water you should not react to anything else you may happen to pass over – minerals, for example. I think you have to train your mind so that it does not confuse things.

Obviously there are different tools of the trade and you will find you have your favourite ones. It is not easy to go along a field waving a pendulum, because the wind blows it. You have to think of the purpose for which you require a tool. If you are dowsing over a map on the table use the pendulum. But if you are going over a field you need something that is simple and tells you distinctly what is there. Some people use angle rods. Well, I find no fault with angle rods but they don't serve my purpose. I am far too sensitive and they respond to other things that I don't want them to respond to. You can't say to them, 'You are not going down here,' but you can get hold of the stick and say, 'You are not going down until we get to the water, and when you reach the water it either goes down or it breaks. So let me repeat – Keep it simple.

My rod is two pieces of whalebone tied together at the end. When I forget my whalebone I cut a stick out of the hedge; it does just as well. You can use plastic rods; rubber tube – this is rather surprising. You can get a piece of rubber tube and hold it and you will find it turning like a snake in your hands when you are going over what you are looking for. A piece of wire spring, which works in exactly the same way; the pendulum; the hands – you can feel in your hands. Those of you who are a little more skilled can put your thumbs together and do the same thing.

I think I should emphasise that I have a note here on the dowser's image. I feel it is very vital for the future of this Society that the dowser safeguards his image. I can see a very pleasing aspect in this Congress. When I think back to the Congress of ten years ago and the people who were visiting it, and then see this Congress, with young people in the audience all eager to try to do something, I think this Society is getting somewhere. Even in our lectures we have heard the younger man's view. In this way I think we shall save the image and get down to sensible constructive use of the dowser and not this wrong image of seeing someone on television make a fool of himself. As we all know, and please remember this, when put to tests dowsing does not work, so if you are ever invited to go on television don't think that you are going on to demonstrate; you are going on to make a fool of yourself. I believe that a dowser should not be put to test or put to gain. If you think you can get the winner of the Grand National by waving your pendulum down the list of horses' names you are not going to score, and if you are put to tests your mind knows that it is not true, so don't be tempted to go on television and make a fool of yourself.

In conclusion, Mr. Chairman, there are three things I have listed to recapitulate what I have been saying.

1. I believe there is a need for representation on the National Water Council.

2. We know that the nation has recognised the value of water. Ten years ago it was just something that ran away, but people are beginning now to recognise the value of water.

3. Please safeguard the image of the Society in the eyes of others.

Appendix IV

Drainage

A talk given at Peebles on 18/9/76 by Edwin Taylor

CCORDING to the programme my talk tonight is on Dowsing and Land Drainage, but that makes me think of someone crossing a field with the stick going down and saying, 'You will find the drain there.' To me that would seem a very uninteresting subject, so I have decided to change it to Drainage, which will give me a little more to talk about.

The chairman mentioned my elevation to the Council. This makes me perhaps rather more careful in what I say, but I hope to make it as interesting and useful as I can. I feel that a knowledge of drainage is vital to dowsing and it is also very important to the countryman. I myself, being born in the country, grew up alongside this particular subject and country matters in general. I think it is important that we have a little knowledge of rock formation, as before we set out into the field of dowsing or draining we should know what is under the crust of the earth.

My talk falls into about half a dozen parts, beginning with natural drainage. But first I should like to tell you the story of the shepherd. Along from Innerleithen to Peebles there was coming the vicar, going on holiday at the Peebles Hydro. Then a shepherd got into the bus. The vicar looked across at him and said, 'My man, what is your occupation?' 'I'm a shepherd, sir.' 'How interesting!' said the vicar. 'How many sheep have you?' 'About eighty.' For some time the shepherd sat and looked at the vicar, then he said, 'What profession would you be?' 'Well,' said the vicar. 'I am a shepherd, too.' 'Oh, how many sheep have you got?' 'About two thousand.' 'Aah!' said the shepherd. 'However do you do at lambing time?'

Drainage

Coming back to serious matters – natural drainage! If we get a picture in our minds of the difference in ground between the western part of Scotland and the south-eastern vale of England we see the tremendous variation in the types of earth, and we have many different kinds of drains. If you pour down a pail of water anywhere in the whole of the British Isles it will find its way out to sea. Had the country been man-made I doubt very much whether we could have fashioned anything as good as nature has done. Again, when we see the natural drainage – the rivers, the mountain sheds, the burns and the streams all running out to sea, I think we have got a tremendous lesson here, and how meek we should feel in our way of life when we see how wonderfully clever nature has been.

In our daily lives as dowsers we often have to work in different districts. The limestone areas of Northern England differ from Western Scotland. Then there are the in-betweens, where drainage is pouring water down into the lower strata, and we have a glacial drift again drawing down into the lower strata – the sandstones, the sand pockets, all feeding the underground streams of water. I think it is important that we consider these under the heading of drainage. Not only are they draining the surface, they are also cleaning the water in the process. The water that we find in our underground sources is usually very clean, because it has been filtered and passed through these various processes. Then again we find volcanic faults, which are also suppliers of underground water. In addition, there are the effects of the running off of water, of hard frost, a quick thaw. i think that in the large floods that the country has known what is actually happening is that you get a hard frost, which seals off the crust of the earth. If very heavy rain follows a quick thaw you have fast-running water flowing down off the whole of the crust of an area and you have these abnormal runouts. When you go down to Berwick-on-Tweed or somewhere else where the outlets run into the sea you can see the marks where they have been about 14ft or 20ft above river level. That is exactly how it works.

That brings me to the subject of natural drainage as it is affected by man. We have catchment areas directing water to reservoirs, and these catchment areas today are very different from those made by nature. For example, we have the Forestry Commission ploughing the hillsides, and I think you can travel anywhere in the North now and see large plantations. Where they have ploughed a deep furrow these are all carrying fairly fast-running water off the hills and returning it to reservoirs, which is different from what nature would have done. I think, too, that the Forestry Commission in the process of planting these large areas is encouraging rainfall, so again you have an area in which man is affecting the normal daily course of nature. We have land drainage for agriculture brought about by man, varying from hill farming to various types of lowland farming, which I will dwell on a little more in a moment. I think we should also remember that with man affecting the general flow of water as it was established by nature there is much more water running off the surface than was previously the case. I have no doubt that this affects the level of underground supplies, so if we are storing large amounts of surface water it is not all gain. We have lost something in the process, as a lot of this water would naturally have found its way down through the various strata and into the underground reservoirs, but instead we have got it in surface reservoirs.

The nation at the moment is trying to devise a grid system. That again comes under the heading of drainage. They are draining water from Tyneside to Teeside at tremendous cost, and they are trying to form a grid system for water similar to the electric grid system. Whether this is in the right direction I am not sure, because it is a very costly system and I should have thought there was quite sufficient water in Teeside without trying to steal the water from Tyneside. This is happening not only there but in other parts of the country, too.

There is such a thing as redistribution of water, which again is passed through pipes, and this talk can hardly be given without mentioning redistribution, because tremendous quantities of water are being wasted daily from our factories and could very well be redistributed and used over and over again. Large amounts of clean water from reservoirs are being wasted on dirty work. Opencast mining cannot be left out, because it is a man-made process which is having some effect, however small, on our underground streams and the water table.

As I am a farmer, you are no doubt expecting my talk to be largely on the subject of land drainage as applied to agriculture. Now I think that the industry of agriculture has recognised the value of drainage over a very large number of years. I think we all appreciate that in this country nothing will grow with its feet in water. It may do so in China in the paddy fields, but we have no paddy fields here and nothing in this country will grow successfully with its feet in water. I think that every department of farming, whether it be the cereal grower, the grass grower or the livestock breeder, will agree that one acre of drained land is as good as three of the undrained. I believe there is evidence that this was recognised right down through the ages. We find remains even from Roman times of stone drains when we are ploughing a very deep furrow or something like that. They were put there hundreds and hundreds of years ago and they are in the same kind of form, with two stones side by side and a platform on the top, and they have been effective for all that length of time. They are only revealed when we have the heavier kind of machine going on to the land and probably going down through these drains.

With the revolution of the 1860s farming entered a new era. A complete new look was taken at food production, and in the 1860s thousands and thousands of acres in Britain were drained with government aid. If you go out into the fields today you will hear someone mention that he has found a drainpipe there, and you can be sure that most of the drains which you find in the fields were laid down by fairly hard labour somewhere round 1860 to 1870. These were the old round tile drains. There was no bottom in them; they were laid in the earth or in the subsoil fairly deep, probably in lots of cases about 5ft down, much deeper than any modern form of drainage and probably less effective than modern drainage. From that period until recent times we have seen a great change in the fashion of drainage. It changed from the red tile type into a larger one, and in the last ten years we have opened a complete new era of drainage with the plastic type. You have all seen those massive piles of plastic pipes rolling along the motorways. They are all heading for the new era of drainage.

In many cases fields which were done in the 1860s have been done all over again in a different pattern. At that time the drains were running down the hill. Since then the fashion has changed to the herringbone type, and now they are running across the hill. They are not nearly so deep as they were at that time; 4ft seems to be about the depth. Now the pipes of the 1860s have stood the test of time; they are as good today as when they were put in. I wonder whether the plastic pipes will do as well. Only time can answer this, but what it all boils down to, as in everything else, more especially in this age, is cost and the return on capital outlay. If, as I said before, undrained land is of no great value, whilst by draining you are increasing the value of your land, plus the increase in the output from the land, you can well afford to spend £100 an acre on drainage.

Now on the hillsides, or the land running up to the hills, as we see it especially coming up to Peebles, there is a fairly high percentage of government aid to those people who are willing to spend the money, and in some cases on the hills there will be 60 per cent, probably 70 per cent grant, so you can well understand that masses of drainage are being done throughout the north of England and Scotland at the moment. There are also the gravel areas of agricultural land which do not need to be drained in this era; they are the high quality land of the past. They are farms on Tweedside and Teeside where the land is in fairly close proximity to rivers, your half land, as it is called – the flood land beside the rivers, generally self-drained – and these were the areas where the abbeys of monks settled in days gone by, in other words, the fertile land before the era of drainage, and I think that even today thousands of these acres do not need draining and are very useful without it.

There is a cheap form of drainage which you have probably heard of – namely, the mole drain. This could be very useful on peaty soil, away from stones. It is something in the shape of a pen, it has a stem underground, and it is ploughed under the ground about 18 inches deep. It is very effective and probably lasts 2–3 years, and then you can afford to do it over again. This is not applied to tillage land or land growing cereals, but is useful on pasture land on the hillsides. There is a fair deal of it done, so one can hardly talk on the subject of drainage without making some mention of mole drainage.

When you are thinking of drainage in any form it is vital that you consider the fall, and there is an art in getting your fall. If you have a level field or what looks level it is vital to put your sights on it and get your fall, because all the drains have to fall away to a single point. It is not just a matter of digging a strip in the earth, dropping in a pipe and sitting about hoping the water will run away. It is important that you get it right, because if you have a ditch in your ground it is obvious that it is going to silt up and in 2–3 years' time you will be back to do it all over again.

I am not a man for machinery, but obviously this work is done by machines, and we have gone a tremendous stride forward in the drainage field. You can see the plastic pipes being laid by machinery. The machines go along at a walking pace, dropping the pipes as they go. The earth is filled in again, and after the machine passes through the pipe is already laid, ready to run your water off.

I doubt whether you can have any advantage in life without some form of disadvantage. We hear about side effects in medicine, and I think drainage too has side effects. We are losing through drainage a tremendous amount of valuable water, which is being shed off and not utilised. It is shed off into the rivers and out to sea before we can put our hands on it, so whatever the gain to the industry of agriculture, we as a nation have lost a tremendous amount of water in the process, and this must be contributing to the loss of level of the underground supplies. Also in a year like this — we do not, of course, always have a year of drought — there is such a thing as over-drainage. Probably all our farmers would have been glad if there had been no drainage of the ground at all.

Now a word about water wastage through natural drainage. At present there is a great cry being made by the Government and at the highest level by people who have never previously thought about water but find there is suddenly a scarcity. Yet we need not go more than 200 yards from this building to see masses of valuable water which by tomorrow morning will be running out at Berwick-on-Tweed. I don't think this nation need ever be short of water; it is just that we are badly organised. If we had another year or two like the present one the house would be put in order.

We also lose water by evaporation from reservoirs. There is no doubt that fairly large amounts of water are being absorbed into the atmosphere because it is stored at the surface. Water conservation is probably a subject in itself, but I think that as a nation we are very poor in our ability to conserve our water and not sufficient thought has been put into it.

Over the last few years I have felt that this Society has some part to play in this somewhere down the line. In the British Society of Dowsers we are not all water finders, but we can make a tremendous contribution to the nation's supply of water. In my own small way I have seen how much water can come out of the ground which otherwise would not have been found, and that probably in areas where it would not mean lowering the water table. I believe there are millions of gallons of water underground which could be found by people like ourselves in this Society and this water could be put to good use. I think that if we went through the right channels we could make a contribution.

Is it we who have failed to regulate the water supply and demand or is it nature? I don't think it is nature, because we have robbed her of much of her water by channelling it off the surface. I think that as a nation we should accept the blame for the failure to regulate our supplies of water. Obviously I am only speaking for myself, but I think we should feel a little ashamed that that is so. Someone this morning mentioned balance, and that is a word which comes to my mind very often. Whatever you do the word 'balance' comes in. If you upset this balance, whether it be in health or in any department of life, the pendulum has got to swing back, but I think again that the balance of the water system of our country has been upset. I am sure that if real thought were given to it we could get an awful lot more use from our water supply.

Now what are nature's aids in drainage? She has provided us with some. Even the mole is a very useful animal in the drainage of the hillside. I know a district – probably some of you know it too – east of Carlisle where the fields are covered with little molehills – just little mounds of soil. You may think the farmers must curse these moles, but no, it is a form of drainage and they don't mind. The mole might be a nuisance under your potatoes but is useful in particular places. Nature supplies us with worms, another vital part of animal life in this country, to see that the water gets down through the crust. The worms are playing an important part there, and when you see the last machines going off an opencast site it makes you shudder to think what must have happened to the worms and to the natural drainage. Plant roots are another of nature's ways of supplying you with a road down through the crust. When the plant roots have died and withered you are left with the taproots and various other forms of root that are siphoning water down through the strata. Then again there are sand, gravel, shale, peat and other water-bearing strata.

You will think that up to now I have made no mention of the dowser in the field of drainage. Well, I am not sure that he has a large part to play here. Knowledge of the subject is vital to his existence as a dowser and I think that is the way I look at it rather than his usefulness to drainage. He is part of drainage, drainage is part of him, and he goes along finding drains, yes, that is useful. He can play some part in the process, but I think the important thing is that he should understand the whole subject of drainage, as it will increase his usefulness as a dowser. He can depth the strata. If there are 10ft gravel and 3ft clay there is no reason why the dowser should not go along and say yes, he can depth this layer and the next, just as you were depthing water this afternoon. If you ask the questions I am sure that in the process you will get the answers.

Most of you have been out on the exercise this afternoon. Many have found drains and some are probably more confused than ever before. I think when you are beginning your career as a dowser you want to stay away from people. You don't want everybody to be looking and saying, 'Oh, here's one of those silly cranks. Let's watch him.' I also think you should keep away from man-made features, such as drains. Go out and look for what nature meant you to look for – the underground sources of water. Get away from pipes and things like that to begin with. I think you will be far wiser to go to a spring and follow it back into the earth, or something like that, rather than go looking for lead pipes down there that must have an offshoot here and there. Get a little nearer to nature to set off with.

Now to sum up the few words I have said – I feel the main thing is that drainage is a countryman's art. He lives with it, he does it, he gets the feel of it; it is a part of his everyday life. It is of prime importance to the industry of agriculture right down the line, whether it be in the high hills of Scotland or the eastern–most tip of England. It is of the utmost use to agriculture. Nature has played her part very well in the process of designing this land. I repeat: Wherever you pour down a pail of water it will find its way out. There is a downward grade all the way to the east, with no hills or hollows. She has fashioned this earth very well indeed, yet man is unable to cope with the simple subject of water and drainage.

Appendix V

Practical Dowsing in Relation to Agriculture

Y OWN county is Northumberland, which is little spoiled by modern civilisation. The character of the British farmer and countryman changes little wherever he resides and, like the dowser, is unchanged from county to county.

The dowser could very well become most important in the next decade of country life in Britain. His services to mankind in the past have been tremendous, but have not so far earned the rewards and recognition they deserve. Now the scientist tells us that dowsing is no longer a myth and if this is true it is the greatest milestone in the history of dowsing, for it opens up the field of equality of profession. The attitude of modern science is trained to be sceptical, for it is not easy to prove the simple nature of the divining ability which works so accurately with a hazel twig cut from any hedge. But if we are able to overcome the difficulties there is no doubt whatsoever of the possibilities which lie in front of the skilled dowser, and this is where a closer and more definitive line should be adopted by the practising dowsers of this Society.

If we analyse the fields of scope open to widespread dowsing which will be useful to the community as a whole, we will see that they lie mainly in the supply of water to agriculture and remote country dwellings which are outside the range of a mains water supply. The number of potential users falling into this category could be amazingly large. Others include locating water for light industries and the less-sought-after requests of finding lost property, missing people and diagnosing the centre of ills in both man and beast.

We dowsers profess to be able to walk into a field and mark a spot where we say, at × number of feet down you will find × number of gallons of water per day. No wonder the audience or onlookers say 'Impossible, this person must be nuts,' but after a careful explanation of the methods used to do this, it is then quite easy for people to understand that it is done by calculation and not by guesswork.

How can we be of use in this age when man has achieved a landing on the moon and has been able to return – which is even more remarkable, and dowsing in its simple form has not changed for thousands of years. Can we make this the time of achievement and usefulness in Britain when such a shortage of water is becoming a reality and a danger to the smooth running of the nation? A great role could now be played by the British Society of Dowsers, first by unifying the hard core of its practical dowsers in the field, by pooling the knowledge and formulating a definite plan of action as a service to the modern need. This certainly exists, especially in rural areas where water supplies are obsolete, and in many cases not there at all. The fact that the need is there should be sufficient for the geologist, the dowser and the national Agricultural Advisory Service, to get together and explore the needs of country dwellers on a national basis and insure that these are not the reasons for a further drift from the countryside.

We have maps carefully compiled by the Geological Survey, a full set of maps of Britain in large scale, wonderfully detailed by the Ordnance Survey; why could there not be the same carefully drawn-up map of the underground water courses which produce over a given quantity? This would be a national asset well worthy of Government grant aid. Or failing this, a service by the N.A.A.S. to offer to farmers or estate owners a map of their holdings giving details of their potential values and quantities in underground water courses. If we consider the cost of taking mains water to country places, it would be greater in many cases than a private supply found by dowsing. There is no better example than my own case, where mains water was within half a mile and we found it much cheaper to install a private supply found by dowsing, drilling to one hundred feet and extracting seven thousand gallons per day. If we are to consider cost at over four shillings per thousand gallons, this could mean over five hundred pounds per year in charges by a water company over the cost of installation. If this is an example there must be thousands and thousands of cases where separate supplies could be harnessed by the water companies on a national scale throughout the British Isles in co-operation with dowser and geologist and be much cheaper than mains and on a basis similar to electric and telephone installations. Finer details of such a proposal could be quickly worked out by practical, experienced and proved dowsers in regard to the most suitable points for drilling. I have found in hilly districts, where boreholes are sited on hilltops, water can be successfully siphoned to lower-lying farms and homesteads and if suitably sited can supply several users very cheaply. The drilling equipment needed for this shallow well exploration need not be so elaborate and expensive and therefore could, in fact, reduce some of the cost to the consumer sinking a well. It would be most interesting and revealing, to launch a pilot scheme in a district where there is no main water. I mean a scheme sponsored by the Government and paid for by the Treasury. This could be one of the services that our Society should pursue and profit by in these times when it needs evidence of its ability and value.

Whatever service is done today our minds are trained to be cost conscious and it is necessary to make some comparison. First, have we ever stopped to consider the value of the service of divining when asked to locate water on some country estate, and compare the value before and after finding a good supply? Take for example a dairy farm of two hundred acres without a reliable supply of water – this would be, on average national land values, in the region of thirty-five thousand pounds. With a good supply it would be about forty thousand pounds. Now an interesting comparison can be made on the same farm with *mains* as against a private supply.

A daily consumption of four thousand gallons per day at four shillings per thousand gallons on the mains would equal £292 per year. If the job were done privately locating and boring to one hundred feet would be £600 pump and pumphouse would be £300. This would qualify for a fifty per cent grant on water supplies, which would reduce the amount of £450. Spread over a twenty years' expected life of the machinery makes it about £22 10s. per annum, thus giving a private installation a lead of £259 10s. This is without the cost of bringing mains water to the farm gate. This is an important point.

There are very large areas in the British Isles which will never be supplied by mains water and it is these areas which will have to be catered for in a long-term plan and now is the time to begin thinking.

I remember a few years ago doing work for the Forestry Commission (a Government department). This was to locate water by divining to supply a few farms in South Northumberland, where an existing well had become inadequate, so an appointment was made to meet their land agent with a view to surveying for a new site to drill. On arrival at the site for exploration, I questioned the agent as to the whereabouts of the old supply and he was quite prompt in telling me it was no use. So I insisted that we first look at the old well, because the tank and pipes leading to the farms were already installed and if possible would be better made use of. My survey of the old well, which was a pipe from a surface spring, told me that there was ample water in the spring and it was at a depth that workmen employed on the estate could well dig down – my estimate was six feet deep. A few days later my telephone rang to say 'We are nearly to the depth and the ground is bone dry.' I immediately visited the spot, and on arrival saw that water had been found and was gushing down a ditch, almost sufficient for a small town. How easily a large amount of money could have been spent in this case if a new well had been drilled and the old one abandoned. This is a perfect example of the work of divining.

I must now give one more example to illustrate the importance of co-operation between the geologist and the dowser in the field.

A farmer in East Northumberland who was needing a new water supply asked his county agricultural committee for help and advice as to how he should go about getting his farm watered. He was told that the Geological Survey Department would give him all the advice needed. They were called in and marked a point on his farm where an ample supply could be found. Drilling was done and the supply was installed, the depth of the borehole being two hundred feet. Three years later the poor supply progressively worsened, until it dried up altogether. The farmer then telephoned me and told me of his trouble and asked for my help. The drilling company equipment was in his farmyard and he had again been advised to redrill the borehole. On arrival at his farm that evening, I examined the borehole and surrounding area and found no sign at all of any underground course. His supply had been only seepage and drainage which had dried out. After establishing that the old bore was a failure, he asked me to find a new place to drill. I found water running north-south at forty-five feet down, another east to west at eighty-five feet down and marked my point to drill where the two streams crossed. This mark was within a hundred yards of the old failure and I told the farmer he would not need to drill half so far for this one. The following day the drilling was done and at four o'clock in the afternoon he telephoned me and said that the water was running down the field. I called about a month later and his wife answered the door, and on enquiring about the water, she said, 'This is the first time we have been able to bath the children one at a time.' So it is very often important for a dowser to mark the point to drill.

Some mention must be of old wells and the siting of farmsteads. If we make a general survey of old farms, villages, castles and other forms of old country life, a well will most certainly be found in a very convenient position to the particular need, such as the well at the back door of the farm house, in the centre of the courtyard and the castle or in the centre of the village green in a country village. These wells are not here by chance, divining is an old and practised art going back in Britain further than we realise. The well was found and then the farm was built, and in the case of castles and other dwellings. If you are journeying through the countryside and wonder why a farm was built there, this could be the very answer to the question.

Not much has been said of ordinary depthing in sand, gravel, peat or any other sudden change from one kind of strata to another. The following method can be useful in estimating a quantity of gravel in an area for sale, or depth of peat in a draining scheme, and I find that strata levels throw back a ray at 45 degrees and can be estimated in a similar way to finding depth of water, the only difference being, for example, a peat field to be drained. Stand at any point where you wish to know the depth, pace forward and where your rod goes down, the distance you have travelled is equal to the depth of peat or gravel and so on. This is very useful and something I have not read of in the Society's readings.

Good husbandry demands a constant watch on land drainage. If you are lucky enough to have a farm on gravel or able to be on porous ground giving land a natural drainage, you may be fortunate. Where I live in Northumberland, with a predominance of boulder clay, land drainage is essential. If one is able to find burst drains, whether burst by modern heavy machines or by a normal collapse of a drain pipe, to be able to locate a pipe line by divining is a great saving. Many times an outburst of water needs running into a field drain. On land where livestock needs watering it is useful to harness small springs in fields to watering troughs and if one has a reasonable reputation neighbouring farmers often make use of your ability and in this way you feel a service is being done to a local community. It is in this small way that you become known as a Dowser.

Most Dowsers have their own choice of medium. My own particular one being a whalebone which I bought back in the 1940s and with which, up till now, I have found many thousands of gallons of valuable water. My second choice is the normal, simple hazel forked twig, which may be the better. Copper or brass rods are too sensitive for me and they pick up everything – it is similar to using a broadcasting mast to receive on a transistor radio. I can use also a piece of rubber tubing, a flexible spring and even my hands without any other device.

It might be generous to point out to would-be or potential Dowsers the dangers that can happen in the countryside. Experience is a great teacher, but to be forewarned is to be forearmed. Overhead cables, both electric and telephone, can be a distraction if they are near where you are calculating – take care not to be confused. If you are dowsing for water in limestone country the fissures that carry water in heavy rain or in winter give the same reaction when dry and can cause great disappointment. I have found over the years several wells which are very intermittent and on investigation discovered they are three to four yards off their mark, obviously found by a dowser who was not confident enough to check and re-check or maybe not aware of the width of stream. Imagine what could happen to the inexperienced dowser on approaching an underground supply if his rod dips down too soon because he is not holding it firm enough. Could this be what went wrong with these 'off the mark' wells? It would be interesting to hear other views on this.

We are entering a new phase when the townsman's interests have changed considerably from the mass pilgrimage to the sea-side, which today has so much pollution, to the fresh air of the countryside. The country cottage has come into its own and a great need is coming to provide these people with a good water supply. This is another chance for the dowser to give his service and the Society to give a lead and let the public know that this service is available. Details could be given from the Society's office and the names of competent dowsers passed on. This could even be a source of income for the Society's funds, operated on a commission basis.

Walking on Water

How the Water Resources Act affects potential users of water in any kind of quantity should be explained in some form and as a guide to what can legally be done when extracting water from nature's resources. From the 1st April, 1965, it is an offence to abstract water from any source without first obtaining a River Authority licence, and before so doing, a press notice is to be inserted in the local newspaper at least twice in two weeks, and once in the *London Gazette*. However, there are minor exceptions to the above ruling.

1. Abstraction in one operation or a series of operations of a total quantity not exceeding one thousand gallons.

2. Abstraction from an inland waterway for domestic or agricultural purposes other than spray irrigation.

3. Abstraction from underground strata by an individual for the domestic purposes of his household.

4. Abstraction in the course of land drainage.

5. Abstraction for firefighting purposes.

Even when a licence is needed the charge is still quite nominal at five pounds per annum for a farm supply and if joint domestic and farm it is just one pound.

Is this the thin end of the wedge? Typical of so much legislation introduced in an unimportant disguise, or is it the price to pay for our larger population?

I read with great surprise and interest that the annual consumption of water in the United States of America is ahead of their national rainfall. We should not be surprised when we consider the daily consumption is 200 gallons per head of their total population. If we compare this with Great Britain, where our daily consumption is 50 gallons per head and nine-tenths of our good, clean, soft rainfall ends up in the sea before it has been used, this must warrant a major enquiry, especially when our underground water level is falling at an alarming rate.

I remember drilling a particular borehole where it was agreed to supply and provide water for the drilling rig. The depth was to be about one hundred feet, but at about thirty feet in the terms of the driller's speech 'they lost the water' and it took thousands of gallons to lubricate the drill. This gave me the idea that water could be returned to underground reserves in massive amounts by drilling and directing large quantities of water underground in high rainfall periods of the year. Where does the Dowser play his part? These inlets to underground can only be pinpointed by the skill of the dowser with the backing of an organisation like the B.S.D., or by patiently building confidence over a long period of time, which would be too late to give the highest service to the British population.

Let us look a little more seriously at this possibility of returning water underground. I know great problems exist with returning polluted water back and upsetting present clean supplies, but there are many untapped possibilities here if they can be harnessed to the best advantage. These surface water courses must be above the level of industrial pollution and also away from the main catchment areas for existing reservoirs. This still leaves massive areas in Britain where this challenge could be exploited – so how do we apply it?

Select by analysis the clean water on the higher regions with a view to drilling by the edge of streams and directing water from the stream at given points all the way downstream at places selected by a skilled dowser and in the rainy season if some of the drillings misfire and come out in the wrong place they can be plugged and left. However, put into practice and with experiments, a scheme of this nature could unfold many new regions of reward for our nation which according to our rainfall figures, should have no shortage if it were fully utilised.

To sum up there are five points I would like to emphasise:

1. That the major role of the Dowser lies in the countryside, with agriculture receiving the greatest service.

2. Over three years a team of scientists have experimented and proved 'That the phenomenon of dowsing exists'.

3. The Society has an opportunity to gain a greater recognition than ever before by pressing for a chance to demonstrate its ability and launch a pilot scheme in co-operation with various organising bodies.

4. Costs seem to dominate the present way of thinking which is unfortunate when one wants to obtain the best out of the nation's intelligence. This can aptly be applied in the field of dowsing.

5. Serious wastage of clean, good water, running to the sea. Remember the possibility of returning valuable water to the nation's natural reserve.

Appendix VI

Dowsing for Water

A talk given by Edwin Taylor at the Golden Jubilee Congress held at Oxford in July 1983

HAT A pleasure it is to again take an active part in the Society's Congress. Each gathering becomes a milestone and I find myself much wiser after each one.

My way of life is farming; living with Nature, the land and the livestock, who are all individuals when you come to know them and their temperaments and how they respond to kindness – as does Nature and the countryside.

The deep roots of my family in a small locality have farmed in an unbroken line since the late 1600s. This inherent character seems to have passed down to the next two generations as I have a son and two grandsons working on the land.

You will, therefore, not be surprised that my way of life includes the art of dowsing as a natural asset. I am very conscious of this gift and it gives me a great sense of responsibility.

I am a great believer in giving value for money and to be correct. You must look through the other man's eyes to be able to give him the best service from which he can be a satisfied customer. Living in the country, having farming as a career and being close to Nature has given me a vast amount of knowledge which can be used to help clients in need of a new water supply. In many instances I have to become the adviser for their new system besides finding the water they need.

Many dowsers tend to complicate their task so unnecessarily by little fads picked up from seeing others doing similar things, such as they cannot do their dowsing in Wellington boots or holding a sample bottle of water when they are locating water.

Thirty years of dowsing has taught me to apply some caution. Do not be afraid to take time and 'tarry a while', start again and again if need be. Build your picture from a distance; you cannot see the wood for the trees when standing too close. The same thing applies in dowsing. Find your proposed stream to be used and if you are amongst buildings get out into the open field or a clear area and assess it from there. You will find that the picture becomes much clearer and it is less likely to be a failure.

Locating water by dowsing is not a game of chance although the general opinion is that the strength of pull on the rod is the basis of calculation. If that was true dowsing would be a game of chance but success in dowsing is the result of careful calculation, applied rigorously and done on site. It is most important to make more notes than you seem to need at the time and later when you are rewriting them to put them on record, you realise the value of those extra notes. Where markers are put in for measuring quantity and depth (which will be explained later) do not trust your memory – write them down at the time of measuring.

In my experience, clients do not make notes or keep any written record of your visit other than the stake you have put in to mark the point to drill. This point must be marked on your plan with measurements in case the driller decides to move a few yards to the left or right to miss some obstruction. In such a case you would then have on record the point marked where to drill, relieving you of the cause of failure.

On many occasions, I also find that where the drilling is done several months after the dowse your client asks again for the details of your visit, which proves the importance of those written notes.

I am inclined to think that our image is divided into three. That of the 'general public', your 'client' and the 'professional'. The image of the dowser to the general public is of a strange person with a hazel rod walking in a field searching for water and he is also shrouded in some measure of mystery.

When I think back over the years and generalise the views of the clients, I find their expectations and pre-assessment of the dowser is far from reality. They vary so much from expecting you to arrive on a push-bike to someone who will walk over the area of the farm and not in any way be sure of the end result and how it is achieved. Some even think you have a magic wand that will bring water to the surface.

My third image is different. As dowsing cannot be explained or measured by an instrument, the 'professional', and I say this with respect, finds it hard to believe that dowsing is anything other than a myth. On at least two occasions I have asked persons of this category to hold the rod correctly and walk over the ground where there is an underground stream and in their hands the rod has turned down. On these occasions I have witnessed an expression of shock rather than amazement.

Also in this category are those who 'need you' and those who 'do not need you'. The former give you the benefit of the doubt and in the end, because of the result, respect you and many become members of the B.S.D. The latter, among which are the non-believers, who say water is found anywhere, and those who say without an explanation that it cannot be true. I get a kind of side glance from this one.

There are three stages in the task of finding a water supply – before, on site and after. Before begins with the approach, perhaps a letter or a cry for help from a farmer, who needs to increase his existing supply (the most typical) because of higher production and more intensive systems within the industry. I like to know in advance the requirements in gallons per day and the locality. I am then ready to make a visit. Also important is to be able to release yourself from your way of life and in farming this is not always simple as the seasons vary in the demands on my time.

On site is the day that *you* are the professional so therefore act like one. Be punctual, because first impressions mean so much, for or against you. There is a place to begin and this is where the water is needed. At this stage find out the access to a power supply to lift the water, the proposed siting of the water supply tank and its capacity and also if there is the necessary fall to all points of demand, such as field troughs for livestock. Then you will be asked how much it will all cost and if you are not able to answer all the preliminary questions the service you give is not as valuable as it should be.

Now that you know for what purpose the water is to be used you can calculate the requirement and it is now the time to do the all important part of marking out the place to drill and find a supply to match the needs of your client.

Over the years I have found an easy way of locating the streams. I have called it my 'Radar Scan' and I apply it when I am standing at the point where water is most important to be found and saves a great deal of walking. Place the rod in the dowsing position and rotate slowly in a clockwise direction until you have formed a complete circle.

In that process you will find a pull of the rod at one or more places and you will then repeat that process to confirm your first finding. Select your strongest pull and walk towards it marking the point where the rod goes down. Proceed to the second point where the rod reacts and mark that spot too. You can now establish your quantity and, if it fits the demand, proceed further to the next wave band which will give you the depth (Bishop's Rule), being the distance from second to third waveband.

Explore the alternative pull on the rod or the next strongest pull that you found when doing the 'scan' and you can now make a comparison, explaining the merits of that to your client. To go a step further, mark out where those two streams cross and through doing this you have doubled your chance of success. These are wise calculated moves which make you a better dowser.

It is rare that you get the result of your dowsing soon after the survey and your prediction – it is this long wait which tests your patience while you are wondering what the result will be, especially if you are a beginner. But we all have to grow up and go through times of concern in any business or whatever you do in life.

Do not be alarmed if you are called to return at the time of drilling because your client is going through the same state of tension as you are, the difference being that *he* is spending the money while you are advising him how best to spend it. The reasons I have been called back vary but one is that 'We are nearly down to the depth and it is dry all the way'. This is true and will be so until you actually strike the water. Sometimes the drill will get beyond your predicted depth and on those few rare occasions a clay band will be found at the depth given. This does not in any way mean failure. What I have done on the two or three occasions it has happened with me is to reconfirm that the water is still there and that the driller has not moved his rig away from the point you originally marked. You can now redepth the water holding your rod very tightly at the point of the clay band and your rod will react at another waveband giving you the correct depth.

Having explained how to find underground water you may wonder if there is a place today for the skilled dowser. I think there is because if you would look at a map of the British Isles showing the area outside the reach and the area inside the reach, but not supplied, by a public water supply you would be astounded. My requests for help are more numerous from areas where public water is available and I am sure one of the reasons is cost. During the present depression, which is affecting all industries, water charges must be taken into consideration and a user can make a saving by having his own private supply. The cost of water has doubled in the last ten years to around £1 per thousand gallons. A user can quite easily obtain estimates for the installation of a dependable alternative and make his own comparison, spreading the installation costs over a ten-year period.

The other reasons why farmers and larger users of water are seeking an alternative in the form of a borehole is to have a stand-by during an emergency. You may recall the water workers' strike of 1983 and the plight of so many users who were without water. These people have found it essential to have an alternative supply, like the electricity users, for that sort of emergency.

Water is a natural asset going to waste in massive quantities and in time it will become less plentiful, more costly and more valuable. Skilled dowsers could be finding and putting on record exact points to drill with estimated quantities and depths for users needing a supply of up to 100,000 gallons per day. This would, in time, do away with the need to flood valleys and save valuable farm land. This in no way needs to be confined to the British Isles because the underground patterns of water courses are similar throughout the world and needs could be more urgent in other parts.

The track record of the dowser can be very high indeed and knowing this to be true I think he should explain how it works for him to his client, the Society, his family and mankind. Let us remember that our greatest achievements in dowsing are a measure of our capabilities and great achievements become yardsticks, as did the four minute mile.

Dowsers are very thin on the ground and in my experience I am not surprised. A dowser's rise to fame is the slowest possible process for many reasons. The greatest barrier to progress is the inability to give a clear cut answer to how dowsing works. Because of that your client lacks confidence and self-assurance is of no value, so a client seeking the services of a dowser wants the recommendation of previous users. That in itself immediately reduces the field because clients rarely have confidence to employ a budding dowser! It has been word of mouth alone that spread the news in my climb to being a successful dowser. It is a process which is very slow to start but gathers a kind of momentum which I have not pushed because of my commitment as a farmer.

There are highlights in whatever venture you set out to do and dowsing is no exception. I will tell you of one or two that come to mind.

Durham County Agricultural Advisory Service asked me to demonstrate the art of dowsing to a large gathering of farmers, who were all notified by postcard of the talk. At the demonstration and nearing the end of the talk I was puzzled to overhear one man saying 'When is he going to start?' I found out afterwards that he thought the subject was on the 'dosing' of cattle or sheep!

A rare occasion in a dowser's career is to find an artesian well. It was my good fortune that it happened with me at Low Trewhitt in the Coquet Valley in Northumbria, where the water spouted up into the air from a depth of over 100ft. There was quite enough to supply several farms.

Yettlington School, at the foot of the Cheviot Hills, had been sold as a private building with planning permission to convert it to a dwelling. The new owner asked me to find him water, which I did, but it was about 9ft. outside his small area which included the school yard. The building was in an exposed country area far from another dwelling and I said I would write to the adjoining land owner offering as a gift some of the water when the drilling was completed. The answer came back 'No', and I later found out that he had supplied the school previously and then cut the supply off. I paid a second visit to the building and found a small supply under the wall between the boys' and girls' playground. My estimate was that there would be 300 gallons per day and when it was drilled my estimate was correct.

For a number of years I was chairman of the local District Council's Rural Water Supply Committee. I received a request to find some water so I took along the District Engineer, who was a real non-believer of dowsing. I shared with him the whole procedure from beginning to end but he would never admit that it was anything other than chance.

It is widely known that some underground streams can be harmful to both man and beast if they live over them for any length of time.

The dowser is often being called in to investigate houses where occupants have an illness that cannot be explained, or is of a kind which is common in some houses which have a reputation for illness.

When I think deeper into the art of dowsing and its capabilities in the hands of skilled people, I liken it to the Universe as it is beyond our ability to measure.

Dowsing in my experience can be so accurate in finding underground water, the depth and the quantity which are all vital to success and proving without doubt the truth of it, and this same truth and ability can be found in other departments of dowsing such as homeopathy, medicine, archaeology, oil and others.

Television channels have highlighted dowsing in different ways from the 'sublime' to the 'ridiculous'. My experience has been to praise the BBC for their presentation of my work as a water diviner portrayed on a farming programme earlier this year. It was put over in the way of how important a skilled dowser can be to the farming industry and showed my map where pockets of ten or more bores have been put down in localities over a wide area. It also transpires, after the television programme, that people are keen to know more about the subject. Even the Agricultural Training Board have included the art of dowsing in their classes in the next series of Country Crafts to be held in Northumberland.

When I think of the enjoyment derived from being able to dowse for water a chapter or a book would not cover the joys, it would need a volume. Every request is a chapter with the circumstances, the characters, my adaptability to the situation – not without anxiety and concern – and the satisfaction in the end result being the reward. I can still hear the words 'They found a great supply at Sandy Ford' and 'You were spot on with the depth at Homesteads.' These kind of remarks are the pleasure.

In any profession you accumulate a vast number of friends, mainly business friends and I have also found this to be true in agriculture. Dowsing has proved different because dowsers come from every walk of life, too many to mention, but you have all been delightful to meet.

After attending ten or more of the Society's Congresses this 50th Anniversary Congress must be a world event and is a great climax. To conclude and sum up I would like to divide my dowsing into three parts – the Past, Present and Future.

The Past has given me a tremendous amount of experience and has taught me a lot, with unlimited rewards being the pleasure. It has given me great satisfaction in being a dowser and to make full use of my abilities.

The Present speaks for itself. We witness a great occasion with a climax of events within the Society. A gathering of you all so interested in the subject and enjoying yourselves. If I can make a comparison between this meeting and a Congress of about twenty years ago at Cambridge. The atmosphere here is so different to that Congress, there are different attitudes now. Where there were people then walking around and I could not understand what they were doing, and I suspect they did not know either, now common sense is creeping in. This is progress.

The Future holds a great and untold potential if dowsing is applied sensibly and with guidance from those with experience and dedication dowsing will succeed.

The following questions were asked:

Q. What planning permission is needed before drilling commences and what do you do about the potability of the water?

A. In Northern England, where I am, it is very doubtful that you would get bad water because it is coming off the hills and is fairly well filtrated before you find it. So I have not really been troubled at all over this point. With regard to permission, you need a building licence obtainable from the Water Authority to drill. You also need a user's licence or a consumer's licence; if you are a householder it will cost you at the moment £1 per year and if you are a farmer it will cost you £5 per year. These licences are issued for the authority to have information on where and who is using water from underground.

Q. Can you give us some idea of the costs of drilling?

A. In reasonable drilling conditions the cost is about £15/metre for drilling. If the drill has to go through granite the extra costs of breakages etc. will be passed on to you. The top thirty feet is sleeved and sealed at the top, there are travelling costs to the site and these also have to be taken into account.

Q. Can you tell us something about pumps?

A. We are so up to date with the pumps produced now. The modern pump is like a cylinder and it is put down to the bottom of the hole. It goes under the water and is used to push the water that is there; it does not draw the water from under the ground. The modern pumps are very efficient but you must be careful and make sure the pump is suitable for the situation. If the pump is too big for the amount of water in the hole your supply will run dry in a very short while.

Appendix VII

Water Dowsing for Irrigation

A talk given by Edwin Taylor at the Congress in Carlisle in October 1986

HEN THE British Society of Dowsers was formed over fifty years ago, water divining was the main interest and I feel somewhat concerned to see our position as water finders giving way to the other departments with the medical group leading the field.

I do not for one moment resent their lead but there is a greater need for water dowsers in Britain of a higher standard to match up to professionals in the water supply industry.

You all know the word irrigation in terms as far as the dictionary goes, it is the watering of plants but for this morning's purpose it is a little different and I think that I should try and explain to you what we mean by this word in the sense that we are trying to apply it this morning. In the last few years, I have been asked several times to go to farms and find a supply of water for this purpose. Basically, the reason for this is that if a man has to keep to the maximum in his business of say, for example, potato growing, he has to keep up with the times and to keep there he has got to do some irrigation to keep in the front line. If he doesn't someone else will and, therefore, he will be behind.

So in this progressive kind of farming, the farmer has done his sums beforehand and comes and asks for my service. Economics is the reason for coming and water for irrigation can be a very valuable asset; it is an investment and also an insurance. It increases the yield of the crop in many instances by 25 per cent which is at the profit end of the scale. The crop is also ready for harvesting earlier and catches the market before other crops become plentiful and before prices in the shops begin to fall. The principle applies to all other vegetables that receive water in this way and for the same purposes, greater yield at a higher price is the aim of the growers.

In his particular role, the dowser has a very responsible and important part to play in accepting the challenge to find underground water for this purpose. Quantity being the great difference from the water dowser's normal requests of a few thousand gallons per day. The normal requirement for irrigation is 6,000 gallons per hour to maintain the general water spraying system and use it to its greatest advantage.

In a ten-year span of farming we may well get three drought years and irrigation is a form of insurance for those years of drought, especially in potato growing. So you can see that with irrigation crops would be very much more valuable in those three drought years.

I think it would be wise to give you a little outline of the costings for irrigation. If you think in terms of £5,000 for a borehole, £20,000 for irrigation equipment, and if it is needed a reservoir which would cost another £20,000 plus £5,000 per year maintenance you are quickly into £50,000. The point that I have got to make is that I can see this year there are quite big changes in the attitudes of the dowsers at this Congress; they are taking up more responsible positions and fitting the part more of what they should be and I think that this Society is leading towards a more professional type of person. I would like to emphasise that the water dowser has got to be in the same category of going forward as a responsible person and being conscious of the very fact that you are asking someone to spend £50,000 on the point where you are telling him to drill.

Where does the water dowser come in here? This is where he comes in, because the farmer does his sums and then thinks 'All I need now is the water'. So the approach is made and the farmer says that he is going in for irrigation and needs 6,000 gallons of water per hour. Rather a tall order, and not to be taken lightly. I think unless someone feels confident in dowsing for water they should not do it; it is not a place in dowsing that one should begin at.

It is vitally important that you fully understand the need and that you can advise on the alternatives if you have to. For example, if you are in an area which will not produce a well to yield the full amount you could advise building a reservoir to hold about ten million gallons, which could be filled during the out of season time, or make the quantity found fit the circumstances. And for it to be successful it is better if the dowser is able to give the necessary advice on all matters relating to each scheme.

To carry out a dowsing survey for irrigation is much greater and time consuming than the normal dowsing operation; it is also a greater cost to your client who is spending a large amount of money on your advice, but at the same time he is encouraged by the prospect of quite an increase to his income. Also comparing the cost of water through a meter at present day rates makes large amounts from a bore very reasonable.

I will go through the process of the survey. After receiving a request for a water supply from a farmer, I make an appointment to see him. I do nothing beforehand, no map dowsing and I want to hear nothing about it whatever. I like to go with a clear, open mind knowing nothing whatever, except that he wants, say, 6,000 gallons per hour. That means that I know in the back of my mind that we are going to need a much stronger underground water supply than is needed for the cottage or the ordinary farmstead that is needing 5,000 gallons a day. There is more work in this survey and more travelling.

If you can imagine that there is a farm of either 200 or 500 acres within a ring fence, the first question would be 'Where is the irrigation to be supplied from?' That is the part where you begin, so around that point I do the initial survey. This survey is done by scanning with my V rods and when I get a reaction with them I know in which direction I will find the water. I make notes of all that I find and hopefully this area is giving a sample of the rest of the property I am on.

To save long distances in walking, I ask for some kind of vehicle to cover the whole area of the farm in the form of a cross. There is little point in walking and dragging over a whole area of ground like that when you can do it just as simply and neatly in a vehicle. I prefer a Land Rover or similar vehicle where I can ask the driver to stop at each band of water that I cross. I get out, take measurements and write down what I have found. It is helpful to have a map showing all the field. At this stage I attach all importance to the width of the band which denotes the quantity of water. I can soon get a picture of whether it is to be a successful dowse.

The bands of water which are 'non-starters' are left out and I write down each one over 20 metres wide on a rough plan, and a picture begins to take shape. I then concentrate on the better ones especially where they cross marking the point midstream on both, which is very important. The mark is made by digging out a sod and later putting in a stout stake.

A priority in dowsing for irrigation is to go for the best potential supply, unless you have a choice of good alternatives, because it is not so important to be near to a power point when a portable generator could be cheaper and more flexible and, hopefully, it will only be needed in the best of summer weather.

On past experience it is opportune to relate some relevant experience of dowsing done in the field of irrigation. Oddly, where one is called in for irrigation work seem to be those eastern plains, areas of very low rainfall naturally, light soils, and I find especially in the Lothians and in Fifeshire that the potential of the streams is greater on these plains than in other places. Whether Nature has provided in this way, I don't know. In the instance of the East Lothian area and in Fifeshire there has been quite a lot of geological disturbance and earth faults are generally the carriers of water; these earth faults are fairly large in those areas.

My first reference would be to an article in the Scottish Farmer of 31 August 1985, with regard to seeking water for irrigation and finding useful supplies by Dr Roberts. He states there is no evidence to support dowsing, not even as a supplement to the geological or the geophysical approach to ground water operations. I think it is entirely wrong that these people should be so dogmatic about this. I often see their opinions in the press. There have been so many times when I have followed behind geologists and found good water supplies. On the eastern side of Yorkshire a poor farmer had had advice from a geologist and his bill from the driller was £12,000 – for a dry hole with no sign of water.

Irrigation is not confined to the growing of fruit and vegetables. This year I have been asked to find a supply of water in a large development of an eighteen-hole golf course at a country mansion in the area between the Tyne and the Derwent in south Northumberland. You never get two dowses alike, they are all different and this one had its problems. I was called in to mark out a site for water for irrigation of the greens, plus the domestic demands, and it needed a fair drop of water. When the time came for drilling, which was not many weeks ago now, the drill hit coarse gravel, which collapsed. I went back to the site and found another place but unfortunately the band of gravel was still there, so we had to move to higher ground 200ft above and found what seemed to me a very good supply, again making use of the two streams at different levels; the first was at 35 metres and the second at 53 metres. The prediction was made and I made a note in my book of where they would find the water at each level. The driller rang me after the first day's drilling and told me he had got down to both levels. He had put his ear to the drilled hole and said it sounded like a waterfall as one stream poured into the other.

Talking about the lines where the streams cross, the difference in your area of choice is so different when you decide to harness the two streams. If you have an underground stream 20 metres wide you can choose anywhere along it to drill providing you are midstream. Once you decide to harness two streams you are then restricted to an area which can be quite small. There was one time in Fife, on a fairly large farm, where the crossing point I found was right in a farm building so we had to move outside again and all that we could get the drill down to was one stream. The quantity inside was probably twice as good as the point outside.

I always keep a record of my dowsing advice to clients, along with site measurements, estimate depth and quantity. Keeping records is valuable when you have to return to a site and this does happen for many reasons.

There are changes happening all the time in all walks of life and the water industry is not left out of change. Britain is now subject to the rules of Europe which has a higher standard for water for irrigation than those in our public health departments. If enforced in rural areas supplied by near surface springs, it is doubtful whether they would come up to the new standard and could create a demand for drilling deeper wells or putting clean water systems in which could be very costly to isolated houses.

To be successful in the art of dowsing I am sure there are some qualities which are important in achieving that success. Probably the most important being enthusiasm. But time and patience cannot be replaced by short cuts. The water dowser has one great advantage as time goes on as he is rewarded by an end result and it is that end result which is the measure of his success. I was told by a client the other day that he was told dowsing has a 60 per cent success rate. I said that I would be most disappointed if my dowsing was at the 60 per cent level and I do not think I would be dowsing if it was so low. Wherever I go there has to be a well drilled and people are investing money on what I advise. There are other departments of dowsing where there is no real measure of a success rate.

This talk would not be complete without bringing in that very important man on the drilling machine. To think he can find water anywhere is not so, therefore, he has two people to turn to; the dowser or the geologist. Large drilling companies tend to favour the geologist because it is more official and they accept dry holes as part of the process. I have seen one recently costing £12,000 with no comeback for the dry bore.

To conclude my talk and sum up on the subject of irrigation there are three points I would like to emphasise. They are that the dowser is in a very responsible and demanding position, he has to defend his own image and that of the Society. I think he should be conscious of that when he is going out wherever he may be in dowsing, he should try and maintain that image if we want to achieve what we have said. The EEC regulations are changing the present systems, but remember there are 750,000 private water supplies in Britain.

Dependable dowsers will be needed to maintain rural water supplies so I don't think they are going to lay down just yet.

After the talk some questions were asked, as below:

Q. Are you ever asked to predict or specify particular kinds of water? Can you get dirty water which is unusable for farm animals?

A. I do not know whether it is the subconscious working again but you will find what you are looking for, and I think there is an awful lot in this. I am only looking for good water and the dirty water or that not suitable for the purpose I think is discarded. If I have to go back to a site for some reason I can find other streams that I did not see before, because they were not in the category I was seeking.

Q. You do a lot of dowsing and we hear that in certain places the water table is rising, do you find that where you work the level is static?

A.   My field of dowsing is not often in the water table area. If I was in the eastern plains or the London basin or somewhere like that I think I would be finding these areas to be changing. I am never in those areas long enough to have figures in relation to that question.

Q.   With regard to that last question, I am loath to introduce a negative point here, but in West Australia, for example, an awful lot of boreholes have been drilled for irrigation with the result that the water table has dropped to the north of Perth to the detriment of the growth of plants and consequently livestock and I wonder if this backs up the previous question.

A.   (from Cyril Wilson). I would like to answer here. I think you should be careful of what happens in various regions. In one part of the country the water level may be rising and in another it may be falling. For instance, in Ibiza, where I do a lot of dowsing, the water level is falling considerably and where, before, you would get water at 60 metres now you would probably have to go to 90 metres.

Q.   Is that not a serious responsibility that a dowser has to be aware of? That to get water here may be to the detriment of the next person?

A.   I feel that is not the dowser's responsibility, it is a question of the water authority's responsibility as to how much water is allowed to be extracted.

The Secretary then commented on the question of water tables rising and falling. He said that the Society has been approached a few times recently by professional engineers and surveyors because, particularly in the areas of high urban population and industry, they have found cases where in fact the water table is rising much above any architects' or engineers' preconceptions, purely on account of the recession in our manufacturing industry. In industry less water is being used for manufacturing and the rising water table is causing severe problems with the foundations of buildings, which were erected in the days when manufacturing was greater. They never expected this phenomenon to arise and have contacted the BSD for dowsers to help to find the source, if there was one, of this extra water in order to channel it away.

Another comment from Charles Holderness was that in urban areas a lot more hard surface is being put down and the collected run-off water is being put straight into streams instead of allowing it to percolate the soil to establish and maintain the water table.

A further comment from Cyril Wilson was that forestry too had an affect on this as it runs the water off the hills and into the rivers.

Appendix VIII

Many Years of Dowsing

A talk given by Edwin Taylor at Harrogate on 15/4/78

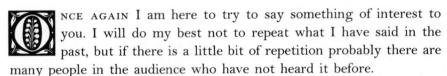NCE AGAIN I am here to try to say something of interest to you. I will do my best not to repeat what I have said in the past, but if there is a little bit of repetition probably there are many people in the audience who have not heard it before.

I always put at the top of my paper the advice that we should preserve the image of our Society. As you have heard from the chairman, I have been coming here for a number of years now and I have watched what I think we could call progress from some of the stick-waggers of ten years ago to the more serious and intent people who are trying to make a business of it. I can see young faces almost bursting with enthusiasm for this subject, which has an increasingly important role in this age.

I see from the programme that the title of my talk has been changed to 'Many Years of Dowsing'. The original heading was 'Work Done'.

There are seventy-six wells in the North of England and South of Scotland which are spilling out water as a result of this little piece of whalebone. I feel very pleased when I look at a certain map I have of the North of England and South of Scotland. I have all little marks on it, and it is amazing to see the particular areas in which this happens. For example, in the Coquet Valley of Northumberland there are quite a number of little red pins put in of work that has been done by myself, and as these patterns unfold they become very interesting.

In the past I have dealt with the broader side of the subject. This morning it is my intention to deal with the more intimate side of individual work that I have done, in other words, to bring in the more human side, the concern of the dowser, the concern of the driller, and obviously also the concern of the client. But I think I should begin

236

where a lot of you people probably are at this moment – at the beginning of a dowsing career. I always feel when coming to a Congress that at least someone down the line should give those people a little bit of encouragement. You may say, 'How do I begin?' so perhaps I should tell you of the first job I did and how I felt about it. I didn't do it straight away. I took probably two to three years studying the feel of the rod, studying how it worked and finding how to depth. I judged how far I was right by going round various wells of which someone else knew the depth to see whether I was following a similar line.

Finally I received a letter from London saying would I find water in the West Riding for a particular company, and I thought, 'Well, the challenge has come.' This was many years ago, ladies and gentlemen. I remember setting out for the West Riding on what i think was the wettest day I have ever seen. I thought, I am going to look for water and the heavens are opening. When it rains in the West Riding you know that it does rain. I don't think we get it quite so heavy on the east side.

I met the estate agent and he chauffeured me to the site, which was about thirty miles further on. Finally we arrived and he led me to the area, two fields, in which I was to find water. He took me into a particular field and said, 'Now, do you find something here?' I thought, I am being put through a little test here. He said, 'We have had a local dowser.' I said, 'Well, there is nothing here of any consequence, not what you are looking for.' I think that impressed him, making him feel that I had a little more knowledge than his local dowser had, plus the fact that I had travelled quite a distance. We proceeded up the field and I felt in my mind that at this first attempt I had to have two strings to my bow. I had got to find one stream running this way and another running the other way, so that when we drilled we should have two for the price of one. They had told me the amount they wanted was 6,000 gallons per day. They wanted it for a village – for the local pub, the school and the bakehouse, in other words, a typical West Riding village. I found a stream that was well worth while running that way and proceeded along this stream until I found another one the other way. I made a prediction as to depth – 35ft or something – for the first one, but told them not to stop at that but to go on to the second one, which was 87ft. I knocked in the pegs and then I had the long wait. Those of you who have done dowsing know that if you don't get the result immediately you have this long wait, and how long it seems if it is the first time, I went through the process of waiting and then finally I got the reply from Richard Turner & Sons of Bentham that, as predicted, they had found water at 34ft and again at 86ft. An eight-hour test had produced 300 gallons per hour, which worked out at 7,200 gallons per day. My prediction and my verbal contract was to find them 6,000 gallons per day, so you can well imagine my feelings on receiving this news. It is twenty-five years ago now and it was the beginning of my water finding career.

The calculation had proved to be correct and from that time onwards they have all, barring the odd exception, proved to be according to the calculation and I think this is the most wonderful thing about dowsing. Just to point the contrast, as the chairman asked me before coming in how we had advanced over the years – I remember a family of dowsers who were in their third generation. There was a man in Swaledale, a member of this dowsing family, who was noted throughout the British Isles and he was finding water in my own countryside. The drillers were down 300ft and they had found no water. They sent for this man to go back again and told him they had found nothing at 300ft, and all he could say was, 'Yes, there is water there. You have got to go on.' I should never have dared to go through that. The important feature is to know your depth, to know your quantity. That man was asking someone to spend thousands and thousands of pounds and all he could say was, 'Yes, there is water there.' Now that would shock me. I am very pleased that I have not needed to ask anyone to go to this expense without giving him some idea of both quantity and depth.

Another interesting case was what I call the Slaley Forest well. It was a known supply on which something had gone wrong. It was a very shallow supply and the client asked me if I could find him a new one. This was quite a few years ago but it would still have been fairly expensive. What I am going to illustrate here is that if the professionals had been called in quite a considerable amount could have been spent on finding a new supply and drilling, the building of new tanks, new pipes and new connections. I said, 'First of all we must try the old well and see what is wrong. We cannot discard this one.' On looking at it I found there were oceans of water in the well according to my calculations. I said, 'It is well worth while to get a man with a spade. At about 4ft down you should have ample water.' Next day the telephone rang and they said, 'We are down about 4ft and there's nothing.' But when I got there a couple of hours later they had struck the water. There was a stream running at least 1ft wide and 6 inches deep, and that to me was a terrific amount of water. It was enough to supply a village or even a small town. That is the value of this rod. Had a dowser not been there they would have thought the well had gone dry.

Now for an example from the Coquet Valley, at the foot of the Cheviot Hills. I don't know if any of you know it, but that is the seat of Lord Armstrong of the old Armstrong Ammunition works of Newcastle, the Krupps of England, as you might call them. On his estate at Cragside in Northumberland there is a farm called Low Trewitt which needed a supply. I took my friend Mr McKay the plumber, who was a typical country plumber, and knew every little corner and all about everyone's affairs for about three generations; we did a lot of work together. Going on to this particular site we marked it out, found what we thought to be a good supply and went through the process of waiting once more. This one was 100ft drill, and when they struck the water it shot out into the air. It was an artesian well, one of the few that have come up, but this one burst out a tremendous amount of water. So it is possible in this country to find artesian wells that will spill out quite a massive amount; this one would have done for a dozen farms in the area.

Another illustration I have headed Sandyford. At this particular time I thought it was most interesting, because I chaired a Water Committee on the Rural District Council and, being in the midst of nonbelievers, I invited the Chief Engineer of the R.D.C. to go with me through the whole process of doing a water finding job.

I had an invitation from Smiths Gore, a national company, to find a borehole for water at Sandyford, so I took Mr. McKay the Plumber and also invited the Chief Engineer to go along. He was throughout the whole process a non-believer, but I wanted to try to prove to him that a dowser had the ability to find water. We went through the process and got the drillers and finally found the water. My notes read: Visit to Smiths Gore, Corbridge, 20th Feb. Arranged to make appointment with Mr McKay of Rothbury (Plumber) to mark out and prepare for drilling a borehole for water at Sandyford on the Roman Wall. Further down I have the result: Got report of water found at Sandyford for Smiths Gore, Corbridge. Estimated depth about 120ft, water found at 128ft rising to 30ft from the surface. Yielding 20,000 gallons per day.

This is typical of many instances and it is one that I hope the Chief Engineer took heed of; he has moved away to some other place now. I got great pleasure out of demonstrating to a professional man that the dowser had an ability to find water; the farmer had no other way of getting his water than this.

I think you have all heard of the Keilder Forest and the Keilder Reservoir, and it seemed very odd that I should be invited to go and look for water on the dam site at Keilder – not to fill the dam, I can tell you – but you can well imagine that in all the eruptions of building the dam and all the various upsets to farm water supplies they found it necessary to call in a water diviner to find water for those people who had lost their supplies in the area round the Keilder dam. I have therefore been on that particular site on more than one occasion, but the interesting thing about one case was that it was one of the times when I worked hand in hand with a geologist. I have always felt that a dowser and a geologist would be a very useful pair provided they could agree. In this instance we got along fairly well. We saw each other's point of view. We went in on equal terms and I felt at the end of the day that we were both much wiser.

For those of you who are interested in finding a small supply, there was the small school at the foot of the Cheviots which had been bought by a butcher friend of mine in Newcastle. He wanted sufficient water for a little cottage, not a very great supply. The old school had had a supply off the neighbouring estate, but unfortunately when they sold the school they cut off the water. The estate itself was short, and I had the tricky problem of looking for water within an area of about half the size of this room, so it was a very difficult one. The stream that I found was just outside the perimeter of the school grounds, and I judged that there would be nothing lost here and we could soon come to some arrangement with the neighbouring estate. In fact, I could see further than that. I thought the neighbouring estate might even get a water supply itself out of it for some field for nothing, and this would be a handy lever to work on. So I marked out the spot just about the length of this table outside the school yard and far away from anything that could be harmed in any way, and proceeded to enquire from the estate whether it would allow a drilling. A plain, flat No! What should we do now? Back to the site and I found within the schoolyard another supply that I would at other times have discarded, but at least there was a reaction. There was a stream running probably 4ft wide, not very deep, something like 35–40ft. When we drilled down we got 300 gallons per day. In other words, a very useful little supply for a cottage, and another man made content.

That was one of the instances of a stream which at other times would have been discarded as being of little use. Those of you who are budding dowsers beware of just saying, 'I have found water. We will drill here.' Get your facts right before you start. If you want a farm supply of 15,000 gallons a day then 300 gallons a day is no use to you. Get your facts correct before you set out into the field.

We had a pub with no water. The interesting thing about this was the expression on the faces of the architect and consulting engineer. They said, 'We are down to the prescribed number of feet or within a foot of it and there is nothing.' There was sweat on their brows, because their reputation and their money were involved. They rang me and one of them met me at the pub door and he said, 'There is nothing.' So we tramped down the field and just as we got on the site they struck water. I forget what his exclamation was, but he said, 'We will go back and have that gin and tonic now.' It was one of those occasions when you like to think that your reputation with your neighbours is not too bad.

A local veterinary surgeon took up farming. This takes me back to the point I made some time ago about finding water at the top of the hill. He asked me to find water and I said, 'We want to be up there.' He was expecting water to be down below the level of the farm on the sloping hillside, and he said, 'However will you find water on the top of the hill?' Well, never mind, we found the water and he rang me up and said, 'You had better come.' I went there and he was coming across the field and he said, 'You're a good water diviner.' I thought, Well, heavens, we have got another happy man.

There is a tremendous satisfaction in doing this kind of thing. My daily business is farming, and I get great pleasure out of going to see other enterprises and other people who need water. I am thinking particularly of a man who had a large milk selling business in Sunderland and South Shields. He bought some farms, again in the upper reaches of the Coquet Valley. It is always a pleasure to me to go to that part of the country and meet this man. He had no water on these two farms. We marked them out and I think after the end of this story you will think there must be other things than water finding in this trade. On one of these farms he had built his country cottage, and after the job was done we had to retire to sample the hospitality of the country cottage, together with the plumber, who was riding with me. The client said, 'You had better have a gin and tonic before you leave this morning,' and he got two tumblers. To cut the story down, when I got back into the car the plumber said, 'By heavens, I was pleased when you said you wouldn't have another.' That is the lighter side!

To return to more serious things, the Houghal School of Agriculture and one or two other people have invited me to demonstrate the art of water finding and I have found a tremendous interest on the part of the students. I am sure that as we are entering this era there is a wide undiscovered field in this dowsing business and students are hungry to know more and more about it. The students at agricultural colleges, being farmers' sons, are naturally very interested in this subject. Two of the lecturers at this particular field exercise were non-believers, and one of them made that so obvious that I said, 'Would you like to try to use the divining rod?' He did so, and I have never seen such an expression of shock as appeared in his face when he discovered that this silly thing did work.

Getting away from water finding, when I was at the Cambridge Congress some years ago I sat with Bill Youngs (who is not here unfortunately this year) and he was telling me in such great confidence how he could set out and find things. By coincidence, when I returned home there was a note telling me that a young woman, who had been married about a year, had lost her wedding ring and would I find it. I thought this was a challenge and if I refused I should be admitting defeat. I decided to accept and made an appointment to go and visit about a week later. I thought, I will go through exactly the same process as I should in finding water. I proceeded in the direction indicated by the rod and finally I came out on to the lawn in the front garden, and there was a pile of garden rubbish. There were three sacks of rubbish neatly placed on top of the garden rubbish and the rod led me to one of the three sacks. I thought, it is going down. It is very distinct. This looks like it, and kept my fingers crossed. I tipped the sack out, spread out the contents and went through it but there was nothing. Was this defeat? I went back and the stick took me again to the same point in the garden, right on top of the pile of garden refuse. The movement of the rod was distinct enough, so we had another try, and when we got some way down in the pile of rubbish the ring was showing. I looked round and there stood the young lady with a tear on her cheek, so it was another of those satisfying cases. The farm staff had been looking for the ring on and off for a week, and I found it within five minutes of getting on to the site. Looking for gold rings is not, however, something I wish to do, because there are problems. You are never sure whether it was there in the first place, and once you start doing that sort of work, half the nation will want you to find their gold rings.

Another experience away from water finding was a request from a large engineering company to find the source of pollution in a particular river. I thought, how can I deal with this? Obviously the pollution was getting in through an underground stream, so I went by the river and found a stream about 8ft deep that seemed to be running between factory and river and to the point of pollution, and I thought that must be it. I tracked it back and found it inside the factory yard, running right under the main buildings and right under a settling pool that they had for their old oils, sumps, etc. The question then was, how to advise them to get rid of it. Well, I told them to cut it off and pump it out before it got into the water, and I think this was carried out successfully. Well, that was another use for the dowser other than water finding, and I don't think the problem could have been solved by any other means.

Another thing I was once asked to do was on the Tyne, where there are one or two fairly large dry docks. There was a fairly large dry dock on the north side, which was 300ft long, and on the south side there was a company wanting to build one in competition, if anything a little bit longer. They had a plan for one at 150ft long but they wanted to extend this. Their problem was what they termed a sand pocket loaded with water, in everyday language, a quicksand. This was right in the path of the proposed new dry dock, and I had to map out the area, so that they could pump it out and then they could proceed. They did proceed and the dock was in operation within two to three years. Whether any credit was given to me I have no idea, but it was another interesting use for a dowser's skill.

There are dowsing groups being formed at the moment. A gentleman now sitting at the back of the room will be getting together with me to try to do something in the Newcastle area. The problems I have found are the distance between this gentleman and myself, the distance between the potential clientele, wondering what kind of clientele we ought to invite or whether we should just leave it to our members. I am a little lost at the moment as to the best procedure in forming a group. Timing is an important factor. If we put out an invitation we might get half the nation and we don't want that, it would be embarrassing, but there is an opportunity for something to be usefully done in most areas of the country by getting the right kind of approach. I am not certain in my mind what the correct approach is. Those of you who have got groups going might be able to give me a lead on this.

How does dowsing work? This is the old, old question. We all have our theories. I have had many theories over the years. Some people think it is in the muscles, others think it is in the divining rod. I am sure now that it is in the mind. I believe the subconscious mind is the major part. There was a time when this was proved to me by looking at someone else crossing the lawn. This is an exercise we can try out this afternoon. Let someone else walk out while you hold the rod. Your mind is travelling with this person. I found when my mind travelled that as he crossed the stream the rod went down, and that I think was the time that changed my view right round to the fact that the mind has this kind of ability. We are not sure how to measure it but there is something there for thought.

I think I mentioned before that we have a complete, undiscovered field in the future of dowsing. It seems such a contrast with the Congresses of years ago that we now have all these young people who are getting in at ground level. If this interest can be maintained I am sure that in years to come they will have a lot of ground to cover and will have more means at their disposal then we have had. I think this might be a happy note on which to end.

Thank you all very much.

Appendix IX

Twenty-five Years of Practical Dowsing

A talk given at York on 3/5/74 by Edwin Taylor

I HAVE BEEN an active dowser for twenty-five years and I would like to give you a view of some of the highlights. I think the proper place to start is the beginning and to tell you how it all began.

It was either in 1948 or 1949 that I had a visit from a friend who lived in Canada. I didn't know that he was a dowser, but he turned up with his little piece of something or other – I think it was fencing wire – and said, 'I will show you where there is water on your farm.' Due possibly to some latent desire to see how the thing was done rather than to know where the water was, I felt that I must watch the operation. After his departure I was very quick to find a piece of fencing wire – which obviously any farm possesses – and do exactly what he had done. To my very great surprise, as you can imagine, I found exactly the same reactions as he had done. I set out with a piece of wire, it went down, and each time I went over the farm I found new places where it went down.

That was when the seed was sown for those twenty-five years of dowsing. It seemed very important to me that I should pursue this matter, and pursue it I did by becoming a member of the British Society of Dowsers. I think one of the great advantages of membership was that we were able to read the Journal and compare notes on what others had done. I made full use of the Society's library and read up what past masters had accomplished and their methods. I found that the responses I got were similar to those described by those masters

245

and I was doing things in the same way. Depthing and various other results were identical.

I began to get more and more confidence in what I could do as a dowser. I built up confidence by going round local farms, getting to know their wells and finding that without exception every well I saw had been found by a water diviner in some bygone period. I also followed springs. They would come out on to the surface and I would follow them back into the earth, measure their quantity, measure their depth, and likewise in reverse find underground streams and track them out on to the surface. Having done this and proved beyond doubt that it was possible, I felt a kind of confidence that I could go out and predict that I would find a supply of water for some needy person, wherever he might be.

In passing, I would mention that this gives you a new picture of the countryside. When you see a field on the farm and you know that there is a stream running that way, and another running this way at a certain depth, you have a different outlook from ordinary people, because you know these particular patterns are there, apart from the features which all can see.

You have to study farms, their wells, go round boreholes, find their depth and verify everything which you discover. I think that in days gone by the local dowser was a very important person in the district and countryside. He was a very busy man, too, because all the wells I find even today have been located by dowsers. Usually they are spot on, although occasionally you may get one that is on the side of the stream, that is, on the first of the wave bands.

I don't know whether it happens this way with other dowsers, but after this continuous build-up of confidence opportunity was presented to me in the form of a notice from estate agents in the West Riding of Yorkshire, asking whether I would find a supply of water for the village of Bolton-by-Bowland in that district. To me it was a long way from home and quite a challenge, but I set out with a fair amount of confidence because of all the build-up I had done over about one and a half to two years. I think it was the wettest day I had ever spent; I didn't know that it could rain so hard in the West Riding. When I arrived I was led first by the estate agent to some particular spot. I felt sure that I was being tested, for he said, 'Do you find something here?' I said, 'Yes, there is something there, but obviously not good enough for what you want.' What they required was a supply for a village – the pub, the local farms, in other words, the complete village. As a countryman, I fully understood what was needed. I found two streams. I had read that one of the tricks was to locate one stream running this way and another running that way, and then to try to find the point where they crossed. That I did. A month or two later I had the result. The geologists gave me the full list of the strata they had gone through. At 45ft they had found water and at 96ft they had found water, which was within 1ft of what I had predicted. Again my confidence rose, and I felt that I could depend on my findings. You need a fair amount of confidence before you can tell a man where to drill, because the cost very quickly runs into four figures.

The tools of the trade are many, and most dowsers have a particular liking for one of them. I use a piece of whalebone which goes right back to the days of Portugal Street, the original headquarters of the BSD with Colonel Bell. Then there is the old hazel twig, which is mentioned in the history books. I cut this one yesterday; it won't break and it is as supple and good as ever you will find one, springing back, and you can use it over and over again if need be. There is the piece of ordinary fencing wire, as used by the man from Canada. And there is a little tight spring, which will work perfectly if you are trying to amuse someone. The tools are all cheap and simple. You can, of course, use your hands if you can't find anything else. Use your thumbs; they go down exactly the same, or you can feel pins and needles in your hands if you decide that when you are going over a reaction you will feel it in your finger ends.

There must be beginners here tonight. Over the years I have seen one thing lacking in these Congresses, and that is someone to explain to the real beginner what to do and how to do it. I have no secrets and am willing to tell anyone anything: How it is done, how you depth, what to do when you go on a farm. To find water, get the feel of your divining rod. And look around; it will tell you where the water is. When you go to see a client and he says, 'We want to find water,' it seems a silly question but the first thing I say is, 'Where would you like to find it?' He may want it beside electric power. Go to the place where he wants it and you will soon feel where the nearest point is. Then you will not be long in finding it. You find it at right angles, then cross it and find the width of the stream, and this width will tell you the quantity. Proceed from there until you come to the first wave band, holding your rod firmly, and there you have got the depth. It is as simple as that. All you have to do is to build up confidence by going around and verifying your reactions.

You will always find water on a hilltop. It seems odd but that's the way it works. I think the reason is that the hilltop is there in the first place because of a fault in the earth. You have a rising and a break in the strata; generally in that break in the strata you have a crack in the earth, and water.

Most of my work had been in the County of Northumberland, and in the last year I have made an interesting find at the little village of Blanchland. A field had been divided off into six smallholdings all in a row, and they all belonged to lead miners. One owner asked me to tell him whether there was water. I found his old well, and the interesting thing was that each of the six dwellings had a well, and every well was sunk on the same stream of water. That was something which nobody could have found except by using the simple divining rod. Obviously a diviner had been at work finding water for the lead miners.

At Low Trewitt I had an interesting find, exact again in depth, but one of the very few that I have had which came right out of the top, and yet it was 100 or 96ft down. It supplied a number of farms.

At Slaley Forest I had a find which I very often liken to the story of Moses passing through the desert with his Israelites. The Forestry Commission needed water for half a dozen farms in the Forest at Slaley and asked me if I would find them a new supply. I said, 'Let's look at the old one first,' I always like to do that, even if it is an old well, because very often they are not deep enough. In Slaley Forest I estimated there was any amount of water, and I advised them to dig the cheap way, in other words, two men for a couple of hours in the afternoon could get down to confirm my findings, which was cheaper than drilling. When they reached 5ft. I had a telephone call to say they had found nothing, it was bone dry. An hour and a half later I went to the spot and found a little stream of water running the full width of the ditch, in other words, enough for a small village. Apparently between ringing me up and the next foot they had found the water. This is one of those coincidences. In bygone days people were said to perform miracles, but when Moses struck the rock was he not doing just what happened on this particular occasion?

Another interesting job was at Long Horsley, on the A1 through Northumberland. In this particular case I was against the geologist. A well had been sunk over 200ft down, (and 200ft is an expensive well), and about three years later the farmer rang me up and said the water had gone dry in the well and could I advise him. It was a Sunday night and we did the 30-mile journey to his well. He had his driller in the yard and he was ready to start drilling the following morning. Looking at the point where the geologist had advised, there was absolutely nothing. I found a point within the length of this hotel from the point where the geologist had advised to drill. I said, 'You will not need to go half the depth for this one.' I predicted 75 or 76ft down. On the following afternoon I got a telephone message to say, 'We have found the water exactly where you said, and it is running down the field.' That confirmed to me that the professional in his capacity of geologist is not always right. He can be wrong, we can be wrong. But I think the two would make a grand team – the geologist finding the area and the dowser pinpointing where they should drill. At that same place I called back a little while later when the water was in use. The farmer's wife came to the door and I enquired after the supply. She said, 'It is the first time we have bathed the kids one at a time.' Evidently she had been used to a poor supply of water all her life.

There was a case at one of our own farms which I think is worth mentioning. We sank a well and had an ample supply of water, but between the time of finding it (when it was tested) and using it it became polluted. It was heavily polluted and we discovered what it was polluted with, but we couldn't understand why, because it was about 150 yards from the farm. However, a soakaway had been built for a new building put up to house animals, and this soakaway had been built exactly on another stream, which was running in the opposite direction but exactly on top. It was through this that we sealed up the soakaway and cured the problem, but this was another case where the water diviner found out something which nobody else would ever have known – the location of the other stream running in the opposite direction.

Just a word about the dangers and pitfalls of siting wells when working near clay. This was one of those odd occasions when I failed in the depthing. I predicted water at about 80ft and the driller was down another 10ft and had found no water. Naturally they were very concerned. I immediately went over and confirmed firstly that the water was still there. What had gone wrong? I tried the depthing again and halted at the point on the wave band where the clay band was struck, and discovered there was a very strong pull of the stick at that point. This had led to a miscalculation. So beware of that clay band when depthing. When you are going over it, if the stick wants to go down keep hold of it until it *really* goes down. On that afternoon I predicted the depth would be 165ft after holding the stick over the clay band, and this turned out to be exactly true.

I am not a speaker, I am a practical farmer. But over the years people have come along and said, 'We are interested in your subject. Will you talk to us on water divining?' I don't know whether it is that they can't get anyone else to speak and we are willing! But it has pleased me very much to see the Ministry of Agriculture recognise the dowser. They have asked me to demonstrate to farmers in two counties the art of divining or of finding water. I have also spoken at the School of Agriculture in Durham. It is being proved more and more every day that the water diviner is a useful person, and I am sure there was an age when he was *really* recognised, and that day might very well return.

I don't know whether we have the Press in tonight, but I think it worth mentioning that I have found them to be useful. The local Press have recognised my services to the district and have never spoken other than favourably. I would like to give them praise, because they have served me well, not because of any personal friendship, but because they too have recognised that the art of dowsing is useful. Radio and Television have not come along; I haven't invited them. But Radio have twice asked me to give a talk on divining, and that I enjoyed doing and I am sure that they too were very interested.

Who are your clients if you become successful? Nearly all *my* clients want me to find water. What amazes me is the willingness of people of position to agree that there is something in dowsing. In the last few years four titled people – four lords and one duke – I cannot mention their names, for they would not wish me to – have come along to me and said, 'Will you find water on my estate?' Golf clubs, farmers, estate owners, government departments, the Ministry of Defence, the National Trust – those I *can* mention. They are all willing to recognise this art of finding water and to let me be of use to them. The latest client is the townsman, who buys a country cottage with no water supply. Over the last year or two there have been quite a number in that category.

Apart from finding water, we are asked to do other things. One very interesting job was at South Shields in the County of Durham quite a number of years ago. There was a dry dock on the north side of the Tyne, 300ft long, capable of carrying a ship of that length for repair. A firm in the south side decided that they would like to compete, but the obstacle in their way was a water-loaded sand area. Of all people they called in a water diviner to map out for them the area of water-loaded sand. I found myself in a completely new field, but I didn't feel afraid. They built their dock at 301ft and I think they would end the day quite happy that they had the largest dry dock on the Tyne.

The President and I have talked this evening about doing things outside one's normal sphere or one's normal interest within the art. After being at the Cambridge Congress a few years ago I met Bill Youngs, a Council member of the Society, and he seemed to put into me a kind of confidence that one can do things beyond finding water, and I decided that if ever the challenge came my way I couldn't do other than accept it. I had not long to wait for that challenge. Within two days of my getting home, there was a message that a friend and neighbour, a young lady married less than a year, had lost her wedding ring. You can imagine that she was upset and she asked whether I would find her ring. How does one answer this straight question? If I say No, that is defeat. So I said Yes, not knowing what the consequences would be, and arranged to go to her farm. They had searched for more than a week with the farm staff, but nothing had turned up. I adopted exactly the same method as for water, and I got a response in a particular direction. They took me into the garden. They had been gardening, and there was a pile of garden refuse and rubbish and one thing and another, and tidily on top of the pile were three fertiliser sacks full of weeds. I was taken to the middle one of the three and down, down, went the rod. I thought, 'Well, it's now or never. My reputation is either going to survive or there is going to be some ridicule. But never mind.' I picked up the sack and went through all its contents very, very carefully, because I knew that the name was at stake. And to my sorrow, in the sack there wasn't a thing. So I tried again, and I was again taken back to exactly the same spot, but this time the stick went down where the sack had been. I went down on my hands and knees and carefully went through the rubbish in the very small space to which the stick was responding. The husband was leaning over my shoulder and he said, 'There it is,' and, sure enough, the ring was there within a square foot. I had found it within five minutes of arriving at the farm. I was amazed that that was possible.

For several reasons I am a little afraid to accept this kind of challenge. There is sometimes some doubt as to whether the article is lost at all. If you are looking for water you know it is either there or it is not there. But if you are looking for a ring there are many pitfalls such as side effects and wishful thinking, so you have to leave your mind a complete blank.

I have been reading some interesting things about the new Water Act of 1973. It covers land drainage, and whatever is done goes through the mechanism of this Act.

Over the last year or two the Hexham Rural District Council, of which I am a member, have formed a Water Supply Sub-Committee. This opened my eyes to the great need in the district for people who understand the problems of country water supplies. It became more and more evident that something should be done by the people with the ability to go out and find water. They are not being put to their proper use. I never want to 'sell' myself, but there are a number of people in Britain who have this ability but are not allowed to put themselves to good use, and there are thousands of people without a decent water supply. There are three short items in the Water Act of 1973 which I should like to read to you, as I think they are very relevant:

1. It shall be the duty of a Water Authority to supply water within their area.

2. If it is not practical to provide a supply in pipes, but is practical to provide such a supply otherwise, at a reasonable cost . . . (This is where we as a Society could come in if we have dependable people.)

3. The Secretary of State may also collaborate with others in collating information on the demand for water and on water resources.

In other words, it would be quite within the modern law for anyone to collaborate with others on this subject. This is food for thought. I think there could, in fact, be an opening here for the BSD.

What are the untapped resources that we haven't explored? I think there is a tremendous field which we haven't touched upon. You all have your own thoughts. I will mention only one commodity and that is oil. If a man can confidently find water there is no reason whatever why he should not go out and find oil.

Finally, there is a little saying which I have had instilled into me all my life, and which I think is worth making a note of: 'If you want to be successful, get enthusiastic about it.'

Appendix X

A Gift Appreciated

A talk given by Edwin Taylor at the Harrogate Congress in November 1984

IT IS MANY years since I presented my first paper to a British Society of Dowsers' Congress and it has been my pleasure to have given several since. It is difficult not to repeat some part of the subject from time to time and because of this it is important that I change my style for this occasion.

George Orwell said that 1984 would be a great year and for me it has been, not because of the drought, but because of some gathering momentum over the years that seems to have come to quite a climax this year by so many people coming to me to have work done.

Experience has become a great teacher in so many ways and must not be ignored; time alone has made me much wiser and appreciative of the gift of dowsing. Today I see no difference in my intake of knowledge than I did on the very first instance thirty-five years ago. So never let us think we know it all, we mellow with time and also become more humble. It has been said that the wiser we become, how much we realise how little we know.

When I check the old wells, sunk two or three hundred years ago, they prove to me that the dowser of that era was a very wise man; he was spot on the stream when siting his wells.

The highlights produced in 1984 have spread over each month of the year. The most interesting ones I would like to relate to you, not for personal pleasure but to give the budding dowser a foretaste of what could be in store for him or her as they become more skilled.

My particular field is dowsing for water and it is in this sphere that I relate my experiences. But it also means that to be successful as I have been with dowsing the same can apply to any department of the subject. In each of the experiences I am going to tell you about, there is a lesson to learn, especially for the budding dowsers.

The journey for water has taken me long distances within our islands and I would like to begin in February with a visit to the eastern side of Northumberland, where I don't think the cold wind blows any colder in Britain. On this farm the water supply has been disturbed by a gaspipe line having been laid. I went there to find a supply and marked the site where the drilling was to be done. All the necessary plans had been put in motion – the licence to abstract water, the driller had been contacted together with the plumber and drainage officer. But still the unexpected happened.

The driller got down to the water and then the embarrassment arose, as it was an artesian well and there was no place for the water to go. It had not been calculated for drainage to take away the surplus water.

Like the example given, the experiences over the year are to illustrate points relevant to the art of dowsing and could be a guide to other dowsers.

My second call, in March, was on that very wild area of the Roman Wall – those of you who know Roman Wall country will wonder why the Roman soldiers ever wanted to be up there! It was a fairly extensive hill unit with large numbers of cattle and sheep and a good water supply was very important to a business of this scale.

The farmer met me and gave a guide to his requirements in thousands of gallons per day; he told me that the old well was no longer in use and his present supply was going dry in times of drought.

My first thoughts when visiting any farm is to check the old well because they have usually been found by a dowser, a wise man in days gone by. With the exception of about 5 per cent they are spot on, the 5 per cent or so being located on the edge of the stream and not deep enough.

The yield showed 20,000 gallons per day and the depth for drilling was 70ft. There was no need to search further with the potential so good, near to where it was needed and at a point where power was available. I marked the spot for the new supply and the drilling was done.

The driller told me he had found a good supply. I always make notes of what I do – quantity expected, place to be drilled etc., and it is very important to be able to refer back to these figures. However, I received word from the farmer that he was worried about the supply as it was beginning to go off.

I returned the next day and found the farmer concerned because what started off as a good supply began to dry up. My concern was to see the reason why. This is where the lesson lies. Now, I predicted water at 70ft at about 20,000 gallons so I checked the measurements I made at my first visit. I asked at what depth the water was found and was told at 30ft! I then checked and found that a small spring was running in a different direction but by chance crossed the site where the drilling was down. The driller had hit this and had pulled out thinking that all was well. I assured the farmer that everything was all right and that he should get the driller back and go down to 70ft.

The driller did return and found a great supply at 70ft. How easy, without dowsing, that would have been regarded as a failure.

My next visit was to the more fertile valley of the Tyne, west of Hexham. This particular dowse puts the emphasis on cheapness, or more to the point, value for money. The farm had a poor supply fed by gravity from a surface spring yielding about 800 gallons a day. Because of expansion of the farm business the demand had increased to 4,000 gallons a day.

As all the pipelines, tanks, troughs and installations were there, I knew it was wiser to try and harness existing assets and the first thing I did was to check the potential of the existing supply.

The result of the survey showed that the spring could yield much more if lowered a further 8ft, quite within the reach of a JCB digger. The owners agreed that the scheme should proceed and followed my advice, which is given here in detail. 'Before digging, have on site two tons of 2″ gravel and three concrete pipes, 3′ in diameter and 3′ long. Then start digging down to 9′ below the surface at midstream. Place in the bottom 2″ gravel and stand the first pipe on end. Begin to fill in around the pipe, then continue with the next pipe. When the water has found a level in the well put in the supply pipe 3′ below the water level taking it to the supply tank.'

It proved to be a very satisfactory result with an overflow spilling out. That could have been very expensive to drill for a new supply and yet, at the end of the day, it cost probably little more than £100 for a new scheme and plenty of water.

A Gift Appreciated

A few years ago I presented a paper to a Congress on land drainage and my next visit would have been very fitting to illustrate the value of dowsing in such circumstances.

On a neighbouring farm was a twenty-three acre field in the middle of which was a large mound, with water seeping out on the southerly and easterly slopes wetting and spoiling six acres of the area. The mound was a sand hill and at the bottom of the mound was a clay band. There were great drainage schemes done here in the 1870s, which failed and it was drained again in 1942 and it failed again. This year I was called in to give advice on the best method to dry up the field.

I dowsed over the wet parts and found nine places which were centre points of spillage, each 9' to 10' deep. This was quite deep to put in a land drain but with plenty of fall in the field it was possible. So this was done and thousands of gallons of water per day were taken out and for the first time in the life of the field it is now dry and producing to capacity.

It was still winter time when I was called to 'Gap Shield', a high lying stock farm situated in the gap of the Pennine Range between Newcastle and Carlisle.

At the time of dowsing, I was not told nor did I realise that mine workings were under the land near the farm. A site was chosen in the usual way and marked out for drilling. It had all the good signs of the amount needed – about 7,000 gallons per day.

The driller began his task and at about 50ft the drill passed through some old mine workings, causing the drill to get slightly off track and then getting rapidly worse, which forced the driller to give up. A second attempt also failed with a similar result, then abandoned.

The situation was not one that could be left unsolved and a meeting was arranged with the landlord, the farmer, the driller and myself, as dowser. Different alternatives were considered, including a public supply costing about £15,000. Drilling too far away from the power supply was also costly. My advice was to explore the present poor supply to see if it had a potential of producing more. The pipes, tanks and other equipment were already there.

My advice was accepted and we all went to the old well site. I found there two sister springs running side by side, number one was 6 metres wide and 3 metres deep and the second was 4 metres wide and 3 metres deep. They were running on the same strata, collected in a tank and gravitated to the farm. I assessed them both and thought they should do much more than they were. I suggested they dig down on one of the springs, leaving the second as a reserve, put in the pipes with the gravel on the bottom, as I mentioned before. I don't know why we bothered with looking for a new supply elsewhere but they were so determined to find a new supply at the farm. I called on them some while later, when I was passing, and they had loads of water coming out and were very happy people.

This shows that we should look at the easy way out before trying to spend a lot of money.

My next journey, getting into summer now, was to that very beautiful part of east Yorkshire, near to Ampleforth and in sight of the Abbey and Colleges. The request on this occasion was a much greater demand to fulfil the needs of a large pig fattening unit which had 9,000 pigs all the year round needing water for drinking and cleaning out.

The annual cost for water at £1 per thousand gallons and using 35,000 gallons per day made the owner consider a private supply and my task was to find the water. So it was very important to explore the site very carefully to get a yield of this volume and also important to call in past experience to ensure a good result.

As always, I try to get a supply as near to the place of consumption as possible and with that in mind I began my survey. Also in mind is that all important figure of 35,000 gallons per day, plus. In this sort of district you do not find streams yielding that amount unless you get down to a water table.

I picked up stream No. 1, which was no use in itself. No. 2 was much better at 13 metres wide and the two together might produce half the amount required. By the time I had nearly done full circle round the unit, with hopes fading, I found a much larger stream which crossed No. 2 and would yield in excess of the 35,000 gallons. Economics had got to come into this and I was very conscious of this when doing my dowsing and this applies to wherever I go.

The Agricultural Training Board in Northumberland asked me if I would consider giving classes throughout the county on dowsing. That in itself is not easy because we are all individuals in dowsing but I did agree to give some basic instruction.

There were three single classes to be taken and I was left to not only teach the students but organise the classes at the same time. First of all I would give them a basic history and background information as most people do not realise the importance of dowsing down through the ages to find water, minerals etc.

I showed them what to use as tools of the trade, which have to be simple not because of the farming community, but because of the fact that they are able to utilise the simple formula of the hazel stick from the hedgerow, a piece of wire or even the thumbs on their hands if needs be. Dowsing is simple and is meant to be simple, as the daily way of life.

I gave them a demonstration by performing a mock dowse using the place of meeting as the site and going through all the motions of finding, quantity estimate, depth estimate and costings. Most important was to emphasise the value of dowsing to agriculture in the daily way of life, such as finding water pipes, field drains and pinpointing the source of wet areas in fields to get the right place to put in pipes for drainage.

Also explained was the importance of choice in forked stick, the hazel being the first choice with each limb of equal size for balance and the knots being shaven off smooth so as not to cut the inside of your hands when the rod pulls down over water.

There was time given for questions and the meetings were concluded with all making an attempt at dowsing, many of whom are potentially good.

Pipelines are something we have been troubled with in the north of England, because the British Isles comes to a narrower part just south of the border, so whatever comes south has to pass through that narrow point. When you take out Newcastle, the Tyne valley, the populated area and Carlisle the other side, the hills in the middle, there are not many places left for pipelines to come through. So they all seem to be concentrated in small areas and when the pipelines go through farmers get upset, naturally, because water supplies go amiss. This was my journey back in July to an area of Cumbria where supplies had gone dry because of the drought and others because of the pipelines. Other little problems had happened such as a spring coming up in the middle of someone's lawn – things like that. It was through the pressure from farmers to the Gas Board that I was called in as a kind of referee or ombudsman to put into categories those water supplies lost through the actions of British Gas and those by an act of God.

It was a most interesting day travelling by Land Rover through the county following the pipelines. This shows another way in which the dowser can be brought in to adjudicate as to whether the Gas Board has caused the problems or not.

In mid-August I received a request to visit that great county of Fife, noted for its high quality farms which are some of the very best in Scotland.

With land of such high quality in a low rainfall area, water for irrigation becomes a valuable asset to the production of high yields of both potatoes and cereals.

It is asking a lot for a dowser to fill this demand, which is in the region of over 200,000 gallons per day for one site. But nature has made some contribution through volcanic disturbance in that area of Scotland which has created earth faults able to yield higher quantities of water than we could expect in most parts of the British Isles. With this in mind, I set out for the Kingdom of Fife with a little more enthusiasm.

There were three farms needing a supply of this kind and the first one set the pattern for those to follow. This farm needed 200,000 gallons per day and the signs were showing up good as I dowsed, with streams measuring up to 50m wide. It was important to find two streams in this category and then hopefully find where they both crossed. A site of this kind was found within reasonable distance of a power supply for pumping.

The most interesting thing on this site was that there had been another dowser called in. The farmer asked me if I would like to know where this other dowser had said there would be a supply. But I had no wish to know anything of what he had found until I had completed my survey. The reason for this being that you could be misled, as a dowser, by wishful thinking or suggestion. Keep your mind clear and start your work with a clean sheet.

After I had done my survey, I was shown the site where the other dowser had said there was water. He was spot on as far as the dowsing goes but the quantity was only 7,000 gallons per day and would not have met the needs of the farmer. Now this man was just seeking, by dowsing, a site to put in a borehole but he was not stipulating quantity or depth.

Farm number two was situated by the side of the trunk road leading over the Tay Bridge to Dundee. Once again this was land of high quality needing a large quantity of water. On this occasion a little more comfort was provided in the form of a new jaguar car to ferry me over the land. On that farm the farmer was not worried about the water not being found near the buildings and we were able to mark four sites around the farm. He was willing to take the electric power to those sites to lift the water out.

There are two points with the third farm. I found two very good streams and when it comes down to the area in which to drill where two streams cross the size is quite small. Now that small area involved was bang in the middle of one of the stone buildings in the middle of the farm and it could not have been in a worse place. So we had to be content on that occasion by getting out on to the better of the two streams and being satisfied with half the quantity. That had all the signs of being a good one if it was situated better.

The other point was that the farmer had had advice from a geologist, who told him a large fault ran down the side of the entrance road to the farm. He kept asking me if I could find any water along the side of this road but I could find nothing. He took me in the house and showed me the report of the geologist in which it said that the fault was running down the side of the road and if the farmer drilled there, water would be found. It quickly came to my mind that I had found the earth fault, not where the geologist had said but where I had found the good stream, which was running parallel to where he said but about 200 yards away. So the dowser and the geologist may well be a good team together.

The highlight of the year was a request from a London firm to do some work, which was very vague, for a large stone quarry firm in Europe in Lismore, one of the western isles of Scotland. I tried to get some more details and I agreed to go as it was a challenge and the western isles can be very lovely in autumn. So I started to lay the plans for this trip and got a little more detail and found they needed about seven sites on Lismore. A date was fixed for 17th September.

My wife rang the weather office and said we were planning to go to the western isles on the 17th September and what would the weather be like? They said: 'There could be better places to go!' They advised that over the few days around the 17th the weather would be very wet with gale force winds. I don't know whether the dowsing instinct came in here, but as I had already committed myself to a date and plans had been made for me to meet the Rural Development Board – the chairman and secretary – the various people concerned, we decided to go.

When we set off from home it was raining but by the time we reached Oban in the evening it was a beautiful night. I worried about the wind rising overnight but Monday morning came with a drizzle and we boarded the boat. The sea was like a mill pond. The stage seemed to be set for a good and fortunate trip.

We reached the island and as I got off the boat I quickly eliminated each person in turn as the one who had been sent to meet me. An unlikely farmer, who was loading sheep for the return journey, came across to me and said: 'You'll be the dowser.' He said he wasn't wanting much as it was only a pipe he wanted me to find. I asked him if that was all he wanted, thinking that wires had got crossed and things had gone wrong, but another man came up and said he had been sent to take me to the chairman of the RDB. We got into a little old Fiat and we hadn't gone two yards when there was a most awful bang from the bottom of it, but he never flinched. Every few yards there were such awful creaks and groans and bangs from the bottom of this car as we went over every bump in the road. I asked where we were to meet the chairman and it seems that he was back at the jetty waiting for us so we had to turn round and return to the jetty!

It took about half an hour to get to the first site and the bush telegraph must have been working as heads were peering out from windows. Amongst the delegation that met us was an American lady, who was a writer, and she was living on Lismore and writing a book about life on the island.

After completing the first dowse, we were all invited in for coffee. Not knowing what the arrangements were for lunch, it seemed like a good idea. On entering the house, there were piles of a child's clothing everywhere and the old gentleman sitting in the corner in his pyjamas – I think he had been there two or three days. It was a different way of life, people just living in a placid way. The coffee arrived and then followed the greatest plate of banana sandwiches ever seen!

It was about the third site that I found out what was probably the purpose of my going there. We introduced ourselves to the lady at the house and I said I was there to find a site for water and she said: 'I am not sure that I want it.' Then the quarry man explained to her that there would be no charge and it would all be done free. It began to dawn on me then what was really happening here on the island of Lismore. It was very poorly supplied with water and this multi-million pound company was moving on to the opposite bank on the mainland and they were trying to sweeten up the islanders by pleasing them. By doing this they would have got over the first hurdle and probably the one after that and another again!

My last visit was to a little country croft where there was a man and two ladies. The man wanted me to find the water up the hill and I told him that 'up there' was no good and the place to drill was near the house. He insisted he wanted it 'up there' and I left him a very disappointed man.

I marked out fourteen points to drill and when we caught the ferry back to Oban I was ready to sit down. The weather man had got it all wrong for the sun came out at the first dowse and stayed with us all through. Lismore is ten miles long and about two miles wide; it rarely ever gets snow and livestock, both cattle and sheep, thrive. From a dowsing aspect it allowed me to try to find underground water during the boat crossing, a thing I have never tried before and to my great surprise the reaction was the same as travelling over land.

In conclusion, I realise more and more that there are large areas in Britain without water and I think there is plenty of scope now and in the future for a dowser to be employed continuously.

Appendix XI

The Place of Dowsing in the Eighties

A talk given by Edwin Taylor at Carlisle on 24/10/80

HEN I WAS asked for the subject of my talk I suggested one which should give me a tremendously wide field. I am getting away from the usual tonight and trying to use my imagination a little, but I hope that what I say will show foresight rather than just imagination.

I should like to start by giving a message to dowsers. I am sure there must be many new ones here and there are also those who will say, 'Here he is again with another talk.' Well, I think it takes a particular kind of person to be a dowser. He or she has to be a kind of passive individual with patience and a sense of humour, but the message for those of you who have a good memory, or a pencil and paper, is that if you want to make a success of dowsing you must get enthusiastic about it. If you bear this in mind you should achieve what you are setting out to do.

Being a dowser brings many rewards. It means you have at least one extra sense and you have a feeling of achievement. This is a very good talking point on nights like this and a lot of good comes out of it for us all, but why have we not made full use of dowsing in the past? I think the whole crux of the matter is that the human being has become so professionalised (I don't know whether there is such a word in the dictionary but it does express my meaning) that he has someone above him and someone below him; he wonders what they are thinking and therefore feels that his hands are tied. He cannot be quite his own self, and if you wish to be a dowser I think one of the essential things is that you be yourself. I am sure that dowsing cannot succeed in the climate of thinking of one above and one below and considering what they might be thinking about it. This is probably the reason why, if we are not careful, dowsing could lose hold again today.

As dowsers we have another disadvantage if we want to sell our wares in the water or any other field. We haven't got a marvellous array of technical terms that we can set out in our shop window. In other words, what we are really searching for is how it works. Even though we know it is working perfectly well we cannot say that it is done in a particular way, and in the professionalised world that we have it is difficult to convince sceptics that we are professionals at our own trade, although we have masses of evidence. In my particular field I can go round and see millions of gallons of water flowing where wells have been put down, where the depth and quantity have been predicted with absolute correctness. So there is no question that we have evidence that dowsing works, but we have got to go on from there, we have to find out how it works and I trust that in the eighties we shall find the answer to that question.

How can we begin to give the world this information? Are we not dowsing in our daily life? We dowse for many things by habit. Have we never thought that we might be just a little more clever than we are giving ourselves credit for? We do many things automatically, and when you are a dowser you look at these things and say, 'Well, there is some kind of link here,' and you go into these things and wonder why you do it. I think we may be using the dowsing faculty unknown to ourselves. We all know people who are successful in business. I think it possible that they may be good dowsers, who formulate the right questions and get the right answers. All down the line I think it may be not by chance and beyond coincidence. I do believe there is a link which makes some people successful at whatever it may be and dowsing could very well be playing a part.

We cannot pass the eighties without thinking of occasions when telepathy may be involved. Can we not all remember a time when we suddenly thought of Old So-and-So at twelve o'clock lunchtime and by one thirty he had telephoned or knocked at the door? Here again is a source that is untapped and I believe the eighties may very well see big strides forward in telepathy between one mind and another. It is there now in forms that need to be cultivated. People do think about others and they in turn think of them, and I think this is a sphere that could be cultivated to advantage.

I have often thought that the British Society of Dowsers, if it had sufficient funds, should be thinking of a research fund and a research project. We are convinced that we have the ability but we need money to progress in different directions, to do particular things. I have many times thought the Society might well dig down its hand into its pocket after nearly fifty years of having all the proofs that are needed, but to date that has not been done. I am not saying that the Society has ever refused to help in this direction, only that so far nothing has been done.

What I am coming to now in connection with the telepathic mind is that I have had a call from overseas – from Sweden, as a matter of fact – from someone who seems to be answering this kind of call. He is a big business man in Stockholm with interests in South America. He has a research fund in Sweden for exploring certain subjects and the dowsing faculty could very well come under his wing. This summer he has been in Britain for two weeks looking round various dowsers and trying to find out more about the subject. He is not a dowser himself but he is very, very keen and believes, as I do, that there is a great future in dowsing. He is willing to put money into the study, so we set out to try to achieve something in this respect.

As a beginning we have already put into action a kind of plan. My friend has gone round to two or three of the prominent people and has finally settled and given me the honour at this stage of working hand in hand with him and offering a service of 'no water, no pay'. I think that to offer a guaranteed package deal means sticking one's neck out in the dowsing world, but after looking into my track record he is so confident that he is willing to say to the client, 'We will guarantee you what is in effect a package deal – × gallons of water at such-and-such a price.' That is not all he has at the back of his mind. As I said to someone sitting beside me at dinner tonight, 'If we can be so successful in the field of water there is no reason whatever why we should not be equally successful in any other department.' There is no reason why we should not be successful all down the line. We have invited people anywhere in the United Kingdom to take part in these schemes. We have made offers on the above basis and have already had some enquiries, which I hope will bear fruit. This is what I call Stage One.

Stage Two need not be confined to this country, because if we can find water why should we not find oil and the valuable minerals? The thought of all the possibilities just about sets the mind dancing.

There is also the question of illness. At this Congress the majority of the speakers are on the healing side, and I am sure we could be as successful with the one as with the other.

If we consider the last half century or so we have seen unbelievable achievements. At one time they used to go round the corridors of this hotel with candles, and electricity was looked upon as a marvellous introduction to the modern way of life. I don't think I had better give my age away by saying I remember running to the top of the school yard because a motorcar was going past the school. In the last sixty years we have seen the coming of the motorcar and the aeroplane, the early days of radio, and now we have television and men have walked on the moon. These sixty years have seen great advances. Now the point I am trying to make is that the pattern of the future is the pattern of the past. We have seen a gradual build-up and then in the last century the wonders of the world have come in very thick and fast.

When we look at things in this light we can see great possibilities in the dowsing world, in other words, there should be room for this new science in the eighties. So do not let us underestimate ourselves as dowsers and do not let us underestimate our chances of doing good work in the field of dowsing. I think there is a tremendous opening here for us.

Those of you who are just budding dowsers at present I think should get cracking, go on and make a success of it. The skilled dowser should be a valuable person in the eighties and onwards. I think it is important that you set about it in the right way, that you demonstrate your skills as able people and, as I said at the beginning, get some enthusiasm built up. You will probably say to me, 'Give us a lead and show us how to make a start.' I am sure there must be people who are anxious to get going but just need something as a guide on how to begin. If there are any in this room who have that feeling I think the first question is – Can you get your divining rod, or whatever instrument you use, to work? If the answer to that question is yes, you are free to consider your course of action. I think the next thing is to develop your skill and practise the feel of the rod. In other words, you want to be getting to know what it feels like when you find somewhere where it is working. Keep going at it until you know what it feels like and there is no mistaking it. You are getting a response from the rod, so keep going again and again.

If you are interested in water the advice I would give is to try to find a spring of water in your garden or elsewhere, go over it and try to find what direction it is coming from. If it is coming up out of the ground it has got to be coming from some direction. If it is on a hillside don't think that it follows the slope of the hill, because that doesn't mean a thing. It depends entirely on the underground strata and it could even be coming from the opposite direction. Try with your divining rod to find which direction it is coming from and then track it back into the field. At the same time estimate your quantity by the width and estimate the depth as you are going farther into the field and see if you are correct. After you have convinced yourself of that lesson from measuring the delivery at the spring and estimating the quantity, go on to the next step and find the lines. Go into the field and find the spring, not very deep, and be prepared to walk a couple of miles and track it out on the surface, and then if you have got it out to the surface I am sure you will be convinced that your rod is working. I think you need something like that to convince you that you have achieved something. If you have tracked it for a mile or more you will feel that you can guarantee that it is working for you and you have got an end result.

The North of England is very short of dowsers and very short of people to show them how to do it. I don't know whether I should stick my neck out but I would be very pleased to help anyone in the North of England. This is the first time I have been on home ground to talk to a Dowsing Congress. I live in the Border Country and if there are people who are very keen on dowsing I would be willing to offer all the help that I could to get them started. After thirty years of dowsing I am still finding something new all the time. One keeps learning new ways, new techniques and I think it all comes from practice. Those of you who are professionals in your own field will probably back up that statement.

Homeopathy is not my subject, but I don't think you could mention healing in the eighties without that word coming into it prominently. I am sure that the achievements under this heading will become tremendous in the eighties, when great strides forward should be made in the world of healing. I think it would be fair to say that a large number of our population in Britain today are beginning to get fed up with the synthetic and are trying to get back to nature's way of doing things. I know it would be impossible to convert the whole world back to natural ways of doing things, but there are many fields where I think they will return. In the healing world and in the world of common sense I hope we shall get away from the synthetic and come back to good sense and the way that nature meant things to be done. Let us hope that we have nearly completed the circle and are returning to a more natural way of thinking.

To conclude, I would like to put the emphasis on foresight rather than imagination for the summing-up as I did at the beginning. The research project could be a winner and I think we could get a lot out of it. It allows us to do experiments and confirm facts. There is a tremendously wide field for checking, I think there would be possibilities and I have hope for the eighties on that score. To you people in this room I would say get in on the ground floor. Those who can dowse will, I think, find opportunities in the coming era. So try to get in some practice and make use of it. There may be a need for teaching and, as I said before, I am not setting up as a teacher but I am willing to help anyone if there is any advice I can give.

Edwin Taylor Senior on the occasion of his 80th birthday together with his son, Edwin at Mosswood Farm.

Edwin Taylor, grandson at Durhamfield Farm.

Edwin Taylor, son, with machinery at Durhamfield Farm

Epilogue

t is very appropriate that in the last few days of my eightieth year I sit down to put words together to fit the occasion.

I have been very fortunate, when I now look back life has been good to me, in a country way of life that I loved so much. When I look at the family tree and find my family tree goes back 400 years in the same way of life, it is not surprising to find joy from a life that nature meant it to be.

The outstanding parts of my life are worthy of mention. I look back seventy-five years for my first love, in the month of April when the lambs were born, that pleasure has stayed with me to this day.

Nine years later, at the age of fourteen, I left school and began my life as a farmer. It was in that first year that Old James the horseman retired, and left a vacancy which my father gave me the opportunity to take on the duties of horse man, which was all the work with a pair of horses, build the stacks of hay, and corn. The ploughing I remember well thinking of the poems of Burns when he was a ploughman and his lines 'to a mouse'.

It was in the Autumn of 1933 that I first witnessed the meaning of Burns' poem 'To a mouse'. I was ploughing stubble for the next years crop ploughing in a single furrow walking behind the pair of horses in the furrow which was being turned over. Sadly in the process the mouse had made its winter bed, and grain gathered from the previous crop. Suddenly disaster struck, the furrow turned with the bed, and its occupant running in panic.

> Wee, Sleekit, cowrin' tim'rous beastie,
> Oh, what a panic's in thy breastie!

271

Thou needna startawa' sae hasty
  Wi' bick'ring prattle!
I wad be laith to rin and chase thee,
  Wi' murdering pattle!

The Second World War began September 1939 when life changed overnight. The work horse was first to go. The tractor became the power on the farm to plough large acreages to feed the Nation.

The price of wheat rose from £3-19-0 to £20-0-0 on day one, per ton.

My wife Anne and I married in December 1943 in the days of food rationing when there was no special occasion, even the honeymoon was a short distance carrying our gas masks. We were to travel by train through Darlington Station on the 4.00 p.m. train. At 4.00 p.m. the previous day a bomb was dropped on Darlington Station.

In 1949 I became very interested in the art of Dowsing for underground water. I joined the British Society of Dowsers and have now been a member for fifty years. About 1850 there were two dowsers who each wrote a book of there lives as dowsers and well sinkers, telling of their success, and methods. I tried their methods and found that it worked for me. I only wanted to follow success with a track record I could depend on.

I used my spare time during the following two years to master the methods of my copy lead of one hundred years ago. My findings were very heartening, but not proof. At this time I received a request from a London firm of land agents seeking a dowser to locate 6,000 gallons of water per day for a village in Yorkshire's West Riding.

My confidence had been strengthened so much by the guide of my copyhead that I accepted my first challenge to put my judgement to test.

The day came for the survey with the agents and I followed the rule of my self training. Finding two rows of water on site. To play safe I marked the point to bore where the two veins crossed, and predicted the yield to be in excess of their needs. I asked them for a log of the drilling. The log of the borehole drilling arrived to me four months later for my dowse number one. I could not believe my eyes. Water found at two levels as predicted test pumped to yield in excess of 6,000 gallons per day. The water at two levels were both within three feet of my prediction.

The country village I dowsed the water for was Bolton by Bowland, in the West Riding of Yorkshire. It was the first of several hundreds

Elliot James Taylor, my grandson, dowsing.

of sites successfully formed, and now fifty years later I am still called upon to mark the point to drill for water.

I am so pleased that my second grandson has inherited the skills of my dowsing ability, and has proved it by using my methods which have done so well for me over so many years. Elliot James Taylor is now in his twenty-second year and after leaving Wye College, University of London, has returned and joined the farming business as his older brother Edwin did five years ago. A repeat of what has happened for the last 400 years, and hopefully will continue. Following the pattern of continuity as nature planned.

The conclusion spells out that I must return to the farming enterprise of today with three generations of the Taylor family with an Edwin involved in all three.

The acreage of inby-productive land being farmed extends to 2,600 acres of which 2,000 are growing wheat, barley and oilseed rape. The livestock includes a dairy herd of British Holstines, a sheep flock of 700 breeding ewes, also a smaller herd of beef breeding cows for the beef market.

In this year, just months away from the year 2000, it is my son Edwin who is in the driving seat of the farming unit. I have passed through that stage, and most of the 'Seven ages of Man'. All of which have there joys in life.